LINGUISTIC THEORY:

What can it say about reading?

Roger W. Shuy, Editor
Georgetown University

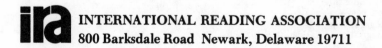
ira INTERNATIONAL READING ASSOCIATION
800 Barksdale Road Newark, Delaware 19711

Copyright 1977 by the
International Reading Association, Inc.

Library of Congress Cataloging in Publication Data

Main entry under title:
Linguistic theory.

    Bibliography: p.
    1. Linguistics.   2. Reading.   I. Shuy,
Roger W.
P121.L516   410   77-1834
ISBN 0-87207-720-9

Contents

Foreword

As Noam Chomsky has said in so many ways over the past decade, linguistic descriptions that capture our unconscious knowledge of language are several steps removed from how we actually make use of that knowledge in language performance. The potential set of inferences from linguistics to the applied problem of reading must be explicitly delineated and argued; they are not necessarily straightforward or immediately apparent. Performance models of the adult reading process which embed linguistic knowledge structures within their total functioning are but one example of the attempt to make use of linguistic theory. Another is trying to structure initial reading materials in line with one or another linguistic theory or generalization. Dr. Shuy is undoubtedly correct when he warns of the dangers of facile generalizations from the theoretical descriptive science of linguistics to the culture-specific task of reading. Fortunately, this volume gives equal weight to both the level of linguistic description and the problem of drawing inferences to reading.

This publication also reflects a shift of emphasis in linguistic studies away from syntactic issues confined to the sentence and toward an elaboration of extrasentential considerations needed for effective interpretation of language, such as discourse constraints, context, intentionality, and referencing. These issues have generally been raised in the context of semantic studies and are due, in part, to efforts to construct adequate performance models for understanding language. Especially in computer simulation studies, it has been found that a characterization of semantic context is needed in addition to sentence parsing routines. Selected aspects of our "knowledge of the world" must be formalized and, as theory in this area has begun to devlop, it was inevitable that inferences to reading would be forthcoming. A number of the more prominent cognitive models of reading (such as the works of Kenneth Goodman and Frank

Smith) have emphasized the role of semantic expectations in reading comprehension to such an extent that one can predict a relatively easy accommodation of these models to the new linguistic formulations. From another point of view, it has long been recognized that cultural differences may be responsible for a significant proportion of reading failures; again, as linguistic theory articulates these contextual variations, we might expect some additional insight into the relative importance of numerous sociolinguistic differences as they affect reading acquisition. As Dr. Shuy intimates in his introduction, this type of vital interaction of semantic-contextual theory with problems in reading may be especially useful in helping us think about teaching strategies for the development of reading comprehension in the middle grades.

Yet another way of thinking about the conceptual distance that separates linguistic theory from reading is the problem of linguistic accessibility. This has been the subject of much psycholinguistic, information-processing research of the past few years. In learning to read an alphabetic language such as English, many developmental theories depend upon the accessibility of rather abstract linguistic units such as phonological segments, morphological elements of lexical items, and trace elements in complex syntactic surface structures or logical form. Since these awarenesses are not initially present in children, we can presume they develop only as their attention is drawn to these distinctions through a combination of tutelage and maturation. Furthermore, as these initial awarenesses in reading are subsumed in later stages of reading development and automaticity of functioning ensues, the child's attention is freed to consider larger semantic-contextual issues. But just what combination of factors is needed to bridge this gap between linguistic units and psychological access to these units for children learning to read remains somewhat of a mystery. This book certainly appears to be a step in the right direction.

ERIC BROWN
NEW YORK UNIVERSITY

Introduction

It has always concerned linguists that professionals in the field of reading would allow the notion to develop that there is such a thing as "a linguistic approach to reading." One of the more obvious aspects of the act of reading (in most languages at least) is that, in some mysterious way, the knowledge a reader possesses of his language is called upon and made of use. There can be little question about this activity among most readers who are speakers of alphabetic languages. This is not to say that such readers do not also call on other skills. Undoubtedly they make heavy use of psychology, but we have yet to hear of "the psychology approach to reading." It seems rather clear that readers call upon their social and cultural knowledge, but there has been no discernible rush to establish a "sociological approach to reading." The major principles of information processing are utilized in the reading process, but no movement seems to be fomenting for "an information processing approach to reading." Why linguistics has been singularly blessed with such a burden is not at all clear, but the phenomenon is certainly apparent.

At first blush it would appear that linguists could be happy to be so highly valued by reading teachers, but a closer examination of the situation will reveal that the attention paid by reading specialists to linguistics usually has been superficial, fragmented, and misguided. Reading specialists are not entirely at fault for this improper view of the field. Linguists also must share the blame, largely because they are generally unaware of what is going on in this field under the name of linguistics. But here, as on every other occasion in which the excuse is utilized, ignorance is certainly not excusable.

For example, linguists have known for some time that their field involves a great deal more than phonology. Yet all through the fifties and sixties, for most people, the term *linguistics* was synonymous with letter-sound correspondences in reading research, materials development, and teaching. Such awareness was often accompanied by sighs of relief that, however esoteric this new linguistics might be, it at least bore some similarity to more comfortable phonics, giving birth to the enduring confusion between phonetics and phonics—a distinction made by Charles Fries but missed completely by those who chose not to see it.

Another trivialization of the presumed linguistic approach to reading came about as a result of efforts to apply the orthodoxy of language teaching to the reading process. Repetition drills were very popular at that time and it was naturally assumed that sentences like "Nan can fan Dan" would bring systematic, predictable, regularity to the otherwise chaotic chore of learning to read. Now *linguistics* came to mean two things: noisemaking and repeated noisemaking.

Largely through the efforts of Kenneth Goodman, Frank Smith, and their colleagues and students, a countermovement developed toward the obviously overdrawn focus on language units smaller than a word. The new evidence, impressively researched and eloquently presented, argued against overusing decoding and for moving immediately to syntax processing. Thus, the influence of linguistics was again redefined to include sentence and discourse level processing. The major objection to this healthy infusion of new blood into the analysis of the reading process was that it tended to reject categorically other legitimate language processing units. To be sure, letter-sound correspondences were grossly overemphasized in most reading programs and it may well be that, by paying continuous attention to only the phonological language access in reading, more students were lost from boredom than from ignorance or willful slothfulness. In any case, borrowing their premises from classical generative grammar, Goodman and Smith saw reading as syntax or discourse processing of meaning units, not the one-to-one decoding of sound units. This healthy advance in understanding how language processing takes place in reading was generally referred to as psycholinguistics and reading.

Not to disagree with the excellent notions of Goodman and Smith but to supplement this concept of linguistics, this collection of viewpoints on linguistics and reading was assembled. It is our contention that many aspects of linguistics, besides those of phonology and grammar, can be brought to bear on the act of reading. Sociolinguistics, for example, is one such area. Another is a rapidly developing field of study shared by anthropologists and linguists, generally referred to as the ethnography of communication. In addition, we need to know a great deal more about the interrelationship of children's language acquisition to the ways they acquire reading skills and processing. Recently, the term *pragmatics* has come to be used by linguists to refer to the task of recording and explaining a portion of linguistic reality. Pragmatics is generally concerned with the broader role of context as it is related to the benefits and attitudes of the participants in a communication event. It deals with status relationships and the purpose or intent of this communication.

In one sense of the term, learning to read involves the learning of certain skills which, once learned, must be almost immediately shelved for more cognitive strategies. What happens in the learning-to-read process is that, at the onset of reading, the more behavioral processes tend to dominate; but, as the reader learns more and more about reading, he calls more and more on cognitive strategies, especially those which involve processing larger and larger language accesses. More precisely, at the onset of reading, the reader processes letter-sound correspondences, a skill which one learns primarily in order to begin to deny it in favor of other more cognitive strategies later on.

A schematic illustration of this view of the language accesses involved in the reading process is the following:

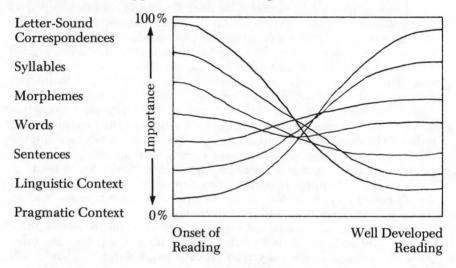

It should be clear, however, that this schematic illustration is not a description based on research but, rather, it is a reasonable estimate of what is likely to be the case once the necessary research has been done. Of particular importance is that it displays letter-sound correspondence as crucial at the onset of learning to read, then decreasingly important as the learning to read process develops. Similar progression can be noted for each of the other language accesses, with particular focus, in the case of pragmatics, on the increasing significance of context and discourse. Note especially that both accesses are available and important at the onset of learning to read but of relatively low cruciality at that time. As the learner continues to progress, however, he calls less and less on the word to subword level accesses and more and more on the language accesses that are larger than word level.

At this point, it should be noted that most language learning activity parallels the learning to read progression, insofar as the early stages of learning are relatively clear cut and show obvious gains, whereas the middle level and advanced stage of language learning are less well known and obvious. That is, in almost every case, the stages in the beginning courses in language learning are relatively well known and measurable but, as the learner progresses, the exact stages in his program become less clear. From a commercial viewpoint, we know considerably more about how to construct introductory courses than we do about how to construct advanced ones.

The parallels to reading instruction should be clear. Historically, we have developed reasonably good onset reading programs but increasingly ineffective advanced ones. Most children who are learning to read show predictable gains during the first year or so and then demonstrate, according to our admittedly weak measurement system, progressive fall off the next few years. One contention of this volume is that a reason for this fall off is that the teaching program continues to focus on onset skill development at stages in which more appropriate strategies would involve larger and larger chunking of the language accesses. A second contention is that a teaching program in reading should be constructed to develop middle-level reading skills, a program which will call on a child's knowledge not only of syntax (as Goodman and others are doing) but also one which will make use of the child's pragmatic knowledge—his knowledge about how language is used.

Among the things that have plagued the relationship of reading to linguistics, the following might be noted:

1. The independent development of the two fields. In one sense, at least, it is necessary for fields to develop independently.
2. It has been difficult for reading specialists to catch up with fast moving developments in linguistics.
3. Linguistics has been viewed myopically as phonology, phonics, or at other low level decoding levels.
4. Linguists have not provided adequate attention to reading as a legitimate field of study.
5. Far too often, linguistics has been viewed as a set of methods or techniques rather than as a content area of reading. This results, at least partially, from the tendency of the field of reading to view itself as a set of methods or techniques.

This volume intends to dispel some false assumptions. It is hoped that linguists will be encouraged by this volume to enter into the arena of reading research and development. For far too long, reading has been ignored by most linguists, permitting many false assumptions about their field to develop. Five areas of linguistics have been singled out for presentation here. Several are somewhat familiar to the reading specialist (phonology, grammatical analysis); others may be new (sociolinguistics, pragmatics). All may present what is thought to be old territory in new light. The authors are all linguists and, however much they might know about their field, they cannot be expected to know what is needed in daily classroom practice. The intention of this book is to suggest areas in which linguistic theory might lead to the development of such practice. That such a procedure requires a next step is not unusual. Ten linguists have reached out to the field of reading with what they know about language and, in some ways, this places them in positions of vulnerability. These writers offer no final words but they do attempt to help us understand their field.

RWS

GRAMMAR

Grammar:
An Important Component of Reading

Don Larkin
Georgetown University

1. GRAMMAR AND READING

In the following few pages I'd like to outline a few of the things that linguistic study leads us to say about the grammatical organization of languages, using English as a case in point. The aspects of English grammar that will be discussed are those that seem to have the most direct relevance to understanding what exactly it is that people must do when they read English. Although I'll be using examples from English throughout this paper, examples from any other language could be substituted. The arguments to be made here are arguments concerning the grammatical organization of human language in general, and not simply, specifically, one particular language.

It is important, however, to begin any discussion of this sort with a warning concerning the linguist's use of the word *grammar*.

When linguists talk of grammatical rules, they don't mean rules that tell you the right way to do something, like the instructions for putting together a model car, the rules of the road, or the rules of etiquette. Rules like these tell you the correct, legal, or preferred way of doing something that you just might manage to do without adhering to the rules at all. A book on etiquette, for example, might tell me the right way to write a thank you note; but chances are I could write one—however clumsily and tactlessly—without reference to the book at all.[1]

Most of the rules of grammar I learned in school—rules about double negatives, split infinitives, paragraph division, writing *cannot* as a single

---

[1] This is not to deny the possibility that there might be some ways of behaving (like curtseying, for example) which lie wholly within the realm of polite or proper behavior, and which, therefore, might be defined, as well as regulated, by a book on etiquette.

word, avoiding the nonplural use of *they*[2]—were regulative rules of this sort. When we use sentences like

> The grammatical way of saying that would be . . . .

> That's not very good grammar.

> Could you fix this up—check the spelling and grammar for me?

we are using the word *grammar* in this regulative sense.

A linguist's grammar, however, contains rules of a different sort. They're more like the rules to a game than the rules regulating other sorts of social behavior. The rules of chess, contract bridge, tag, and soccer serve to define those games. There is no such thing as baseball, for example, without the rules of baseball. The rules create the game rather than simply regulate it.[3] Although I might write a thank you note disregarding every rule of etiquette, I can hardly hit a home run or strike out without following the rules of baseball, since there is no such thing as a strike out or a home run except as defined by the rules.

Similarly, the rules of grammar define (in part)[4] what a language is. They're rules which state how a language is constructed, how it works. A grammar describes what people have learned, when they can be said to have learned a language. It does not describe exactly what people say, but it does define the principles underlying their ability to say whatever they do—just as the official baseball handbook does not describe how any particular strike out was accomplished; though it does define the principles behind all events that can be described as strike outs.

---

[2]It has recently been suggested that the common nonplural use of *they* (*them, their*) as illustrated in the following sentences

    a) If either of Jerry's parents comes in without the other, tell them I'd prefer not to have to have the same discussion twice.

    b) Anyone who gets up in the middle of the night to plant peas should have their head examined.

should be extended as a way of avoiding the use of *he* (*him, his*) in cases where the sex of the referent is unknown:

    c) A new student at our preschool and nursery will soon find his world rapidly expanding.

In cases like (c) *he* is often called an unmarked or neutral pronoun rather than a masculine one. Yet the fact that it is usually opposed to *she* gives *he* a masculine and, therefore, sexist implication even when used in such general contexts. Note that we sometimes make substitutions for other tainted words when they occur in neutral contexts, such as the use of *young* for *old* in sentences like (d):

    d) Mrs. Robeckson is 83 years young today.

[3]The rules of a game do regulate how the game is played, of course. The point here is that they do more than just regulate; they make the playing of the game possible in the first place; they define what it is to be playing baseball as opposed to playing cricket, football, or doing something else.

[4]A language will be defined by more than just grammatical rules; rules concerning phonological structure or pragmatic interaction would need to be integrated into a total language description.

The rules of English will, in many ways, be similar to the rules of Portuguese, Kom, Malayalam, Korean, and other languages. These similarities will (in part) define what natural language is, what is common to all human languages. The grammars of these languages will also differ; and these differences will (in part) define what English is as opposed to Korean, what Malayalam is as opposed to Kom, etc. More than this, a grammar should describe the various varieties of the same language. The sort of English, Malayalam, or Portuguese used by different groups of speakers, by different individual speakers, or even by the same speaker on different occasions will vary greatly. Since the grammatical rules of a language attempt to describe the internal organization of that language, these rules will also need to capture the variation in some way. Thus an English grammar would also define the various styles, dialects, and modes of speaking that make up what is known as the English language. So, unlike the rules of a regulative grammar, the grammar of a linguistic description would not attempt to set up a single "standard" for the language.

From this conception of a grammar as a body of nonregulative, *constitutive* rules (term from Searle, 1965)—rules which describe how a language is organized—it is possible to draw some conclusions about how grammatical studies might be important to an understanding of the reading process.

First, grammatical rules are unlike the rules of games (such as baseball) in that we can't simply hold a conference and decide on what the grammar of English is or what it should be. The rules of English grammar must be discovered. Unlike games, languages are not subject to explicit legislative control. Most everyone (above a certain age) knows a language, and, therefore, knows what the rules of that language are. The rules are, simply, a statement of what someone knows when they know a language. Unfortunately, we can't simply ask ourselves what the grammatical rules of English are; we must deduce them from our verbal behavior. Whenever people use English they are behaving according to the rules of English grammar. They are using their own internalized grammars in order to construct and understand meaningful sentences of English.[5]

It is, therefore, by observing what people say (or by guessing what they could possibly say), that linguists attempt to construct theories about the structure and nature of language. There is, consequently, a lot of room for dispute. Each grammatical theory or version of a grammatical rule must always be open to question, improvement, or outright attack. And there are a lot of disputes, arguments, and counter-arguments carried on by people working in linguistics. It is largely by means of such

---

[5]In their grammatical studies, linguists have concentrated on the structure of sentences and this paper will reflect this concentration. This is not meant to imply any claim that the rules pertaining to structural units larger and smaller than the sentence are of lesser importance.

argumentation that a field moves forward. And we have been able to move and make progress in the study of grammatical structure. But the nature of our activities (and the almost unlimited complexity of our subject matter) means that linguists will never be able to provide reading teachers with a definitive grammar of English as a whole (if any such thing could exist) or even of one specific style and variety of English.

What we can talk about, however, is a view of language that grows out of linguistic studies. It is such a view of the grammatical organization of English, rather than any specifics of English grammar, that I'd like to outline here, while relating it in a general way to the reading process.

2. GRAMMATICAL RULES

I will be concerned here with what linguistic theory has to say about two aspects of what people know when they know a language. Knowing a language involves at least

1) Knowing how utterances in the language are constructed, and

2) Knowing how the various possible grammatical constructions in a language are related to the meanings they express.

The issues for grammatical theory that are raised by these aspects of knowing a language can be put in the form of questions: What syntactic rules are needed to describe the utterances that speakers of English can make? What is the relationship of the meaning of a sentence to its grammatical structure? Grammatically speaking, what is it that speakers and readers do when they communicate successfully in English? Let us take a look at the way that current grammatical theory attempts to answer these questions.[6]

First, it is easy to show that the actual structure of English sentences does not accurately represent their logical content. Consider sentence (1):

1) Several trains were said to have been delayed by the storm.

Here, any description of what is understood by this sentence would include a statement to the effect that *several trains* is, in fact, the object of *delayed*. The answer to the question, "What was delayed?" would be, "Several trains were." But the sentence as it stands, as it appears in the text, represents *several trains* only as the subject of the whole sentence, and not as the object of *delayed*. Five words separate these two terms in (1), and we would be hard pressed to show how this sentence captures the semantic relationship between them if we had to rely only on the structure of the sentence as it appears here. A more "semantic" representation of what this sentence means might be paraphrased by something like (2) or (3):

---

[6]The theoretical outlook is that of generative grammar, generally, and generative semantics, specifically.

2) [Some unspecified person(s)] said that the storm delayed several trains.

3) There are several trains about which [some unspecified persons(s)] said that the storm delayed them.

These paraphrases are rather cumbersome, of course, but using the structure of either of them, it would be fairly simple to show how *delayed* and *several trains* form a meaningful unit. This unity is not directly represented in the structure of (1).

So, in this case, we would want to associate the structure of (1) with the meaning represented by the structure of (2) or (3). As we shall see, that is precisely what grammatical rules, or transformations, attempt to do.

But first, let's define a couple of terms. The actual structure that sentences have as they appear in texts is known as *surface structure.*[7] The grammatical structure of (1) is a surface structure. The structure which captures more accurately what a sentence means is known by several names, *deep structure, semantic representation, base structure,* or *logical structure,* etc., depending upon what school of thought a particular linguist belongs to. For our purposes, let's just use the more common term *deep structure* and treat it as a neutral term. The grammatical structure corresponding to (2) or (3) would be something like the deep structure for (1). So in example (1) *several trains* is a surface structure subject, but a deep structure object.[8]

Grammatical rules (transformations) relate base structures to surface structures. These rules, therefore, capture what speakers and readers of English know about the grammatical structure of sentences, and about how a particular sentence is associated with a particular meaning.

When we talk about relating surface structures with deep structures, it is customary to talk as if we start with a deep structure and then, by successively applying transformations to it, we derive a surface structure. But in reality this is just a manner of speaking. Each sentence simultaneously has a phonological form, a surface grammatical structure,

---

[7]This is a slight oversimplification. Sentences as they appear in texts don't have structures; structures are assigned to them by analysts using particular theories. It might be more accurate to say that the structure of a sentence appearing in a text, as it might be diagrammed, is a surface structure.

[8]Although examples (2) and (3) are given as surface sentences, it would be incorrect to assume that one sentence is the deep structure for another sentence or even that the surface structure of one sentence is the deep structure of another. It so happens that, in certain respects, the deep structure of (1) coresponds more or less directly to the surface structure of the sentences given in (2) and (3), at least as far as the point about *delayed* and *several trains* is concerned. But it also happens that some deep structures have no direct (relatively untransformed) correspondence to a surface sentence. This paper will avoid using examples of such sentences, however, since to do so would involve presenting a whole theory of deep structure representation. Rather, I will use surface sentences to invoke the relevant points of closely related deep structures.

and a deep grammatical structure. The function of grammatical rules is to relate surface to deep structures and to define what is and what is not a possible structure. But it's easier to talk as if we went through a derivation from deep to surface, so I'll continue to talk that way here too.

One way to demonstrate grammatical rules of this sort is to pair sentences that are (almost) identical, except for the fact that a particular rule or set of rules has applied to one member of the pair, but not to the other member. The two sentences will, therefore, be very similar in terms of deep structure, but will show a particular difference in their surface structures. The difference between active and passive sentences, to take a familiar example, is that the rules which form passives have applied to one member of the active/passive pair, but not to the other.

That is, the deep structure of both (4a) and (4b)

4a) Jerry carried the equipment bag.

4b) The equipment bag was carried by Jerry.

would specify *Jerry* as the agent (the subject) of *carry*, and *the equipment bag* as the object of *carry* (what was carried). But in (4a) *the equipment bag* has been transformationally moved to subject position while *Jerry* has been made the object of a preposition.

(In addition to the deep similarities between actives and passives, there are of course certain meaningful differences. Active clauses would sound awkward at best in a sentence like (4c):

4c) With all the speeches that have been given, all the resolu-
     tions that have been passed, and all the editorials that have
     been written, nothing at all has been changed.

I'll limit myself to those aspects of meaning that can most clearly be captured in deep structure representations.)

In the examples below, the first member of each pair has had a rule of Raising applied to it. This rule takes a noun phrase, which in deep structure is the subject of a subordinate cluause, and raises it up to become a member of the main clause (as either subject or object).

5a) I believe Kim to be a genius.
 b) I believe that Kim is a genius.

6a) Kim appears to have been delayed.
 b) It appears that Kim has been delayed.

7a) We appreciate Kim coming in to help out.
 b) We appreciate Kim's coming in to help out.

In the (b) sentences of these examples, Raising has not applied and the noun phrase *Kim* remains in the subordinate clause. In the (a) sentences, however, *Kim* is not a part of the subordinate clause in surface structure at all.

In (5b) and (6b) *Kim* retains its base structure position as a subject of the subordinate clause in surface structure. In (7b), however, it has been transformed into a possessive noun phrase, though here too it retains its status as a constituent of the embedded clause. It has not been raised into the main clause, as it has in (7a).

Skeptics might question whether *Kim* really has been raised to the position of object in the main clauses of (5a) and (7a). These doubts have traditionally been countered by a couple of observations. First, when a nominal occupies the position that *Kim* does in (5a), it can be passivized,

    5c) Kim is believed to be a genius.

and the Passive rule cannot move anything to subject position but an object. Second, if we substitute pronominal forms for the raised noun phrase of (7a), we find that they must be in the objective case:

    7c) We appreciate him/her coming in every day.

    7d) We appreciate his/her coming in every day.

Since example (7c) parallels (7a), and (7d) parallels (7b), we reason that *Kim* must be a surface object of *appreciate* in (7a) too.

Rules have applied in the derivation of the (a) sentences of (8), (9), and (10) which reduce relative clauses, stripping away the *wh*-word and deleting a form of the verb *be*. The (b) sentences have not had these rules apply to them, and their relative clauses remain intact.

    8a) The car in the garage is a Volvo.
      b) The car which is in the garage is a Volvo.

    9a) Sam was a happy man.
      b) Sam was a man who was (characteristically) happy.

   10a) I had an argument with the woman standing by the Coke machine.
      b) I had an argument with the woman who is standing by the Coke machine.

In sentence (9a) an additional rule has repositioned *happy* to the left of *man*. And (10a) demonstrates that the operation of grammatical rules can introduce an element of ambiguity into sentence structures. Since the tense-carrying verb *be* has been deleted from the (reduced) relative clause in (10a), this sentence doesn't explicitly commit itself as to whether the woman is now standing by the Coke machine, as in (10b), or whether she was standing there at some previous point in time, as in (10c) below:

   10c) I had an argument with the woman who was standing by the Coke machine.

Thus, we see that grammatical rules can account for the ambiguity of surface structures, and relate surface form to underlying meaning.

3. THE DIVERSITY OF DEEP STRUCTURE

So far, we have looked at pairs of sentences that have similar (though not exactly identical) deep structures but have very different surface structures due to the fact that certain rules have applied to one member of the pair but not to the other. It would be wrong to conclude from this, however, that grammatical rules serve to associate a limited number of deep structure patterns with a greater number of surface structure patterns. In general, the opposite seems to be true: The variety of deep structures in English (or in any language) is far greater than the variety of surface structures. The things we can say and do and mean in language are greater than the grammatical patterns that we have available to express those things. To demonstrate this, let's look at some more examples. One way to derive the surface structure pattern *modifier plus noun* is by reducing a relative clause, as we have seen by example (9) above. This reduction is relatively straightforward. However, some surface adjectives are deep structure verbs and adverbs. Consider the examples below. (I use an asterisk to indicate an ungrammatical or absurd sentence.)

11a) The former Secretary of State was vacationing in Sumatra.
b)*The Secretary of State who was former was vacationing in Sumatra.
c) The person who was formerly Secretary of State was vacationing in Sumatra.

12a) The captain's a real bore.
b)*The captain is a bore who is real.
c) The captain is a person who is really boring.

13a) This joint venture will be the first of its kind in the Western hemisphere.
b)*This venture which is joint will be the first of its kind in the Western hemisphere.
c) This thing which is jointly ventured (i.e., undertaken) [by some unspecified persons] will be the first of its kind in the Western hemisphere.

14a) George was an occasional visitor.
b)*George was a visitor who was occasional.
c) George was someone who visited occasionally.

Whereas the (b) sentences of (8), (9), and (10) seem to preserve the sense and the grammatical integrity of the (a) sentences, the parallel (b) sentences of (11), (12), (13) and (14) clearly have very little to do with the (a) sentences at all. Rather, the (c) sentences of these last four examples show that in their deep structure representation, the adjectives in question are not adjectives at all. The transformation creating the modifier plus noun surface patterns exemplified by *joint venture, real bore,* and *former Secretary of State* here must also create adjectives from deep verbs and adverbs. Although lexically *jointly* appears to be derived from *joint* plus the adverbial suffix *-ly*, grammatically or semantically the reverse seems to be the case.

Still other adjectives that participate in surface modifier plus noun constructions are derived from nouns that have been preposed and adjectivalized.

15a) Sam has a nervous cat.

  b) Sam has a cat which is (characteristically) nervous.

16a) Sam has a nervous disorder.

  b)*Sam has a disorder which is nervous.

  c) Sam has a disorder of the nerves.

17a) Better urban planning is essential if we are to avoid such crises in the future.

  b)*Better planning which is urban is essential if we are to avoid such crises in the future.

  c) Better planning of cities is essential if we are to avoid such crises in the future.

In (15a) *nervous* appears to be derived as *happy* is in (9a), by a simple reduction of the relative clause. But in (16a) *nervous* must have a different analysis, as the ridiculousness of (16b) shows. Here, *nervous* appears to be a simple adjectivalization of the noun *nerve(s)*. Similarly the adjective *urban* in (17) seems not to be a deep lexical item at all. Rather it appears to be transformationally derived from a deep nominal meaning something like *city*. We can also note here the parallels between adjective plus noun constructions of this sort and noun plus noun constructions where a deep noun has not been adjectivalized on the surface:

electric stove (*electricity stove)—gas stove
financial statement (*finances statement)—bank statement
mechanical engineer (*machines engineer)—traffic engineer
wooden table (wood table)—wood pile (*wooden pile)[9]

This, of course, does not exhaust the various sorts of modifier plus noun patterns in English. It would be possible to extend our list of deep sources for this construction by considering examples like *main route, costume jewelry, reverse discrimination, agricultural expert,* or *racial disturbance.* In all these cases, an identical (and relatively simple) surface structure pattern masks a wide variety of (often complex) deep structure patterns. But to see some of these complexities, let's look for just a moment at the simple adjective *short.* When it is preposed, this adjective can usually be related to a full relative clause:

18a) Bring me three short sticks.

  b) Bring me three sticks which are short.

But look at a sentence like (19a):

---

[9]See Levi 1976 for a fuller discussion of constructions of this type.

19a) In a short three hours we saw five Scarlet Tanagers.
 b)*In a three hours which were short we saw five Scarlet Tanagers.
 c) In three hours we saw five Scarlet Tanagers, and that's a short time to see that many Tanagers.

In this sentence, the adjective *short* participates in a more complex semantic construction—illustrated in (19c)—than it does in (18a). But now consider the difference between the following two sentences.

20a) We were able to meet with Mao for a short three hours.
 b) We were able to meet with Mao for three short hours.

Sentence (20a) seems like (19a) in that the speaker seems to be saying that three hours was a short time to be allowed to meet with Mao, that the speaker would have liked to have spent more time with him. Sentence (20b) seems to say that the meeting was engrossing, that the time went quickly. But in neither sentence does *short* derive conceptually from a simple relative clause as in (18).

Similarly, relative clause reduction is not the only way to derive a noun phrase consisting of a head noun plus a gerund (as in sentence (10a) above). Consider the examples below.

21a) The rule causing all this discussion is silly.
22a) The rule forbidding parties after 11:00 is silly.
21b) The rule which is causing all this discussion is silly.
22b)*The rule which is forbidding parties after 11:00 is silly.

Sentence (21a) can be derived by simple relative clause reduction, as the possibility of an unreduced (21b) shows. But (22a) has a different sort of meaning. There is no full relative clause for the gerund in this sentence, as the impossibility of unreduced (22b) shows.

The point here is simply this: It is not possible to just *read* the meaning of a sentence off of its surface structure. There seems to be a conspiracy of sorts within the English language (and within other languages) to use a limited number of surface structures to overtly express an amazing array of underlying conceptual structures. It is a conspiracy to package a wide variety of very different meanings in very similar surface containers. What we have said here about modifier plus noun constructions and nominal plus gerund constructions would apply to every other surface construction in English. We, as users of English, must do a lot of unpacking to understand what we read. Sometimes the unpacking will be relatively simple. But at other times, the grammar of the sentence will be sufficiently complex or sufficiently unfamiliar so as to cause us problems.

4. UNPACKING SURFACE STRUCTURES

The question now arises as to what tools we use to understand what we read. What information do we have available to us that indicates how a surface structure should be *unpacked*?

Knowing the meanings of the words that are on the page before us and having some knowledge about the real world and the subject matter being discussed helps, of course. We wouldn't expect a disorder to be nervous in the same way a cat is, for example. But this in itself is clearly not enough. Although we bring knowledge of the world to our reading, we also learn about the world from it. It would be strange (not to say nonsensically circular) to say that we must know what something means before we can understand it.

Moreover, the unpacking of surface structures into deep structures is not random; it is not constrained just by what something could possibly mean or what we might imagine the author to mean. The unpacking of surface containers proceeds according to grammatical rule. So, knowing how the sentence we are confronted with is put together on the surface, e.g., knowing that *clean* is a verb in (23a), but an adjective in (23b),

  23a) Kitty likes to clean dishes.
   b) Kitty likes clean dishes.

ought to be an essential ingredient of our ability to understand what we read.[10]

But knowing the surface grammatical structure of a sentence and knowing the meanings of the words in it (and something about what the real world is like) are not in themselves sufficient to tell us what the sentence means. There is some other knowledge involved, the knowledge that is captured in the grammatical rules which connect deep and surface structures.

In order to demonstrate that knowing the meaning of the words in a sentence and some surface grammatical facts about the sentence (like what parts of speech are involved) is not all a reader needs to know in order to unpack a surface structure, let's consider some more examples of sentences with parallel surface structures which don't have parallel understandings.

Consider first the case of two transitive verbs, *resent* and *doubt:*

  24a) He resented the report that the police were corrupt.
  25a) He doubted the report that the police were corrupt.
  24b) He resented it that [some unspecified person(s)] reported that the police were corrupt.
  25b) He doubted that [some unspecified person(s)] reported that the police were corrupt.
  25c) He doubted that the police were corrupt, which [some unspecified person(s)] had reported.

Sentence (24a) means something like (24b); but (25a) doesn't mean anything like (25b). Rather, it has a deep structure more along the lines of

---

[10]I'm not suggesting that a successful reader needs to know the names we give to these word classes, just that the grammarian's distinctions capture some knowledge that a reader must have.

(25c). The parallelism between (24a) and (25a) is, therefore, limited to their surface structures. It is not as if (25b) is an absurd or unreasonable thing for (25a) to mean; (25b) expresses a perfectly understandable idea—unlike the "disorder which is characteristically nervous" of (14b). It is just that (25a) *doesn't* happen to mean what (25b) does. This fact cannot be read off from the surface grammatical structure of (25a) directly. Nor can it be read directly from the meaning of *doubt* (at least not insofar as we usually conceive of the meanings of words).[11] It is rather a fact about the grammatical organization of English. In order to understand sentences like (24a) and (25a) we need to have internalized a knowledge about what sorts of rules may apply to sentences that contain words like *resent* and *doubt* and what sorts of deep structures these words figure in. It is not enough to know just the surface syntax and the meanings of the words in these sentences. A reader must figure out the deep as well as the surface grammar of a sentence.

Let's now consider the case of an adjective and it's lexical negation, *possible* and *impossible*. In some constructions, as in example (26) below, *impossible* seems to be the opposite of *possible*.

26a) Under present conditions, an election is possible.
  b) Under present conditions, an election is impossible.

But it is not always so. Look at example (27).

27a) She's a possible candidate.
  b) She's an impossible candidate.
28a) That she will be a candidate is possible.
  b) That she will be a candidate is impossible.

Sentence (27a) means something like (28a). But the meaning of (27b) is not parallel at all. From (27b) we know that she is already a candidate, not that she might or might not be one. Moreover, we kow that she's hard (or impossible) to deal with in her role as a candidate. Here again similar lexical items are participating in very different deep syntactic constructions with very different grammatical rules. And here again (28b) makes perfectly good sense; but not the sense that (27b) makes, because the grammar of English does not permit a derivation connecting structures like (28b) to (27b).

Sometimes the surface structure of a sentence and the words in it give us very little indication of how it should be unpacked, or how it might be used. Consider the two sentences in (29) and (30), which differ only in that one of them has the indefinite article *a* whereas the other has the definite article *the*.

---

[11]It may well be that it is some fact about the meaning of *doubt* that makes the derivation linking the structures of (25b) and (25a) impossible. In this case, the relevant grammatical information would not be framed in terms of the particular lexical items but in terms of some element of meaning, which might be shared by a number of different lexical items.

29) There's always a quarterback.

30) There's always the quarterback.

The real difference between these sentences is more than just that. Sentence (29) is a relatively straightforward existential sentence. It might be used to answer someone's question about the composition of a football team. Sentence (30) would be used in a quite different situation. It might be used where the coach and his assistants are running out of uninjured players to carry the ball and, as a last resort, someone says, "Well, there's always the quarterback." In this case, we take it for granted that everyone already knows the composition of a football team. Clearly, a reader who mistakes one of these meanings for the other might have done more than just mistake one article for the other.

Similarly, the difference between the conjunctions *and* and *or* seems clear enough. But how does that difference account for the fact that the author of (31), below, wants the joke to be told; but the author of (32) doesn't? The first sentence has an imperative as the first clause but, despite appearances, the second sentence doesn't.

31) Tell that joke again or I'm leaving.

32) Tell that joke again and I'm leaving.

In these pairs of examples two very different deep structures show up with very similar surface structures. It can also happen that two different deep structures are merged into the same surface structure:

33a) Mary asked what I did.

b) Mary asked a question which I also asked.

c) Mary asked: What did I do?

34a) Mohan and Megan are married.

b) Both Mohan and Megan are married.

c) Mohan and Megan are married to each other.

35a) The story that John wrote in England is ridiculous.

b) John wrote a story in England and that story is ridiculous.

c) The story is that John wrote in England and that's ridiculous. (He wrote in France.)

Sentence (33a) may either have a meaning like that given in (33b) or like that given in (33c). That is, the *wh*-clause in (a) may either be a headless relative clause (b) or a subordinate question (c); sentences (34a) and (35a) similarly have multiple "readings." The deep structures corresponding to the meanings given in (b) and (c) sentences have been transformed into the same surface structure, this time without leaving an obvious trace.

We use many different kinds of clues to unpack such sentences: The context, an understanding of the mood and opinions of the speaker, the meaning of adjacent sentences in the text, intonation, knowledge of what is possible or likely in the real world and what isn't, the type of discourse the sentences appear in, etc. A major problem for the area of linguistics that goes by the name *pragmatics* is to discover how the sort of grammatical knowledge being discussed here manages to link up with these other factors to yield a model of linguistic understanding. We need to know how linguistic forms depend on or invoke other sorts of knowledge and how that knowledge is applied to the task of understanding what is said or written.[12]

But no matter what sorts of clues we use to unpack surface structures, the unpacking itself is not random or capricious. It must proceed according to grammatical rule. When we read we do more than recognize letters, words, and grammatical structures. We also understand; that is, we unpack the words and surface grammatical structures we are presented with into something meaningful, into a deeper structure. A grammar which specifies the relationship between deep and surface structures will specify how surface structures can be unpacked. Such a grammar is something akin to a map; it specifies the routes which connect the forms a reader is presented with to the meaning encoded in those forms. Just learning a bit about what such a map is like, or even realizing that there is such a map, is an advance for linguistics.

5. DEEP GRAMMAR AND READING

Now, let's turn to three areas in which the view of grammar that I've just outlined could affect our understanding of certain reading errors or *miscues* (Goodman 1967).

First, it is at least possible that some errors could be best understood in terms of the grammatical rules that relate deep to surface structures. That is, some reading errors might really be unpacking errors, where a reader understands the surface structure of what he reads but fails to connect it with the correct deep structure.

We might imagine several sources for such unpacking difficulties, but it would be reasonable to expect them to occur most typically in two sorts of situations: 1) where the derivation of a particular sentence is especially complex or 2) where it is somewhat unfamiliar. A derivation could be complex either in the sense of having a large number of rules connecting deep with surface structure or in the sense of there being a great divergence between deep and surface structure—that is, what rules there are are complex ones, causing drastic differences in the two structures. Either sort of complexity might contribute to a reader's difficulty. Similarly, if a reader is unfamiliar with a rule that connects the surface with the deep structure of a sentence he is attempting to read—if he has not yet internalized that rule in his own grammar, for example—or if he encounters a familiar rule in unfamiliar surroundings, then too we might expect some reading miscues to occur.

So a reader who is thrown off by *three short hours* or *a short three hours* might not be experiencing the same sort of grammatical difficulty

---

[12]See Peg Griffin's chapter in this volume for a discussion of some of these pragmatic problems.

as one who is thrown off by *three short sticks.* And a reader who substitutes *Kim's* for *Kim* (or vice versa) in a sentence like example (7), *We appreciate Kim coming in to help out,* or *or* for *and* (or vice versa) in a sentence like (32), *Tell that joke again and I'm leaving,* might actually be substituting one whole grammatical package for another. The difficulty might have very little to do with possessives or conjunctions per se, despite surface appearances.

The point here is simply that it is impossible to understand what readers are doing, grammatically speaking, from the surface alone. The grammatical knowledge we apply to texts includes more than the ability to understand surface structures; it also includes the ability to unpack them into deeper structures.[13]

A second area in which the view of grammar outlined above could possibly contribute to an understanding of the reading process concerns a class of miscues that might be termed *misexpressions.*

Once a sentence is successfully unpacked and its meaning is obtained, it is often possible to repack that meaning into a different surface container. Thus, if I am faced with a sentence like (10a) and I read it off as (10b), or vice versa,

> 10a) I had an argument with the woman standing by the Coke machine.
>   b) I had an argument with the woman who is standing by the Coke machine.

it would be clear that I had understood what I read. I would have simply substituted a different surface package—one simpler either in terms of the rules that applied to it or in terms of its surface constitutents—for the one in the text. But in order to make such a substitution, I must have first successfully read (unpacked or understood) the surface structure in the text.

There are, of course, constraints on when and how variant repackagings or misexpressions of this sort can be used. The constraints seem to be mostly contextual. It depends upon what's being talked about, under what circumstances, how, and why. For example, if someone substitutes *wooden* for *wood* in a sentence like (36),

> 36) This picture needs a wood frame.

we could safely assume that the sentence has been successfully read. The same sort of substitution in a sentence that talked of *wood screws, wood stores,* or a *wood pile* would be more disturbing. The adjective *wooden* derives from a reduced relative clause (*wooden table/table which is wooden*) and the modifier *wood* is derived from a deep nominal source (*wood pile/pile of wood*). When we talk of frames, this grammatical difference doesn't matter, but when we talk of postures, screws, or salespersons, it does.

---

[13]Ralph Fasold's and Yetta Goodman's papers from this conference delve more deeply into this question.

Similarly, a substitution of *but* for *and* in (37) would not be a serious misexpression. In fact, since *but* is more explicit than *and* as to the contrasting relationship between the two clauses, it would actually be an indication that the reader was understanding very well indeed.

37) Mary took the train, and I flew.

A similar substitution in (38) however would not fit nearly so well (in most contexts).

38) Mary took the train, and I was sad to see her go.

Misexpressions (substitutions of one surface package for another) might even be a source of encouragement for the reading teacher. We would know, for example, that the reader who substitutes (10a) for (10b) has successfully understood what was being read—successfully enough to allow a repackaging of the meaning in other words. We would know that the reader was not just attending to the text word by word or phrase by phrase. We would also know that the reader had successfully applied the grammatical knowledge he already possessed to the reading task, that the rules which relate full to reduced relative clauses were also a part of his reading competence. Even where a reader uses an inappropriate misexpression, we would know that he is doing what successful readers do—attending to the meaning and deep grammatical structure of the text and not just the surface structure of the words it is composed of. We might also be able to learn something about what he conceives the text to be about.

Finally, any grammatical study leads us to a view of linguistic structure as something that is extremely complex and extraordinarily subtle. The grammatical knowledge that speakers of English have (the grammatical knowledge that we apply to the reading task) is far more intricate than any present theory allows us to describe. It will always be an error, therefore, to try to understand what happens when people read in terms of a narrow grammatical theory. That's probably true even of the sort of transformational grammatical theory I've used here. But it is certainly even truer of any grammatical theory that is concerned primarily with the description of surface structure, or of a theory that seeks to set linguistic standards. We need to approach reading with an idea of grammar that tries to understand the intricacy, variety, and inner workings of natural language.

REFERENCES

Goodman, Kenneth S. "Reading: A Psycholinguistic Guessing Game," *Journal of the Reading Specialist*, 4 (1967), 126-135.
Levi, Judith N. *The Syntax and Semantics of Nonpredicating Adjectives in English*, Indiana University Linguistics Club, 1976.
Searle, J. R. "What is a Speech Act?" in Max Black (Ed.), *Philosophy in America*. George Allen and Unwin, 1965.

Grammar and Reading in the Classroom

Yetta Goodman
University of Arizona

Jennifer Greene
Georgetown University

ONE CHILD'S READING: AN EXCERPT

This article begins with a sixth grader's reading because we believe that the best way to understand how readers use syntactic knowledge is to observe and evaluate their oral reading responses. The excerpt is from Tim's reading of a chapter from *Bristle Face* by Jeffrey Ball. The markings indicate the miscues which Tim produced as he read orally. Miscues are the observed responses which Tim produced which were different from what we expected to hear. We call them miscues rather than mistakes to call attention to the fact that they are not random; they are variations from the text which reflect readers' expectations about what they are reading.

Tim's excerpt is marked so that you can follow what he did. Any substituted word or phrase is written directly over the text. Omissions are circled and insertions are indicated by a caret ($\wedge$). In addition, whenever the reader regressed a line was drawn to indicate the point at which Tim started to regress to the point where he started his repetition. If the repetition was for the purpose of correction a © was placed in a circle and if Tim regressed to anticipate a problem an (RS) was placed in the circle. The (RS) suggests that Tim regressed to give himself a running start in order to move into a subsequent structure.

By the time I got out and over to where they were, he had the cat out of the water and was standing over it watching to see if it was going to make a move. It didn't. I knelt down by my dog, and that was when I saw the blood

all over him   *a*   *rip*
on him. I looked (him over) and found (he was) ripped down both sides and one ear
ⓒ I
(was) chewed almost off, (it) looked like. Blood was dripping from underneath him
o
and I saw (that) his chest and belly were ripped bad.
that   *was going*   ⓒ *him*
    I was afraid at first (that) the panther's claws had gone clean (into) his
that it   *then I*
belly but when I looked closer I could see (they) hadn't. But they had sure-
ⓒ *it*
enough gone deep, (all) right.
at the
    I thought the cat was dead but right then it kicked its legs○ Bristle Face
down
let out a growl (and) was on it and had (it) by the throat quicker (than) I could have
OFF
snapped my fingers.
   it ∧   *and*   *W*
    Now (that he) was out of the water he could do his best°, (and) when those big
down   *crush*
jaws clamp∧onto the cat's throat I could hear the bones crunch. He held
on and (just) kept holding on, biting and biting. I let him do a good job (of it)
while he was at it.

UNDERSTANDING SYNTACTIC STRUCTURES
AND THE READING PROCESS

     Tim made a lot of miscues. His oral performance only approximated what was actually written, and often not very closely, at that. Listeners might well be tempted to judge him a very weak reader. Yet in his retelling of the story, he demonstrated not only that he had understood the bare essentials of the plot, but also as the exchanges in (1) and (2) suggest, that he had become very involved in the unwinding of the story and had developed a noticeable sensitivity to nuances in mood and tone.

1a) Question: Did the boy like his dog?

1b) Tim: Yeah, I guess...but, at first, he thought he was a no account dog—you know, good for nothing—'cause he wouldn't help him catch bait but would just stomp on the worms and stuff...but then after the dog killed that mountain lion...I mean the panther, I think it was, well, then he really felt bad that he had thought bad things about his dog and he really thought that Bristle Face was a really brave dog.

2a) Question: Why do you think that?

2b) Tim: Well, it said that when he thought that the dog might be sick or even die or something that just thinking about it made him almost bust out crying.

That is to say, on some level not superficially (aurally) discernible from his reading performance, Tim was using the clues he found in the chicken scratches of print to successfully interact with the author and actively create the intended message of the story.

Through miscue analysis research it has become evident that Tim's performance may be closer to what actually goes on in silent reading than what we hear in a smooth oral reading performance. It is impossible for us to know, of course, how many of his miscues Tim corrected silently, but what we must conclude from his performance is that he did not need to orally reproduce exactly what appeared in print in order to understand the story. And this in itself is an extremely important lesson. The more we observe the reading process, the more we realize that readers who work on getting meaning bring all of their knowledge of language, all of their relevant life experiences to bear in an effort to make sense out of a heretofore unfamiliar story. To say it a little differently, faced with sentences they have never seen and happenings they have never experienced, they use all they know about language and life to make sense out of the unfamiliar. A lot has been said of late about the burden placed on children who are forced to try to learn to read in the context of experiences they have not had. A child who has never been out of the city trying to learn to read from a book about life on the farm is bound to have trouble. What we have been less aware of until more recently is that young readers use their knowledge of language in a way somewhat parallel to the way they use other life experiences. They use what they know to make predictions about what will occur in print. And because of the nature of language, specifically because similar meanings can be packed in different syntactic structures, they do not need to produce precisely the same syntactic structures that the author wrote in order to understand the author's intended message. Just how much deviation is allowable is impossible to determine out of the context of a specific child reading a specific story. The point here is that as long as we can trust that children are trying to understand what they are reading, we can also trust that they are going to make sure that the language makes sense. In a way, the fact that written language has such an obvious, visible linear order is misleading, for it is too easy to assume that readers must reproduce that linear order exactly in order to understand what they are reading. If that were actually all that was required, the process of reading would be much more passive (require much less of the reader) than we know it to be. Reading is a very demanding activity, requiring the reader to interact with the author to create meaning from the chicken scratches on the page.

There is still surprisingly little known about what actually happens in proficient readers' minds as they are reading. Similarly, very little is known about the steps involved in the acquisition of fluent reading. Some children learn mysteriously easily while others have tremendous difficulty (a fact which could be taken to suggest that teaching methods currently employed don't really have very much to do with the learning strategies children actually use). The ease with which many children learn to read implies that reading is a natural language process requiring the use of the same human cognitive abilities that are involved in speaking and understanding. In order to make learning to read easier for more children, we need to understand the kinds of things that can disrupt this natural process. In the following section we will look at 1) some potential linguistic problem areas for developing readers, 2) the kinds of knowledge they have to enable them to overcome these problems, and 3) why and how we should aim to avoid linguistically overburdening children in the early stages of learning to read. Then, in following sections, we will discuss a specific problem which occurs frequently, explain why it occurs, and suggest some strategies for dealing with it.

WHY LEARNING TO READ CAN BE DIFFICULT BUT OFTEN ISN'T

Militating against children as they are learning to read is the fact that the variety of spoken language they have learned (whether a standard or nonstandard dialect) is going to be different from the written language. Adult written language tends to be syntactically more complex and compact than children's spoken language. Formal-style linguistic patterns which occur frequently in written language are learned late in the acquisition process. The following are some examples of the differences between typical oral and written styles:

3a) Oral: He walked like he was drunk.

3b) Written: He walked as though he were drunk.

4a) Oral: He is allowed to pay his book fine so he can register for classes.

4b) Written: He is permitted to pay his book fine, thus making it possible for him to register for classes.

The following are differences a nonstandard speaker might experience:

5a) Oral: I asked her did she want to help me.

5b) Written: I asked her if she wanted to help me.

6a) Oral: She's the one what gave me a penny.

6b) Written: She's the one that gave me a penny.

In addition to these kinds of differences between oral and written language, there are often differences in order. For example, prepositional phrases, which are usually spoken in final position, are often written initially, sometimes with an additional reversal of subject and verb, as in (7a) and (7b).

7a) Oral: Luis ran down the street and around the corner.

7b) Written: Down the street and around the corner ran Luis.

In addition, there is the fact that specific literary genres, as well as individual authors, have their own idiosyncratic styles. And when we take into account the fact that child and adult language are different anyway (and most published children's stories seem to be written by adults), these dissimilarities between oral and written language can add a lot of weight to the beginning reader's burden.

So, for the moment, we have a rather gloomy picture. But the fact is that the children have a lot going for them to overcome the problem of the mismatch between written and spoken language. The most important is that their receptive competence (their ability to understand language) is significantly greater than their productive competence (the language they actually use). They can understand much more than they would actually say themselves. Second, children tend to learn very early to expect what they find in print to differ from their own language. One kind of evidence of this comes from reports of black children who do not like being given material written in Vernacular Black English because that isn't what is "supposed" to be in books they get in school. We also find such evidence as the following. One youngster read (8a) when (8b) was actually printed:

    8a) Oral: There were no lions about.

    8b) Written: There were no lions nearby.

About used in this sense is almost exclusively a written form, and certainly not characteristic of a child's speech, but this boy was expecting something typical of written language rather than something which would occur naturally in his own speech.

Children expect what they find in written language to differ from what they would normally say, and they have the capacity to understand language they wouldn't actually use themselves. Thus, in at least two important ways, they are prepared for one of the natural consequences of meeting language that is more complex/sophisticated than their own: the expansion of their own linguistic competence. And, of course, it is not by accident that this is one of the goals of education, or that literature is one of the means by which teachers seek to achieve this goal. Although the essential part of language acquisition has taken place by the time children enter school, an important aspect of the role of education is to facilitate the expansion of their linguistic competence, to encourage them to become linguistically more mature and sophisticated. And certainly ideally their experience with written material contributes to this growth. What is crucial is that we avoid making the beginning reader's linguistic task too difficult. We are looking for a unique and extremely delicate balance between two factors. On one hand we have the very important goal of teaching children to read, and on the other we have the goal of expanding their linguistic competence by presenting them with increasingly sophisticated written material. If the material is too difficult, the development of fluent reading will be severely hindered. If the material is too easy, the child's linguistic competence will not receive the challenge it needs for growth. It becomes relevant here to make a distinction between reading and appreciating literature, the latter being a far more demanding art, requiring that the reader be very sensitive to the author's use of language. If our goal for beginning readers is that they get meaning from print, we must be willing to allow them to translate what they see written into language that has meaning for them. This means letting a lot of miscues go as long as readers are getting the main idea. It is by feeling successful at getting meaning that they will come to enjoy reading. In other words, at the start, we want to make their linguistic burden as light as possible. It is only as they become more comfortable with reading that we can begin to use written language to aid the expansion of their linguistic competence.

A FEW ASPECTS OF CONJOINING CLAUSES

In order to give teachers some ideas for practical classroom methodology, we want to turn now to a specific area of syntax-related reading problems. The area involves difficulties young readers have in dealing with complex relationships between clauses as a result of the dependencies created by subordination, embeddings, or complementation of various kinds. First, we will discuss briefly what is going on linguistically and developmentally to cause problems in the understanding of such relationships, and then we will suggest some strategies for dealing with these problems.

Evidence that a problem does exist can be seen in the actual miscues which result from a reader's failure to recognize relationships within complex sentences. In the following miscue examples, collected from proficient secondary school readers, the problem arose because more than one relational word was possible where the miscue occurred, and it was not until much later in the sentence that the inappropriateness of the miscue became evident and was corrected at the point the sentence is terminated by the three dots (. . .).

9a) Text: He went to the store when he was not hungry in order to purchase his food with greater objectivity.

9b) Reader: He went to the store then he was not hungry . . .

10a) Text: It all happened so fast that I could not for the life of me remember that I was supposed to be at the doctor's office at three o'clock.

10b) Reader: It all happened so fast that I could not for the life of me remember what I was supposed to be . . .

Young readers also have difficulty predicting complex relationships between clauses. But their miscues do not show always the same sophisticated processing of the oral reader.

11a) Text: "Don't do that unless you have, to"

11b) Reader: "Don't do that unless you . . . unlis you have to."

12a) Text: He said, "I won't go, though."

12b) Reader: He said, "I won't go through . . .

Cognitively and linguistically they have not reached the level of sophistication that adults have. Mastery of the complex and semantically very precise relationships between clauses linked by such subordinating conjunctions as *although, even though, unless* or *when* comes late and only with exposure to them and practice at manipulating and understanding them. Even when children can read these structures smoothly, they provide evidence when they discuss or retell what they have read that they do not understand the semantic relationships.

This is not to suggest that elementary school children have no means for combining sentences. Very early they acquire the real work horses among the conjunctions: *and, but,* and *so.* And these three are so versatile as to be able to imply many of the meanings of the more precise conjunctions.

In a paper about conjunctions, Robin Lakoff (1971) had some significant points to make about *and* and *but.* Clauses linked by *and* can be either symmetrically or asymmetrically joined. If the conjunction is symmetric (any ordering of the clauses is semantically possible), the clauses must be about the same topic, as in (13), where the topic is housecleaning.

13) Mary vacuumed the living room and Harry mopped the kitchen floor.

If the conjunction is asymmetric (the clauses must be ordered) the common topic constraint can be relaxed somewhat, and the clauses can be either temporally related, as in (14), or casually related, as in (15).

14) Maxwell got up and walked out.

15) Emily saw a police car in her rear view mirror and (she) slowed down considerably.

Categorizing these clauses as strictly temporally or casually related is not quite legitimate; it is true that the reason Maxwell was able to walk out was because he had gotten up, and that Emily would not have slowed down if she had not seen the police car first, but it is fair to say that the relationship between the clauses of (14) is primarily temporal, and that of (15) is primarily causal, and it is certainly true that in both cases, the clauses must be ordered as they are. The unacceptability of (16) is clear confirmation of this point.

16) *The Lone Ranger rode off into the sunset and mounted his horse.

Like *and, but* can also conjoin clauses either symmetrically or asymmetrically. If the conjunction is symmetrical, the semantic relationship between the two clauses involves some kind of opposition, as in (17):

17) Bill is rich, but Phil is poor.

If the conjunction is asymmetrical, the second clause is often the denial of

---

*Lakoff, Robin. "Ifs, Ands, and Buts about Conjunctions," in Charles Fillmore and D. Terence Langendoen (Eds.), *Studies in Linguistic Semantics.* New York: Holt, Rinehart and Winston, 1971.

some expectation that could be assumed to follow naturally from the first clause. For example, the denied expectation in (18)

18) Wilfred is wealthy, but he is unhappy.

is that being wealthy makes one happy. An interesting fact about asymmetrical conjunction with *but* is that although the ordering of the clauses makes a difference semantically, reordering them does not have to result in an anomalous sentence, as can be seen in (19)

19) Wilfred is unhappy, but he is wealthy.

where the expectation is that an unhappy person is not wealthy.

Now let us turn our attention to the differences between coordinate conjunction with *and* and *but*, and subordinate conjunction with *although* and *even though*. We will see that coordinate conjunction is structurally more flexible, semantically less constrained, than subordinate conjunction, which suggests why children have more difficulty becoming proficient users of the latter. Compare sentences (20) and (21):

20) It rained and we had a picnic.
21) We had a picnic and it rained.

Both are acceptable English sentences, cases of simple symmetrical conjunction, but something more complex seems to be going on semantically, in that rain can be understood as a reason for not having a picnic. Actually the sentences are not semantically identical; (20) is a boast about having a picnic in spite of rain, whereas (21) is a complaint about the weather, but what is important to note is that both orderings are good and that *and* is a very versatile conjunction, capable of performing a lot of semantic functions. Parallel kinds of things are going on in (22) and (23):

22) It rained, but we had a picnic.
23) We had a picnic, but it rained.

Both of these are the denial of expectation *but*, the expectations being something like "People don't have picnics when it rains" for (22) and "It doesn't rain when people have picnics" for (23). Further, (22) is like (20) in that it is a boast, and (23) is like (21) in that it is a complaint. Thus *and* and *but* can be seen to be similar in the kinds and number of semantic functions they can perform. Now look at (24) and (25):

24) Although it rained, we had a picnic.
25) ? Although we had a picnic, it rained.

The use of *although* changes the sentences in two important ways. First, a subordinate, rather than a coordinate conjunction has been used, making one clause dependent upon the other. Second, the conjunction is conditional, in fact negatively conditional, in the sense that the clause introduced by *although* gives a condition for the main clause not to occur. The semantics of *although* are significantly more complex than those of *and* and *but*. What (24) says is that it is expected that rain makes people not have picnics, but it rained and we had one anyway. (25) is a possible sentence only in a specific, rather odd context, where people feel that they can control the weather (as children might well); it says that it is expected that having a picnic makes it not rain, but we had a picnic and it rained anyway.

There are definite similarities between (22) and (24), and (23) and (25), in that (22) can (but need not) be understood to imply (24), and (23) to imply (25). However, *although* is far more complex and precise. A quick look at *even though* in (26) and (27) will show that its meaning is very nearly identical to *although*, only somehow a little stronger:

26) Even though it rained, we had a picnic.

27) ? Even though we had a picnic, it rained.

Evidence of this can be seen in the fact that, without the right context, (27) is even more odd than (25).

We know that children acquire proficient use of *and* and *but* before they become proficient with *although* or *even though*. Our purpose here has been to suggest why this might be true. We have focused mainly on the conjoining of only two clauses (It rained. We had a picnic.) in order to demonstrate the versatility of *and* and *but* as opposed to the specificity of *although* and *even though*. Examining the use of the former in a greater number of contexts would reveal an even greater range of meaning. Since *and* and *but* are usable in so many ways and can at least imply the meanings of our more precise conjunctions, children can get by for a long time without the latter.

STRATEGIES FOR OVERCOMING SYNTACTIC DIFFICULTIES

What implications does this discussion about syntax have for classroom instruction? Proficient readers have learned to integrate their knowledge of syntax with the other language systems and do this without the benefit of instruction—many in spite of instructional practices. The motivation to read is overwhelming in a print oriented society and most readers find ways to use what they know about language to develop reading proficiency. However, some readers develop overuse of the graphophonic system as their main focus in reading. They focus on skills such as sounding out, finding big words in little words, structural analysis, syllabication, etc. Often they are using rules which teachers or those who write basal readers believe are true of American English but may not operate in written English even 50 percent of the time. This focus on inefficient rules and on a single cueing system produces readers whose reading is inefficient and laborious. They do not rely on their intuitive knowledge of syntax when they read.

In order to help students become comfortable in using their own language as they read, we must help them focus on the only significant aspect of reading—comprehension. Students must learn that reading is *their* act of communication with an author. They must focus on understanding what the author is presenting to them in the same way that they focus on trying to understand a speaker.

We will propose some strategy lessons which will help readers focus on comprehension. Whenever we plan reading instruction for students and select or write materials for them to read, we must keep two concerns in mind.

1. *Concept load.* If the content of the material is beyond the understanding of the readers, they will have difficulty using the grammatical structures to gain the maximum use of the content.

2. *Complex syntactic load.* If the grammatical structures are unfamiliar to the readers, they have difficulty unpacking the structure or translating the structures into language with which they are more familiar.

Reading instruction can be geared to avoid overburdening children in either of these ways. If the instruction is focusing on introducing new concepts and ideas to the reader, then the syntactic structures should be familiar ones to the reader so he does not have the burden of unpredictable syntactic structures at the same time that he is concerned with new ideas. If, on the other hand, the teacher wishes to introduce unfamiliar or unpredictable grammatical structures, the content of the material should be very familiar to the students.

Our strategy lessons are written for students who have provided evidence that they have difficulty with words or phrases such as *as though, even though, although,* etc.; therefore, the written material used in the lessons will provide students with context which is familiar to them.

Strategy Lesson 1

The following paragraph should be read aloud to the students since it is assumed that they do not often use *as though* in their oral language.

> Leonard plays hockey very well. He always acts as though he is the only good hockey player on the team. He acts as though he is the best hockey player in the world.

Follow the oral reading with open-ended questions which focus on Leonard and his relationship to the other team members. Don't zero in on the target words *as though* initially since the students should focus on understanding the paragraph as a whole first. The open-ended discussion will also provide the teacher with information about which students are comprehending. Through the discussion the students may begin to realize that the word *like* is an appropriate synonym for *as though.* Examples of questions which would elicit concentration on the meaning of the paragraph include: What do you think about Leonard? Do you like him? Why? Why not? Would you like him on your team? Do you know any kids like Leonard? What do you think about them? Is Leonard a good hockey player? Is he the only good player on the team?

After you focus on the meaning of the paragraph, then you can help the students understand that authors have options in writing. They may elect to use certain words or phrases instead of others. Readers also have similar options, as they interpret the author's message. This kind of discussion gives the teacher the opportunity to explore differences between written and oral language which might be similar to the ideas presented earlier in this paper. This discussion can be facilitated by asking the students to explore the different ways the above paragraph could have been written retaining its basic meaning and comparing this to different ways the same message might be spoken.

Strategy Lesson 2

Have the students explore rewriting of sentences so they can continue to see the various options authors have in writing and realize that readers have similar options.

The following is a sample paragraph for rewriting purposes. To extend this lesson, write additional paragraphs which are related to the lives and experiences of the students.

Example

The boys and girls in our class do not like to go on trips together most of the time. The day they went to the zoo they really enjoyed the trip.

Explore with the students how they might rewrite the events of the first pair of sentences into one single sentence without changing the meaning. They might dictate the various alternatives so you or an able student can write it on the board. After a few examples, suggest that they again try to produce a single sentence but this time place the ideas in the second sentence, *The day they went to the zoo they really enjoyed the trip*, prior to the ideas in the first sentence. If none of the sentences include *although* or *even though* add some samples of your own to the list. This should be considered another alternative and not *the* correct sentence.

Example

The day they went to the zoo the class really enjoyed the trip even though they do not like to go on trips together most of the time.

Through the discussion, encourage the students to discuss which of the alternative sentences they prefer and why. They could also explore the way different wordings change the meaning of the sentences and which wordings do not seem to make any difference to the meaning.

Strategy Lesson 3

Use the cloze procedure as an instructional device. The cloze procedure permits the students to use synonyms or even to use a blank for unknown or unfamiliar words or phrases until enough context has been built through reading to understand what the author had in mind.

Use sentences like the following, including blanks where the target structures occur.

Example

Pat's mother said that milk was good for her and she should drink it_____Pat does not like milk.

Tom played ball very well today_____he isn't usually a good ball player.

Explore with the students what words or phrases can go into the blanks and the degree to which different choices change the meaning of the sentences. Point out to the students that they must read beyond the blank to the end of the sentence in order to decide which words or phrases are most appropriate.

Through these three strategy lessons students have been helped to rely on meaning as they read. They were encouraged to use at least four different reading strategies as they participated in the strategy lessons.

1. Concentrate on what words and phrases mean in relationship to the other language cues in the surrounding language environment.

2. Rearrange or transform sentences into language with which they are more familiar in order to understand.

3. Use a blank for words or phrases which are unfamiliar but continue reading to gain sufficient context to decide what the author meant.

4. Use a synonym substitution which would retain the meaning of the written language, for words or phrases with which they are unfamiliar.

In addition to strategy lessons similar to those suggested, there is a necessary part of all reading instruction which will help students expand their use of unfamiliar syntactic structures as they read. Students must have available to them a variety of written materials which may be unfamiliar. As students meet structures which are complex in easy to understand content material, their own language learning capacity will help them expand their receptive control over hard-to-predict or complex grammatical structures. Simply, this means providing students with a variety of reading materials, preferably ones which they can choose themselves. Self-selection assures that the material will be of interest and relevance to the student. Since authors tend to write in unique styles, a variety of written material will guarantee continuous introduction to unfamiliar language structures. Paperbacks, magazines, newspapers, comics, and repair manuals are basic to this approach. There are many reading programs which stress personalized reading with the emphasis on students reading silently a wide variety of materials in an uninterrupted sustained time period. Such programs help the teacher organize and evaluate student silent reading, but more important provide the student with opportunities to expand their understanding of a variety of grammatical structures and thereby to encourage the growth of their linguistic competence.

Developing reading proficiency is enhanced through reader interaction or communication with an author. Language environment must be available whenever reading instruction is developed for students. That is, reading instruction must draw upon language in context rather than using isolated exercises. The strategy lessons use meaningful language situations to give students the opportunity to learn structures with which they are having difficulty. In the last analysis, however, nothing teaches reading better than reading itself.

PHONOLOGY

Generative Phonology: A Basic Model for Reading

Walt Wolfram
Federal City College

INTRODUCTION

There are inherent dangers in attempting to present introductory notions of a descriptive model in a discipline that has undergone as much change as linguistics has over the past couple of decades. Two decades ago, there was a fairly unified version of "structural grammar" thát was, with minor variations, the security blanket for linguistic descriptions. This, of course, was uprooted with the advent of transformational-generative grammar, which challenged many of the tenets held dear by structuralists in the late 1950s and early 1960s. A fairly unitary version of transformational-generative grammar evolved for a few years during the early and middle 1960s. But this has all changed as more specific details and underlying assumptions of the reigning model have come under question. Although this is truer of grammar than it is of phonology, there is little doubt that many qualifications of the earlier interpretation of generative phonology are also in order.

Now this situation presents a dilemma. On the one hand, an honest admission of qualifications that must be made to many of the aspects I would have set forth a couple of years ago might lead to a somewhat frustrating experience for an audience attempting to grab hold of basic principles characterizing generative phonology. I have seen audiences come away from such honest presentations with a deep sense of despair and an inability to grasp even the most rudimentary principles. On the other hand, a clear-cut presentation of unqualified dictums might lead an audience to a false sense of assurance concerning the field. I can still recall my own disillusionment when my second course in linguistics shattered so many of the cherished dictums I had been quoting from my first course.

It would be nice to reach a middle road between the extremes, but realistically one must choose the side on which he wishes to err. I have, I think, chosen to err on the side of limited qualifications and perhaps can cover myself through occasional footnotes and a general introductory remark that many statements that I make should probably be qualified in some way. I hope that the broad qualifying statement as an introduction does not detract from the observation that there are essential underlying principles to be found in looking at phonological systems for a generative perspective.

In a very real sense, the development of generative phonology must be linked with the development of generative grammar. Although it has probably not received as much acclaim as generative types of syntactical analysis, I think it is fair to say that it has changed the way linguists look at sound systems just as significantly as generative viewpoints have affected the way we look at syntax.

WHAT IS GENERATIVE PHONOLOGY?

The initial question asked when confronted with the label "generative phonology" is how one defines such a theory and the way in which it is differentiated from the types of phonological descriptions which were in vogue during the post-Bloomfieldian era of structural linguistics popular during the 1940s and 1950s. In a sense, the remainder of this paper will deal, in detail, with different aspects of this question. But we can preface our discussion by giving a brief introduction to the notion of generative phonology. In using the term *generative phonology*, we are referring formally to statements, rules, or axioms which can produce all but only those well-formed utterances of a language. The goal of such a theory of the sound structure of language is to make precise and explicit the ability of native speakers to produce utterances of a particular language. As mentioned previously, the viewpoint on phonology must be seen as an application of broader claims that have been laid forth with respect to an overall model of language. As such, it extended the units of analysis beyond the limitations set for a phonology during the era of American structural linguistics. The American structural school as practiced by the followers of the Bloomfieldian tradition was largely concerned with achieving what Chomsky (1964:63) classified as the observational level of adequacy. *Observational adequacy* is concerned with giving an account of the primary data, that is, segmenting and classifying the units (the "phonemes" as units in the phonology) of a language. Generative phonology aimed to do more than this by accounting formally for the competence of the native speaker in his language. A description with the goal of accounting for native speaker intuitions attempts to achieve a level of what Chomsky (1964:64) referred to as *descriptive adequacy*. And ultimately, a generative phonology must aim at a principled basis, independent of any particular language, for the selection of a descriptively adequate account of any particular language. The ultimate level of adequacy, *explanatory adequacy,* is consonant with a viewpoint in which linguistic theory is viewed as a special kind of study in psychology in which every capability built into a linguistic theory constitutes a claim that the same capability is built into the language control aspects of the human mind and speech mechanism.

The phonological component of a language model is basically a complex system of rules that apply to a string of elements from syntax and semantics to convert it ultimately to its phonetic form. However one conceives of the organization of other aspects of an overall language model, at least two (and possibly three) bits of information seem essential before the phonological rules can operate. First, there must be lexical representation in which the basic units of the vocabulary (the morphemes) are represented in some form; then, there must be some type of syntactic information which is necessary as the input for the phonological rules. In most cases, it appears that the surface output of the syntax is the input for the phonological rules and, in some models, it appears that there is also some necessary semantic information. The phonological component itself contains rules that can operate on basic lexical representations while taking into account syntactic (and semantic information) in order to arrive ultimately at the phonetic form. Diagrammatically, we may view this as follows:[1]

Lexicon
Grammatical Information
(Semantic Information)
⇩

Surface Output of Syntax
⇩

| Phonological Component |
⇩
Surface Phonetic Information

For our discussion here, the crucial aspects of the above diagram deal with the nature of the rules that make up the phonological component and the phonological form that the lexical units of the language take. These aspects, as a part of a generative phonology, will be discussed in more detail below.

LEXICAL REPRESENTATIONS

The lexical units of a language are an integral part of any description of a language. One aspect of representing each lexical unit (morpheme) is its semantic description or meaning. A particular semantic reading is obviously an essential part of the lexical items found in a language.

---

[1]I have purposely tried (without complete success) to avoid committing myself here to a model that shows the relationship between syntax and semantics. This is a crucial issue in current linguistic theory that is discussed in other articles.

Another aspect of representing the lexical units involves the formulation of syntactic privileges. In other words, a grammar of a language must be able to specify what sorts of units can function as verbs, nouns, etc., in the realization of a grammatical sentence. Still another aspect of the lexicon is the representation of some type of phonological shape for lexical items; that is, each lexical item must have some type of phonetic form. The phonological shape of these units is crucial in understanding how phonological rules operate since it is input for the phonological component. With respect to the phonological aspects of lexical units, the primary question is, What type of phonological information must go into these lexical representations; that is, what should the representations or lexical spellings look like? This becomes an issue of some importance when we observe that some items which we intuitively feel to be related take more than one form. For example, if we look at an item like *electric*, we notice the variation between final *k* and *s* when a suffix such as *-ity* is added, giving us *electricity*. One choice is simply to enter such alternations as a primitive part of the basic lexical item. But if we entered it for an individual item such as *electric*, then we would be confronted with other items such as *elastic*, which show the same alternation when *-ity* is added (*elasticity*). It does not take astute powers of observation to recognize that we seem to have a regular pattern here, in which certain forms ending in *-ic* change a final *k* to *s* when the suffix *-ity* is added. What is more impressive is the productivity of this type of pattern by native speakers of English when confronted with items not usually ending in *ity*. Thus, a native speaker who may never have been exposed to a form like *stoicity* from *stoic* or *rubricity* from *rubric* will automatically alternate the final consonant to follow the patterning of *electricity* and *elasticity*. As we mentioned previously, a generative phonology must account for the competence of a native speaker of a language in the sounds of his language in a precise and explicit way. In attempting to apply this principle to how we represent lexical items, it seems that the most efficient system would be one which places only unique information into the lexical item and allows general principles of sound organization to account for all predictable variations. In this way, we can account for the underlying sameness of certain units and the generality with which processes affecting change are observed to operate. The lexical spelling or representation for each form should, of course, allow us to most efficiently account for all the necessary changes that will take place. Although some of these units may be one of the alternate forms, this is not a necessary requisite; in some cases, a nonrealizable form may serve most efficiently as the unit from which all the variant forms can be predicted. The basic form of the lexical entry is sometimes referred to as the *underlying representation*, since it is the elemental unit in the structure from which other forms can be derived. Although there are rather detailed types of motivations for choosing the actual form that the underlying representation should take, the determination of efficient lexical representations is a cornerstone of generative phonology. In one sense, the notion of underlying representation as distinguished from surface phonetic forms is analogous to the distinction in syntax between deep and surface structure. In this conception, the underlying representation is an abstraction from which the various phonetic forms of an item are eventually derived through the process of applying the various phonological rules.

In structural phonology as practiced in the previous several decades, it was the *phoneme* which was considered to be the basic unit in phonology. Phonology was seen to be clearly separated from grammar and the phonemes of a language were determined apart from any considerations of grammar. This is not to say that linguists during this period did not recognize that certain alternating forms of morphemes were defined on the basis of phonological conditioning, but these alternations were considered to be a special part of the grammar (morphophonemics). When a phoneme was defined, it was not considered with reference to morphological considerations. And although the phoneme was considered to be an abstraction on one level, phonemes were considered to be uniquely realized in terms of one set of phonetic forms. In generative phonology, the level of the phoneme was redefined so that it could match the deeper level of abstraction aimed for in the most efficient conception of phonological processes—one which could account for *all* different types of phonological conditioning found in a language. This redefined notion of the basic unit in phonology has sometimes been referred to as the *systematic phoneme* in order to distinguish it from the classical level of the phoneme.

The important notion to remember here is that the systematic phonemes are the basic units in the lexical representation and that they are represented in such a way to efficiently allow for all the predictable phonological information to be accounted for by the phonological rules. If phonological information is unique to a lexical item, as it is distinguished from the other lexical items of a language, then it is to be represented; but if it is predictable, then it should not be represented in the basic entry. Thus, the difference between *s* and *k* would be represented in items like *sill* and *kill* since there is not a predictable process for arriving at the *s* and the *k*. It is unique information which is crucial to distinguishing different lexical items. But in forms like *electric* and *electricity* and *elastic* and *elasticity* the *s* is predictably derived from *k* when the suffix is added to the related forms. Hence, the predictable change should not be a part of the lexical spelling of an item. As we shall see in the presentation of Vaughn-Cooke, the notion of lexical representation as presented here has important implications for the most efficient spelling system of English.

PHONOLOGICAL RULES

If the task of the lexical spelling in a language is to give only the unpredictable phonological aspects of each item (morpheme) in such a way as to most reasonably and naturally account for predictable information, we still need to account for the regular patterning that can predict the needed information in order to arrive at actual pronunciations. This is the job of the phonological rules—to account for the predictable aspects of pronunciation whether they relate to alternate pronunciations of the same basic morpheme or different phonetic forms that a given sound can take. To begin with, there are properties of particular sounds which are implied by others. We know, for example, that English has sounds produced with the tongue in a more backed position such as *u* and *U*, and ones in which it is produced with the tongue in a more fronted position such as *i* and *I*. As a concomitant of the back sounds, we also know that the lips may be rounded during the production of the sound, but in the production of the front vowels of English, no rounding typically takes place. This is not true of all languages, of course, since a language like French or German can produce front sounds with a rounding of the lips (the so-called umlaut sounds). Since the information about rounding is predictable for English is implied by the position of the tongue, such information is redundant in the lexical representation for English and therefore to be accounted for by some aspect of phonological rules. Rules which account for this sort of information are referred to as *redundancy rules*. In this case, the redundancy rules predict some attributes of a sound segment based on the attribute of another property. The significance of this aspect of a phonological description will make more sense when we introduce the notion of distinctive features later in the paper. At this point, it is sufficient to note that certain aspects of an adequate phonological process are needed to account for predictable attributes or properties of a sound unit. In addition to the prediction of certain properties of a sound which are implied by other properties, some aspect of phonology should relate to predictable information about the permissible sound sequences that may occur in a language. For example, if a three consonant sequence occurs at the beginning of a morpheme in English, we know that the first sound in the sequence must be *s*, the second a stop like *p*, *t*, or *k*, and the third sound *l* or *r*. This is a regular pattern that any native speaker of English would be able to recognize. Given certain potentially new words in the English language, this principle accounts for the fact that the native speaker will accept an item like *splot* or *scrat* while rejecting items like *fplot* or *snrat* as legitimate sounding words in the English language. Rules which account for the placement of redundant information in terms of the sequences of units are sometimes referred to as *sequence redundancy rules* (as opposed to *segment redundancy rules* mentioned above) or *morpheme structure rules*. It is essential to account for this type of information explicitly in a generative phonology since we must account for the native speaker's intuitions about the types of permissible sequences of sounds in his language as distinguished from impermissible sequences.

Although the above types of information are ultimately an essential part of a generative phonology, we primarily will be concerned here with another type of rule which accounts for all the predictable changes that take place in phonological units when certain morphemes are combined into words or certain sound sequences are juxtaposed. There is a general principle which is universal in all sound systems: sounds tend to be influenced by their environment. By environment, we are referring specifically to the influence of neighboring sounds—the position in which a sound occurs in larger units such as a syllable, morpheme, word, phrase, or sentence, and the occurrence of certain suprasegmental units such as stress or intonation. Ultimately, the modification of sounds seems to follow natural principles related to physiological or psychological strategies.[2] For example, some of the explanations may be due to the coordination of different muscles within the vocal mechanism. Others may be due to perceptual strategies that take place to optimize differentiation between units for the speaker and hearer to most efficiently make use of language in communication. There are a number of main types of processes which can be delimited in characterizing the types of phonological changes that are found in language. Since this is the essential aspect of the phonological rules, it is therefore instructive to delimitate some of the main processes with illustrations from English. Similar types of illustrations could have been taken from any number of languages. As we shall see in the interpretation of this paper for the role of spelling in English by Vaughn-Cooke, an understanding of these predictable phonological processes must serve as a basis for determining the nature of regular spelling patterns observed in English.

Assimilation

In assimilation, a sound takes on the characteristics of a neighboring sound. A sound may assimilate in several ways. For one, sounds may take on the position point of articulation of a preceding or following sound. Consider the forms of the negative prefix -in in the following items:

indeterminate	*immaterial*
indignity	*inconclusive*
impotent	*ingratitude*

In the examples, we note that the nasal segment of the prefix tends to change to the point of articulation of the following sound. In the case of a labial sound such as *m* or *p*, the pronunciation becomes *m* as represented in the spelling of *m* before these items. In the case of *k* and *g*, the sound typically becomes an [ŋ], the segment usually represented by the *ng* spelling of *sing*. It should be noted here that the speaker of English will automatically pronounce it this way regardless of the fact that it is spelled with an *n* before a sound produced at the back of the mouth such as *k* or *g*.

A sound may also take on a particular manner of articulation from an adjacent sound rather than the point of articulation. For example, if

---

[2]The delimitations of these natural principles is one of the areas linguists are most actively pursuing at this point in the study of phonology.

we look at how certain plurals are formed, we can notice the assimilation of the voicing specification in the plural suffix to the preceding sound. Consider the following words:

[kæts][3]	cats
[taps]	tops
[pæks]	packs
[kæbz]	cabs
[lɪdz]	lids

The above examples illustrate different plural suffixes that are dependent on the voicing of the preceding segment. This aspect of plural formation is but one part of a more general rule for suffix formation in English in which suffixes beginning in a consonant must match the voicing specification of the preceding consonant. This is true for the addition of regular -ed forms as well as the different types of suffixes involving some form of -es suffixation (i.e., plurals, possessives, and third person singular present tense forms). Note how the rule patterns for the -ed forms in the following examples.

[pɪkt]	picked	[brægd]	bragged
[ræpt]	rapped	[ræzd]	razzed
[pæst]	passed	[ript]	reaped

The same general assimilation pattern we observed to operate for plural forms is found to operate for -ed forms as well. Regular assimilation processes such as these are quite productive in English, allowing us to predict how a native speaker of English would form suffixial forms for new items in English. Thus, given some nonsense verb forms like *blick*, *blag*, *fup*, or *feb*, or some nouns like *wuck*, *wug*, *stap*, or *weeb*, we would expect the past tense and plural formations respectively to be as follows:

[blɪkt]	blicked	[wəks]	wucks
[blægd]	blagged	[wəgz]	wugs
[fəpt]	fupped	[stæps]	staps
[fɛbd]	febbed	[wibz]	weebs

The formation of these forms simply follows the operating rules of assimilation already learned as a part of the English sound system. And note here that these forms predictably would be pronounced with the application of the assimilation process regardless of the fact that the actual spelling of the forms is consistently -s or -ed.

There are, of course, many different types of assimilation processes, so that consonants assimilating to the point or manner of articulation of an adjacent consonant is simply illustrative of a number of different types

---

[3]All the transcriptions throughout this paper represent broad phonetic transcription and are not intended to include phonetic details irrelevant to our discussion.

of assimilation. Vowels may assimilate attributes of other vowels, or consonants may assimilate certain properties from adjacent vowels. Thus, the change of a final *k* consonant in items like *electric* and *elastic* as described previously involves a process in which *k* becomes *s* before a high front vowel of the suffix *ity*. Before a nonhigh front vowel such as that occurring in the suffix *-al* (*electrical*), such a change does not take place. The change to *s*, then, may be viewed as a consonant in the back of the mouth changing to one produced closer to the production of the following vowel. Such types of processes are not at all uncommon in English, as in other languages.

Neutralization

In neutralization, phonological distinctions operating in a language are reduced in certain types of environments. Like other types of phonological processes, the conditioning environment may be related to its position in higher level units (syllable), contiguous segments, or suprasegmental units such as stress. Basic consonant and vowel contrasts may both be affected. For example, in some dialects of English, the contrast between *t* and *d* may be neutralized when occurring between vowels when the following syllable is unstressed. In such cases, a flapped sound may be utilized for both *t* and *d*. All of the following items may be pronounced with this flap regardless of whether the underlying form is *t* or *d*.

[bæ ſe]	batter
[b æ ſe]	badder
[læ ſe]	latter
[læ ſe]	ladder

In the case of items like *batter* and *badder*, it is quite reasonable to assume that an underlying *d* exists in *badder* because of its derivation from *bad* and an underlying *t* in *batter* because of its derivation from *bat;* yet the actual pronunciation of these two items in casual style may be identical.[4] This particular neutralization is affected by the surrounding environment as it intersects with particular types of stress patterns.

In English, a great deal of neutralization can be observed with reference to vowels. Some of these are peculiar to different regional and social varieties of English while others are found generally in all dialects of American English. In many Southern varieties of English, the vowels *I* and *ɛ* are neutralized before nasals like *m* and *n*. A Southerner will therefore pronounce *pin* and *pen*, *tin* and *ten*, and *tinder* and *tender* identically. In other types of environments (as in *bit* and *bet*), the contrast between these vowels will still be retained since neutralizations such as these are typically restricted to certain phonological contexts.

---

[4]There are other dialects of English which distinguish these words by the length of the preceding vowel. In some of these cases, the contrast between *t* and *d* may be neutralized, but the vowel length keeps the words from being homophonous.

One very widespread neutralization of English vowels concerns the reduction of many different vowels to a schwa-like vowel when occurring in unstressed syllables. If we thus take an item like *telegraph* or *photograph*, we note that the first syllable receives primary stress, the second syllable is unstressed, and the third syllable secondary stress. These items are usually pronounced something like [télǝgræf] and [fówtǝgræf], so that the schwa-like vowel occurs in the unstressed syllable. But if we add a *-y* suffix to these items so that the second syllable is now stressed, we get something like [tǝlégrǝfi] and [fǝtágrǝfi]. Note that the first and third syllables are not unstressed; consequently, they are reduced to schwa. Although there are elaborate rules for assigning stress to effect such vowel neutralizations that have been worked out by Chomsky and Halle (1968) and further refined by Halle (1973), the important point to note here is the systematic process of neutralization in which unstressed vowels become a schwa-like vowel. Again we should note here that these vowels will automatically be neutralized according to the stress patterns and regardless of the underlying lexical spelling of the vowel.

Deletion

In the process of deletion, elements which are posited to exist in the lexical representation of units are lost in particular types of environments. In many cases, deletion processes result in a change of the syllable structure in such a way so as to arrive at more "basic" syllable structures. For example, some processes may delete segments in order to arrive at a simple CV sequence since there is a tendency for languages to prefer such sequences. Deletion processes, then, may break up clusters of consonants and vowels in the direction of these more basic patterns. For example, if we look at the alternation of the indefinite article in standard English, we note that the article *a* occurs before items beginning with a consonant and *an* before items beginning with a vowel. By distributing the different forms of the article in this way, we can see how the preferred CV sequence is retained in English, since the distribution prevents the occurrence of CC and VV sequences. If we posit the *an* as the underlying lexical form, the *n* can be seen as a deletion process which arrives at the more basic CV pattern.

In English, some of the deletion processes like the above are quite commonly recognized. Thus, the different types of contraction processes which account for items like *He's made it, He'd fallen, He'll come,* and *He'd come* seem to be derived through general deletion processes. Under certain relatively unstressed conditions, morpheme-initial segments like *h* (*have, had*) and *w* (*will, would*) may be deleted. In a different deletion process, the vowel nucleus of these items (which is changed to a schwa-like vowel when unstressed) is also deleted, along with the vowels of other types of auxiliaries such as *is* and *are*. This process, then, accounts for forms like *He's ugly* and *You're ugly* occurring as contractions along with the previously mentioned items whose underlying forms began with the segments *h* and *w*. Although there are a number of details which would have to be considered in a full account of these processes, the well recognized contractions of this type represent important deletion processes taking place in the phonology of English.[5]

While deletion processes of the above types are often recognized on a conscious level by speakers of English, there are other types of deletion processes which take place in casual speech that are sometimes not pointed out. For example, consider the following forms as they may be pronounced in casual conversation by speakers of standard English.

[wɛs sayd]	west side
[wɛst ɛnd]	west end
[blayn m æn]	blind man
[blaynd ay]	blind eye
[wayl gus]	wild goose
[wayld ɛnd]	wild end

In the above examples, we first note that all the deleted segments consist of the final member of a consonant cluster and the end of a syllable. We further note that the final member of the cluster is only deleted when the following word begins with a consonant. If the following word begins with a vowel, the rule cannot apply. The effect of the rule reduces the number of consecutive consonants so that three successive consonants are reduced to two. Deletion processes of this type are relatively common in a casual style of Standard English, even if they are not always recognized overtly.

There are other types of deletion processes that are sometimes not recognized because of a failure to recognize the relationship between derivative forms in the lexicon of a language. In some cases, the alternations between these forms suggest how particular units in the lexicon should be most efficiently represented to allow for the general phonological processes to operate. For example, look at the relationship between the forms given below:

[sayn]	sign
[sígnəčÙr]	signature
[rɪzáyn]	resign
[r.ɛ̀zɪgnéysen]	resignation
[dɪzaýn]	design
[dɛ̀zɪgnéyšən]	designation

If we recognize that forms like *sign* and *signature, resign* and *resignation,* and *design* and *designation* are related in the lexicon of English, we will note that only when a suffix like *-ature* or *ation* is added is the *g* actually pronounced. If we posit an underlying *g* in an item like *sign,* a

<hr>

[5]For more complete details concerning the actual deletion processes that account for contraction in English, the interested reader should consult Zwicky (1970) and relevant sections of Labov (1969).

reasonable postulation because it is needed in derivative forms of the item, then it must be deleted when these types of suffixes are not added. When looked at in closer detail, then, certain spellings with so-called "silent" letters of one type or another seem to relate to underlying forms to which various deletion processes have applied.

Coalescence

Coalescence seems to be a specialized type of process which involves both assimilation and reduction. In this process, two or more segments are replaced by one segment that shares characteristics of the original units. A typical case of coalescence in English can be observed in the attachment of the -ion suffix to different forms. Consider the following examples:

[rəbɛ́lyən]	rebellion
[dəmɪ́nyən]	dominion
[dɛ̀mənstréyšən]	demonstration
[ərówžən]	erosion
[kənfyúžən]	confusion

In the first three examples, involving lexical items that end in *l* or *n*, we note that the suffix contains the palatal *y*; but in the items ending in *t*, *d*, *s* and *z*, the final segment coalesces with the *y* to form a corresponding palatal fricative, either [š] or [ž], depending on whether the final segment is voiced or voiceless. In the latter case, the segment combines features of both of the original segments while resulting in a segment different from both (ty→š, sy→š, dy→ž, zy→ž).

A different sort of coalescence involves the double consonants. In this instance, double consonants are coalesced into one segment. In casual speech style, double consonants involved in words like *illegal* and *irresponsible* are realized as a unitary segment. In some cases, the coalescence can only operate after operation of other rules which effect assimilation. Thus, when we look at a form like *usta*, we see first that the original [zd] pronunciation of *used* assimilates to the voicelessness of the following *t* in *to* (i.e., *ust ta*). This results in double *t*'s. Once this has taken place, the two *t*'s are coalesced into one segment.

Epenthesis

In epenthesis or addition, a sound segment not posited in the lexical representation of items is inserted through a regular phonological process. Epenthesis seems to occur less frequently than a process like deletion, but it is by no means uncommon. Both vowels and consonants may be inserted in an epenthetical process. One process which a number of linguists consider to be epenthetical involves the formation of plurals in English. In our previous discussion of assimilation, we noted that two different realizations of plural, namely [s] and [z], were dependent on the voicing specification of the previous sound segment. But the observations made earlier do not account for all the regular plurals in English. In addition to the forms mentioned previously, there are plurals that insert a vowel between the final consonant and suffix, as illustrated by the following examples.

[bəsɪz]	busses
[rowzɪz]	roses
[disɪz]	dishes
[maečɪz]	matches
[jeǰɪz]	judges

In the above examples, we note that the vowel (which may be [ɪ], [ɨ], [ə] or even [E], depending on the dialect of the speaker) is inserted only when the sound to which the suffix attaches itself is a sibilant sound of some type. This includes items like [ǰ] and [č] since phonetically they actually consist of two sound sequences, the final member of which is either [š] or [ž]. From the standpoint of perception, it is quite understandable why this epenthesis might take place since the addition of [s] or [z] to an item already ending in the same sound would end in a doubled or lengthened segment, and this might be difficult to perceive as a plural (e.g., [rowzz] or [bəss]). By adding the vowel, the plural formation is quite clearly marked.

The insertion of the vowel in plurals is part of a more general process which applies when a suffix begins in a consonant quite similar to the one in which the base form ends. Thus, forms that add the -ed suffix indicate a similar type of epenthesis even though the consonant forms involved are quite different. We therefore get the following past tense forms.

[weyʃɪd]	waited
[reyʃɪd]	raided
[plæntɪd]	planted
[mayndɪd]	minded

If the base form ends in a *t* or *d* (i.e., an alveolar stop), then the vowel will be inserted to keep a double *t* or *d* from occurring; otherwise, *t* and *d* would be added following the assimilation processes described earlier.

There are also some types of consonantal segments which are most adequately accounted for as a type of consonantal insertion. For example, when certain nasals are followed by a consonant, a stop segment matching the point of articulation of the nasal may be inserted. The *p* in items like *contempt* and *attempt* can therefore be accounted for through its insertion following a nasal and preceding another consonant. Similarly, the insertion of *b* between *m* and *l* in some contexts seems to be a reasonable way to account for items like *trembling* and *humbly* as found in the speech of speakers of Standard English. The pronunciation of *family* and *chimney* as *fambly* and *chimbly* respectively by speakers of some Non-standard English varieties can be viewed as an extension of this general epenthetical process.[6]

Sometimes, particular segments can be derived through a process of either deletion or epenthesis, depending on how the form of the lexical representation is postulated. In some cases there are strong arguments in terms of the overall structure of the sound system for choosing one process over the other, while in other cases, reasonable arguments can be made for either interpretation.[7]

Redistribution

Some processes of phonological change involve the redistribution of segments with respect to each other. In one sense, some of the previously mentioned processes such as deletion and epenthesis involve changes which result in the redistribution of different CV sequences. It is also possible, however, to simply change the linear order of segments in a phonological structure by permutations of one type or another. In English, these sorts of reorderings do not appear to be that frequent, although there are several illustrations found in some nonmainstream varieties of American English. When two segments reverse positions, the process is typically known as *metathesis*. Pronunciations of *ask* as *aks,* as is found in some varieties of Vernacular Black English and Appalachian White speech, represent such a process. Historically, of course, we know that the older forms of English were *aks,* so that the metathesis really took place among speakers of Standard English varieties where the form changed to *ask.* The pronunciation of the Biblical name *Abednigo* as *Abendigo* involves a metathesis of *n* and *d* that can be found among many speakers of standard varieties of English. Nonstandard pronunciations of *relevent* and *revelant* involve a type of metathesis that changes the order of non-contiguous consonants. Although the permutation of elements appears to be quite common in the grammatical system of English (e.g., *He put the garbage out* or *He put out the garbage*), it is much more restricted in the phonological system.[8]

---

[6]For details on the actual conditions under which this epenthetical process can take place, see Bailey (1973:227).

[7]The case of the [ᵻz] plural is a case at point here. Some linguists maintain that the basic lexical representation should be [ɪz] and that [ɪ] should be deleted, whereas others make a case for considering the [ɪ] to be epenthetical. Ultimately, such differences by the naturalness with which it accounts for the data and the efficiency in terms of how the rules deriving the various forms are arrived at.

[8]We should be careful here to distinguish between regular metathesized segments that are part of the rules of a particular variety of English and metathesis as a reflection of a performance factor of some type (a "slip of the tongue"). It is well-documented (cf. Fromkin, 1971) that many types of performance errors, as well as certain pathological speech conditions, are characterized by metathesis.

THE FORM OF PHONOLOGICAL RULES

In the previous sections, we have discussed the status of lexical representations in a generative phonology, the types of rules necessary to arrive at the actual phonetic forms, and the types of phonological processes found in language, as exemplified by English. At this point, we may ask about the form of rules that can capture the various phonological processes that we have discussed. Presumably, there are different sorts of formal conventions that might be utilized in order to capture the various processes, so that the actual formalization is less significant than the actual principles of phonology. Nonetheless, formal conventions that make rules look like "mathematical formulas" can provide an explicit means of capturing the general principles observed in phonological processes. There are several essential aspects which must be captured in any phonological rule in a generative phonology. First, there must be an input in terms of basic elements of the sound system. Ultimately, these elements start with the units in the lexical representations that we discussed earlier. Then, there must be a change to arrive at various alternate forms, the output of a phonological process. And finally, there must be a relevant environment for changes to take place in, since we have already observed the importance of linguistic environment in determing various changes. These facts may be captured in a simple type of convention which takes the form of the following.

$$X \rightarrow Y \: / \: A \underline{} B$$

In such a convention, X is the input for the rule and the arrow indicates that it is changed to or "becomes" Y, the output of the rule. The slant line / indicates that anything beyond that point is relevant environment for the rule to operate. If the relevant environment precedes the sound, then it is placed before the "environmental bar" (i.e. the line____) and if the following environment is relevant, then it is placed following the bar. In other words, the convention captures a change of AXB $\rightarrow$ AYB. The processes we described earlier can be formalized by the use of such a convention. Thus, for example, the rule which neutralizes (changes ε to ɪ before a nasal) might be stated like the following. For convenience here, we shall assume that the rule only operates before n, even though we know it can also operate before other nasals.

$$\varepsilon \rightarrow \textsc{i} \: / \underline{} n$$

The rule simply states that E becomes I when followed by the nasal n. Other types of processes such as deletion or epenthesis can also be captured by such conventions. We thus might approximate the rule which deletes underlying g in items like *sign*, something like the following

$$g \rightarrow \emptyset \: / \: V \underline{} n\#$$

where ∅ is a null symbol indicating deletion in the context of a preceding vowel and a following n plus a special type of morpheme boundary.[9]

---

[9] The "special" type of morpheme boundary is needed here in order to allow the rule to operate when a suffix like plural is added (e.g., [saynz]) while prohibiting it from operating when a suffix like *-ature* is added ([sɪgnəčUr]).

More important than the formal convention for specifying such rules are the particular generalizations in processes that can be captured through the convention. Such rules are written in the form of *process statements*. That is, we start with a basic unit found in the various lexical representations and process it in various ways in order to eventually end up with the acutal pronunciations of the items.

It should be pointed out here that process statements as a descriptive device were not unique to generative grammar. Before the development of generative phonology, there was already an existing tradition in linguistics for describing various forms of a morpheme through what was known as "item and process" descriptions.[10] But there are important ways in which the types of process statements formulated in generative phonology were different from the types of process statements done during the structural period in linguistics. In the first place, there was commitment to this type of description inherent within the theoretical view on which the transformational-generative model of language description was based. Previous types of descriptions often appealed to process statements only for the sake of methodological convenience. Therefore, a justification of the sort, "There seems to be no reason why the linguist should not use whatever method best suits the situation" (Elson and Pickett, 1962:46) was considered sufficient. The emphasis on a convenient methodology for segmenting and classifying units was primary in the structural period, whereas an explicit theoretical model was given primacy in the developments that took place in generative phonology.

Second, the level of abstraction in terms of the basic units of the sound was different in the two conceptions of process descriptions. One of the realized forms was considered to be the base in earlier process formulations. As Gleason (1961:82) put it, "Select one allomorph of each morpheme as a *base form*." Generative phonology was allowed to be more abstract so that no such restriction was placed on the base forms. And in the older framework, the distribution of different forms of a morpheme (*allomorphs*) that were sensitive to phonological environment was viewed to be an intermediate level which was actually part of the grammatical component of a language at the same time it has obvious relationships to the phonological changes occurring in a language (hence, the term *morphophonemics* was given to explain this level). In the structural conception of language model, the phonology was to be clearly separated from the grammar of a language, and justifications of various units was to be made without reference to other levels of language such as

---

[10]Compare Hockett's classic article (1953) on different types of processes utilized in grammatical description. As Hockett points out in his article, item and process types of descriptions were actually older than distributional statements following the tradition of what had been labeled "item and arrangement" (the simple description of elements in terms of their distributional occurrence with other elements). And while item and process statements were utilized to describe the occurrence of some phonologically conditioned variants of a morpheme, the description of the phonemes of a language during the structural period were typically confined to item and arrangement types of statements.

grammar. In terms of the phonology itself, the phoneme was the primary unit and changes in phonemes that interacted with the different forms of a morpheme were somewhat out of place in the phonological level of a language description. In generative phonology, the basic unit in the phonology was more abstract, and all phonological changes, regardless of their sensitivity to morphological variation were considered to be an appropriate aspect of the phonological rules of a language.

The third important difference between earlier process types of descriptions and those found in generative phonology relates to the notion of *rule ordering*. As various phonological processes were looked at in relation to one another, it became apparent that a perfectly concise and explicit model of phonology would have to order at least some of the rules with reference to each other in order to arrive at the actual phonetic forms. By ordering here, we are referring to the placement of rules in a particular sequence so that one rule operates after another one. A number of the processes we described earlier have to be ordered with respect to other rules in order to arrive at the actual phonetic forms. For example, in order to allow certain non-schwa vowels to reduce to schwa, we first have to have a block of rules which move the stress from a vowel in order for it to reduce to schwa. In items like *telegraph* and *photograph*, the stress placement that moves the primary stress to the second syllable with the addition of the *-y* suffix (*telegraphy* and *photography*) must take place before the vowel in the first syllable can be reduced to a schwa-like vowel. And we have already alluded to the fact that the rule reducing consonant doubling in an item like *usta* from *used to* must first have a rule which changes the original *d* in *used* to *t*. If we arrange the rules in this way, we can have a quite general rule which affects a great many double consonants.

To illustrate further, consider the pronunciations of plural forms of *desk* and *test* as *desses* and *tesses*, well-known forms found among speakers of Vernacular Black English and some White Appalachian varieties of English. The derivation of plural forms such as these can best be understood by looking at the order sequence between various rules operating on these forms. If we assume that we start out with lexical representations or underlying forms such as $d\varepsilon sk$ and $t\varepsilon st$, we first note that there is a rule that deletes the final member of the cluster, resulting in $d\varepsilon s$ and $t\varepsilon s$ respectively.[11] Then the regular plural rules that appear to operate on all varieties of English take place. This means that any noun ending in a sibilant-type sound ([s], [z], [š], and [ž]) will appropriately have a vowel inserted between the final s-like consonant and the plural form [z]. The third rule changes the voiced segment *s* to *z* if it follows a voiceless segment. The rule sequence is set up as follows:

---

[11]For a justification of $d\varepsilon sk$ and $t\varepsilon st$ as the underlying forms in these varieties, see Fasold (1969) or Wolfram (1970).

		Underlying Form	test+z	desk+z
Rule 1.	Consonant Cluster Reduction	tɛs+z	dɛs+z
Rule 2.	Epenthetic Vowel	tɛs+ɪz	dɛs+ɪz
Rule 3.	Assimilation of z Plural to Preceding Voiceless Segment	Not Applicable	Not Applicable

By setting up the rules in this sequence, the regular rule for plural formation can be seen to operate in Vernacular Black English in much the same manner as it operates for other varieties of English. The particular plural form is different because the consonant cluster reduction rule has operated prior to the plural rules, thus leaving a final s-like sound for the epenthetic vowel to be inserted between the final s and the z form of the plural. But consider what would happen if the plural rules and the consonant cluster reduction rules were reversed in their application.

		Underlying Form	test+z	desk+z
Rule 1.	Epenthetic Vowel	Not Applicable	Not Applicable
Rule 2.	Assimilation of z Plural to Preceding Voiceless Segment	test+s	desk+s
Rule 3.	Consonant Cluster Reduction	tɛs+s	dɛs+s

In the above order (which appears to be how many speakers of standard varieties of English actually pronounce *desks* and *tests* in rapid speech style), we could not account for the phonetic forms of the Vernacular Black English speaker in a natural way. Note that the epenthetic vowel rule cannot operate before the consonant cluster reduction rule because it does not meet the environmental conditions for the rule to operate (it does not end in an s-like sound). The only way in which we could account for the form if we ordered the rules as stated above would be to have another rule similar to the original epenthetic vowel rule. To have two rules that are identical does not appear to be economical, especially since the same generalizations can be captured by ordering the rules in the way that we previously specified. Concise and explicit rules that are at least sometimes ordered with respect to one another, then, are essential aspects of accounting for the phonetic forms in a process formulation.[12] Formal rules in generative phonology, then, take the form of a

---

[12]The discussion of rule ordering here should not be interpreted to mean there is no controversy about the role of rule ordering in generative phonology. As it turns out, there is presently a considerable amount of controversy over the extent of ordering (i.e., are the rules completely or partially ordered) and the principles that govern the ordering of rules. Currently, there is one group of linguists that feels all ordering can be predicted on the basis of universal principles, while others maintain that some orderings are quite language or dialect-specific. For the former position, see Koutsoudas (1972); for a response to this claim in terms of the rules of English dialects, see Bailey (1973).

series of explicit process statements in which the input of any rule in the series operates on the output of previously applied rules, if they have met the conditions for operation (1. A → B, 2. B → C, 3. C → D, etc.). If a given unit does not meet the conditions for operation (the relevant environment or the input), the the rules are bypassed until the conditions for operation are met.

DISTINCTIVE FEATURES

In the preceding sections, we have only considered the contrastive units in a language in terms of the various sound segments of the phonological system. In some approaches to phonology, units such as phonemes are considered to be the smallest contrastive unit in the phonology. This means that if we wanted to specify a rule that changed ɪ to ɛ before nasal sounds *m*, *n*, and ŋ, we would have to specify the rule something like the following:

$$\text{ɪ} \rightarrow \text{ɛ} \ / \ \underline{} \left\{ \begin{array}{c} \text{m} \\ \text{n} \\ \text{ŋ} \end{array} \right\}$$

While this certainly accounts for the data accurately, there seems to be an important generalization that is not formally handled in this process: namely, that all but only nasal segments can effect the change. While this generalization is certainly implicit in the series of sounds that are included as the relevant linguistic context for the operation of the rule, there is no explicit way in which this generalization is captured. Now a preferred model of language description is one in which such generalizations can be handled in a concise and explicit manner. In order to do this, we must admit that significant units of a phonological description are further divisible into certain properties of sounds. If we, therefore, look at the series listed above in terms of the properties or features of the class of sounds, we observe that a single property unifies this set while excluding all other sound segments from the class; namely, the feature of nasality. If the sounds are then divided into various properties, all we really have to do is capture the general nature of the following environment by specifying the presence of a nasal feature. If we do this by simply specifying the property something like [+nasal], we have explicitly captured the significance of the class of sounds that effect this particular rule. Three different segments can be represented, then, by the formal reference to one property that uniquely characterizes the set. One can see how the breakdown of units on such a basis can lead to more parsimonious, explicit statements in phonology. Similarly, we can take the various attributes of the process of a rule and capture the generalizations in terms of the segmental units affected by the rule. Thus, the consonant cluster reduction rule we specified earlier (where the final member of word-final consonant cluster may be deleted) can be observed to operate on final consonants such as *t, d, k, g, p,* and *b,* but not clusters involving *s, z, s, z,* etc. The process aspect of the rule taking the contrastive segmental units of the language as basic would have to look something like:

$$\left. \begin{array}{c} t \\ d \\ k \\ g \\ p \\ b \end{array} \right\} \rightarrow \emptyset \; / \; \ldots \; ^{13}$$

Now it is quite clear that these sounds are unified by the fact that they are all stop or non-continuant sounds (there is a complete obstruction of the oral mechanism in the production of the sound). This might be captured generally by referring to this property of the sounds, which we might characterize as [+stop] or [-continuant]. The generalization, then, can be stated simply by a rule that utilizes this common property, such as:

$$[+\text{stop}] \rightarrow \emptyset$$

The justification for appealing to a level of phonology in which the ultimate unit of the phonological system is the phonological feature is based on several important observations, all of which are interrelated. As we have observed above, it allows for more economical descriptions of phonological processes and environments in formalizing the rules. In place of a simple listing of the sound segments, we can often state the same observation through the use of a more restricted number of features. The reason we can do this is based on a more essential principle—that the appeal to phonetic features captures important generalities that are observed in phonological processes. Phonological processes do not randomly select from the inventory of sound segments of a language, nor do they operate in linguistic environments where the relevant sounds for the operation of a process are random. Rather, there is a systematic articulatory or acoustic basis for particular processes taking place as they do. The appeal to phonetic components or features of sounds allows us to explicitly and concisely state the regular generalizations that are observed to take place. It stands to reason that a theory that can account for unifying generalities in a natural way should be considered superior to one that cannot. Classes of sounds that are uniquely unified on the basis of their shared features are referred to as *natural classes.* We have already alluded to the fact that a division of sounds on the basis of their features allows us to specify sets that have an internal relationship to each other. In a natural class of sounds, fewer features can be used to specify the class of

---

[13]There are actually more details to this rule than those specified here but we have eliminated them for the sake of demonstrating the principle at hand. For more complete information on how this rule operates in dialects such as standard English and Vernacular Black English, see Wolfram (1969) and Fasold (1972).

sounds that can be used to specify any individual member of the set. Features, then, provide a principled basis for defining what constitutes a natural class of sounds in a language. And we observed above that natural classes of sounds are essential in understanding how phonological systems are organized.

Because the goals of a generative model of language involve a concise and explicit formulation of phonological processes, one can see how the notion of phonological features as the primitive units of phonology would naturally fit into the theory. This, of course, is not to suggest that phonological features of this type were not utilized to some extent in traditional phonological descriptions. Earlier work on distinctive features by Jakobson and others (1952) had been incorporated to some extent into phonological descriptions a couple of decades before the advent of generative phonology. But while they were incorporated into phonological analyses in many traditional studies, the traditional phoneme offer was still often considered to be the central unit of phonology, not the distinctive feature. In generative phonology, features were formally admitted as the central distinctive unit of the system.

Ultimately, the theory of distinctive features is established on a restricted universal set of phonetic features that is adequate for describing the phonological contrasts and processes of any spoken language, although not all features might be relevant as contrastive properties in a particular language. While this notion is generally agreed on by generative phonologists, determining the most efficient set of universal features for doing this task is still not settled. Some earlier formulations following Jakobson's work appealed to the acoustic parameters of speech as the basis for a universal system, whereas more recent formulations have relied more heavily on the articulatory aspects of sound.

Features may refer to major sound classes (consonant, sonorant), manner of articulation (continuant, nasal), place of articulation (anterior), or even suprasegmental aspects (stress, tone). In some cases, features refer to the simple presence or absence of a particular characteristic, such as nasality, voicing, or the involvement/noninvolvement of the tip or blade of the tongue (corona). In other instances, + or - values reflect the extreme points of a feature that actually range over a continuum, such as the various points of articulation that may be utilized in the mouth. The use of features must effectively and naturally distinguish the significant segmental sound units (which may be individual in terms of actual production) as they contrast with each other. Hence the term *distinctive feature*. The + or - values are referred to rather than degrees of individual features in explicitly showing the contrastive phonological units of a language and the processes that change these units in different ways.[14]

---

[14]Although most descriptions in generative phonology still utilize only binary features, there is considerable debate about the empirical and theoretical validity of binary features, at least on some levels of the phonological system.

Following are definitions of features that appear to be relevant for the description of the English sound system, and a matrix of the significant sound segments in terms of these features (primarily from Chomsky and Halle, 1968).

Consonantal—Consonantal Sounds are produced with constriction along the center line of the oral cavity. The only sounds nonconsonantal in English are the vowels and glides *w*, *h*, and *y*.

Syllabic—Syllabic refers to the role of a sound in the syllable. Segments that constitute a syllabic peak are considered to be syllabic while those not constituting a peak are nonsyllabic. Typically, the vowels are syllabic.

For the most part, the following set only applies to consonants:

Anterior—Anterior sounds are produced with obstruction located in front of or at the alveolar ridge of the mouth. Thus, labial, dental, and alveolar sounds are anterior and palatal and velar sounds are nonanterior.

Coronal—Coronal sounds are produced with the front (tip or blade) of the tongue. Sounds produced with another part of the tongue (back) or not involving the tongue (labials such as *p* and *m*) are noncoronal.

Continuant—Continuants are characterized by continued air movement through the oral cavity during the production of the sound. Noncontinuants are produced with complete obstruction in the oral cavity. The qualification of oral cavity is important in order to consider nasals such as *m* and *n* as noncontinuants, since the oral cavity in nasals is completely obstructed while the nasal cavity is open for the duration of the sound.

Strident—Strident sounds are produced with an obstruction in the oral cavity that allows air to come through a relatively long, narrow construction. As the air escapes, the turbulence produces the primary noise source over the rough surface. Most, but not all, of the sounds traditionally classified as fricatives (θ and đ being the exceptions) are considered to be strident and other sounds are nonstrident.

Sonorant—Sonorant sounds are typically produced with a lesser degree of cavity constriction. Vowels, nasals, and liquids are typically considered sonorants while sounds with more radical cavity constriction such as stops (*p*, *t*, *k*) and fricatives (*s*, *f*, *v*) are typically considered nonsonorants.

Voice—Voiced sounds are produced with a vibration of the vocal bands in the larynx and voiceless ones are produced without such vibration. Sounds like *t*, *p*, *s* and *š* are voiceless while sounds like *d*, *b*, *z*, and *ž* are voiced.

Nasal—Nasal sounds are characterized by the lowering or opening of the velum so that air can escape through the nasal passage. Nonnasal sounds are produced with the velum closed so that air can only escape through the oral cavity.

For the most part, the following features are used with reference to the classification of vowels, semivowels, and semiconsonants.

High—High vowels involve the raising of the tongue from the neutral position, involving a relatively narrow construction in the oral cavity. Vowels like *i*, ɪ, *u*, and U are considered to be high vowels and those produced with a lower tongue position are all considered nonhigh.

Low—Low vowels are produced with a lowering of the tongue from a neutral position. (The vowel approximately in the position of ε in *bed* is typically considered the neutral position.) Vowels such as æ, *a* and ɔ are considered to be low vowels. Note that in this system midvowels like *e*, ε or *o* are distinguished by being both nonhigh and nonlow.

Back—Back sounds are classified as being produced with the tongue backed from the neutral position. If it is produced at or in front of the neutral position, it is considered to be nonback. Thus, vowels like *i* and *e* are considered nonback vowels while vowels like *u*, *o*, and ɔ are considered to be back.

Round—Sounds produced with a rounding of the lips are considered to be rounded. Vowels like *u*, *o*, and ɔ in English are rounded while the other vowels of English are typically unrounded.

Tense—Tense sounds are produced with a deliberate, maximally distinct gesture that involves considerable muscular activity. Nontense sounds are produced with a lesser degree of muscle activity so that they are more indistinct. Vowels like *i* and *u* are considered to be tense in contrast to their counterparts *I* and *U*, which are considered to be nontense.

True Vowels*

	i	I	e	E	æ	u	U	o	ə	a
cons	-	-	-	-	-	-	-	-	-	-
syll	+	+	+	+	+	+	+	+	+	+
high	+	+	-	-	-	+	+	-	-	-
low	-	-	-	-	+	-	-	-	+	+
back	-	-	-	-	-	+	+	+	+	+
tense	+	-	+	-	-	+	-	+	-	-
round	-	-	-	-	-	+	+	+	-	+

*For the true vowels, we have eliminated the features that appear to be distinguishable mainly for consonants.

PHONOLOGY

	p	b	t	d	k	g	č	ǰ	f	v	θ	ð	s	z	š	ž	m	n	ŋ	r	l	h	y	w
cons	+	+	+	+	+	+	+	+	+	+	+	+	+	+	+	+	+	+	+	+	+	−	−	−
syll	−	−	−	−	−	−	−	−	−	−	−	−	−	−	−	−	−	−	−	+	+	−	−	−
continuant	−	−	−	−	−	−	−	−	+	+	+	+	+	+	+	+	−	−	−	+	+	+	+	+
nasal	−	−	−	−	−	−	−	−	−	−	−	−	−	−	−	−	+	+	+	−	−	−	−	−
anterior	+	+	+	+	−	−	−	−	+	+	+	+	+	+	−	−	+	+	−	−	+	−	−	−
coronal	−	−	+	+	−	−	+	+	−	−	+	+	+	+	+	+	−	+	−	+	+	−	−	−
high	−	−	−	−	+	+	+	+	−	−	−	−	−	−	+	+	−	−	+	−	−	−	+	+
low	−	−	−	−	−	−	−	−	−	−	−	−	−	−	−	−	−	−	−	−	−	+	−	−
back	−	−	−	−	+	+	−	−	−	−	−	−	−	−	−	−	−	−	+	−	−	−	−	+
voice	−	+	−	+	−	+	−	+	−	+	−	+	−	+	−	+	+	+	+	+	+	−	+	+
strident	−	−	−	−	−	−	+	+	+	+	−	−	+	+	+	+	−	−	−	−	−	−	−	−
sonorant	−	−	−	−	−	−	−	−	−	−	−	−	−	−	−	−	+	+	+	+	+	+	+	+

Although the matrix given represents the various features that are considered distinctive in English, it is noted that, for particular sounds, some of the features are predictable on the basis of other features. Thus, for example, a whole set of features needed for consonants are completely predictable for the vowels. In the most economical statement, these implied features are redundant. For example, in English, if we know that a sound is characterized by being [-back], such as *i* or ɪ, it is predictable that it must be [-round] as well, since only back vowels are rounded. Similarly, if we know that a consonant sound is [+nasal] in English, we also know that it must be [-strident], [+continuant], and [+nasal]. When the values of features are completely predictable on the basis of the values of other features for a particular sound, we refer to them as redundant features. The significance of redundant features in a generative phonology is that the model is committed to a principle of economy in which only nonpredictable information is to be included in representing the basic units and processes in phonology. All predictable information is derived through the various types of rules we discussed earlier in this paper. Some redundancies may be specific to a particular language (such as the prediction of rounding on the basis of backness in English but not in all languages) while others appear to be universal (such as the prediction of [-low] for all [+high] vowels).

To summarize the importance of distinctive features, we first of all see that they serve as a universal basis for describing the phonetic components of the sound systems of language. On a more abstract level, they operate to differentiate the various lexical items of a language, since they are the smallest contrastive units in the phonological system. And finally, their incorporation into a generative phonology allows us to state explicitly important generalizations about the phonological processes of a language, as defined on the basis of natural classes of sounds.

I have attempted to discuss some of the preliminary notions concerning a generative phonology. As we have seen, such an approach attempts to account for what a speaker/hearer knows about the structure of his sound system. This includes information starting with the abstract units in the lexical representation and going through to the actual pronunciation of items. Generative phonology attempts to capture the generalizations on the various levels in an explicit and concise way. While some of the details of formulation will certainly be revised or abandoned as we increase our knowledge of sound systems, it seems obvious that the optimal approach to the symbols on a printed page is one that will take greatest advantage of the awesome knowledge that a speaker/hearer has of his own sound system.

REFERENCES

Bailey, Charles James N. "Variation Resulting from Different Rule Orderings in English Phonology," in Charles James N. Bailey and Roger W. Shuy (Eds.), *New Ways of Analyzing Variation in English*. Washington, D.C.: Georgetown University Press, 1073.

Chomsky, Noam. "Current Issues in Linguistic Theory," in Jerry A. Fodor and Jerrald Katz (Eds.), *The Structure of Language: Readings in the Philosophy of Language*. Englewood Cliffs, New Jersey: Prentice-Hall, 1964.

Chomsky, Noam, and Morris Halle. *The Sound Pattern of English*. New York: Harper and Row, 1968.

Elson, Benjamin, and Velma Pickett. *An Introduction to Morphology and Syntax*. Santa Ana: Summer Institute of Linguistics, 1962.

Fasold, Ralph W. "Orthography in Reading Materials for Black English Speaking Children," Joan C. Baratz and Roger W. Shuy (Eds.), *Teaching Black Children to Read*. Washington, D.C.: Center for Applied Linguistics, 1969b.

Fasold, Ralph W. *Tense Marking in Black English: A Linguistic and Social Analysis*. Washington, D.C.: Center for Applied Linguistics, 1972a.

Fromkin, Victoria A. "The Nonanomalous Nature of Anomalous Utterances," *Language*, 47 (1971), 27-52.

Gleason, H. A. *An Introduction to Descriptive Linguistics*. New York: Holt, Rinehart and Winston, 1961.

Halle, Morris. "On the Bases of Phonology," in Jerry A. Fodor and Jerrold J. Katz (Eds.), *The Structure of Language: Readings in the Philosophy of Language*. Englewood Cliffs, New Jersey: Prentice-Hall, 1964.

Halle, Morris. "Stress Rules in English: A New Version," *Linguistic Inquiry*, 4 (1973), 451-464.

Hockett, Charles. "Two Models of Grammatical Description," *Word*, 10 (1954), 210-231.

Jakobson, Roman, Garner Fant, and Morris Halle. *Preliminaries to Speech Analysis: The Distinctive Features of their Correlates*. Cambridge: MIT Press, 1952.

Koutsoudas, Andreas. "The Strict Order Fallacy," *Language*, 48 (1972), 88-96.

Labov, William. "Contraction, Deletion, and Inherent Variability of the English Copula," *Language*, 45 (1969), 715-762.

Wolfram, Walt. *A Sociolinguistic Description of Detroit Negro Speech*. Washington, D.C.: Center for Applied Linguistics, 1969.

Wolfram, Walt. "Underlying Representations in Black English Phonology," *Language Sciences*, April 1970, 7-12.

Zwicky, Arnold. "Auxiliary Reduction in English," *Linguistic Inquiry*, 1 (1970), 323-336.

Phonological Rules and Reading

Anna Fay Vaughn-Cooke
Federal City College

The phonological component of the model of language discussed by Wolfram in the previous chapter is basically a complex system of rules that a speaker can apply to the underlying representation of a word and arrive at its correct pronunciation.[1] According to Wolfram, the job of the phonological rules is to account for the predictable aspects of pronunciation, whether they relate to alternate pronunciations of the same basic morpheme or different phonetic forms that a given sound can take. At least three types of phonological rules are needed to account for the predictable aspects of the pronunciation of English words: segment redundancy rules, sequence redundancy rules, and morphophonemic rules.

1. RULES OF THE PHONOLOGICAL COMPONENT

1.1 Segment redundancy rules

Segment redundancy rules (also referred to as allophonic rules) account for the predictable phonetic variations occurring in the actual production of sound segments. For example, these rules not only account for the obvious predictable phonetic difference in aspiration between the [p] of *pit* and the [p] of *spit*, they also account for differences not usually recorded by linguists—such as the distinction between the exact physical

---

[1]Wolfram has defined the underlying representation as the "elemental unit...from which other forms can be derived." Examples of underlying representations are presented in sections 1.3 and 3.

I am grateful to my colleague Walt Wolfram for his helpful comments. This is not to say that he would necessarily agree with any of the points I have made in this paper. The research for this paper was partially supported by the Communication Sciences Department at Federal City College.

characteristics of [a] after [p] as opposed to [a] after [b] or [m]. It has been noted that certain predictable variations, such as the front-to-back variation of [k] which is dependent on the following vowel, may be universal (Moskowitz, 1973); that is, the variant pronunciations of [k] may be predictable from the shape of the human vocal tract. Such variations are physiologically determined and do not need to be learned by children. Certain other allophonic variants are not physiologically determined and must be learned through the process of phonology acquisition. Evidence that children acquire allophonic rules is plentiful in the psycholinguistic literature. Studies have shown that children of all languages first produce predominantly unaspirated stops; and then gradually acquire the pattern of aspiration in the languages they are learning (Smith, 1973; Moskowitz, 1970; Leopold, 1947; Preston, 1971).

1.2 Sequence redundancy rules

Sequence redundancy rules (also referred to as morpheme structure conditions and phonotactic rules) delineate the permissible sound sequences that can occur in a language. To use Wolfram's example, if a three consonant sequence occurs at the beginning of a word in English, the first sound in the sequence must be *s*, the second sound must be a stop like *p*, *t*, or *k*, and the third sound must be *l* or *r*. As Wolfram noted, a native speaker's knowledge of sequence redundancy rules accounts for the fact that he will accept items like *splot** and *scrat** and reject items like *fplot** or *snrat** as legitimate sounding words in the English language. In addition to the general rules which describe the predictable occurrence of consonant sequences in words, Moskowitz has mentioned two other types of sequence redundancy rules. One type is a rule delimiting the positional occurrence of sounds in a word; for example /ŋ/ and /ž/ never occur initially in English words. Another type is a rule which prohibits the occurrence of labial and velar consonants after /aw/, for example /awp/* and /awm/* sequences do not occur in English.

1.3 Morphophonemic rules

Morphophonemic rules generate the systematic alternation of sounds in words. These rules account for the fact that the underlying /ī/ in *divine* and *divinity* is pronounced like [āy] in *divine,* while it is pronounced like [ĭ] in *divinity.*[2] They also account for the fact that the plural morpheme /s/ of *bugs* and *books* is pronounced like [z] when it is preceded by a voiced sound, as in *bugs,* but it is pronounced like [s] when it is preceded by a voiceless sound as in *books.* Based on the above words, we can distinguish two types of phonological rules in English which involve morphophonemic patterns. They are internal and external morphophonemic rules. *Internal morphophonemic rules* account for the derivational alternations which are word-internal and occur in items like

---

[2]All phonologists do not agree that the tense vowel /ī/ should be posited for the underlying vowel for *divine* and *divinity.* However, a full discussion of the controversy would be irrelevant here.

divine-divinity, while *external morphophonemic rules* account for inflectional alternations (suffixes) which are word external and occur in items like *bugs* and *books*. When comparing internal and external morphophonemic rules, it is generally assumed that the former are more complex and are learned later by children (Schane, 1974; Darden, 1974).

To summarize, the phonological component of a model of language includes at least three basic kinds of rules: segment redundancy, sequence redundancy, and morphophonemic. The latter rules can be divided into two subtypes—internal and external.

This paper will focus on one of the subtypes of the rules of the phonological component, the type we have called internal morphophonemic rules (hereafter IM Rules); and we will try to show that a speaker's knowledge of such rules has implications for the teaching of reading, particularly the level of reading at which word pairs involving consonant and vowel alternations appear.

First, we will examine the historical changes in English which resulted in consonant and vowel alternations and the subsequent development of IM Rules; second, we will examine the formal representation of IM Rules; third, we will examine some experimental evidence which supports the notion that IM Rules are psychologically real for some speakers; and, finally, we will try to show how knowledge of IM Rules can be utilized during the reading process.

2. HISTORICAL CHANGES THAT LED TO THE DEVELOPMENT OF IM RULES

2.1. The great vowel shift

During the Middle English period, around 1500, the qualities of long, tense vowels in English changed. Jesperson referred to this phenomenon as the Great Vowel Shift and described it as follows (1907: 231, quoted in Wang 1968).

> The great vowel-shift consists in a general raising of all long vowels with the exception of the two high vowels [i] and [u], which could not be raised further without becoming consonants and which were diphthongized into [ei, ou], later [ai, au]. In most cases the spelling has become fixed before the shift, which accordingly is one of the chief reasons of the divergence between spelling and sound in English: while the value of the short vowels...remained on the whole intact, the value of the long vowels...was changed.

Figure 1 depicts the particular changes as outlined by Jesperson.

According to Wang, not all authorities agree with Jesperson regarding the historical details of the shift. He noted the following disagreement (1968:698).

> Some scholars believe that the shift was initiated by the diphthongization of the high vowels, while others contend it was set in motion by the raising of mid vowels. Opinions differ further on whether the dipthongization involves an intermediate state when the nuclear vowels are centralized.

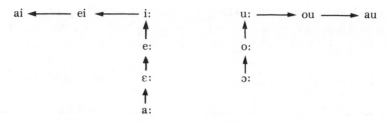

Figure 1. Vowel changes outlined by Jesperson.

Our concern lies not so much with the historical details of the Great Vowel Shift (GVS) but more with the mark it left on English in the form of vowel alternations which occur in words like *divine* and *divinity* mentioned in section 1.3 and those alternations occurring in the pairs exemplified in Tables 1a and 1b below.

A second but major mark the GVS left on English was the non-phonetic spelling of vowels. This mark will be discussed in section 5.0. At this point, it will be instructive to examine in some detail the patterns of vowel alternation resulting from the GVS.

2.2 Vowel alternations resulting from the GVS

The primary pattern of vowel alternations resulting from the GVS is exemplified by the words in Table 1a.

Table 1a. Derived morphemes with front vowel alternations (Moskowitz, 1973: 227).

āy ~ ĭ	ēy ~ ă	īy ~ ĕ
divine-divinity	profane-profanity	serene-serenity
line-linear	explain-explanatory	obscene-obscenity
derive-derivative	grateful-gratitude	meter-metric
collide-collision	opaque-opacity	receive-reception

An examination of the word pairs in Table 1a reveals that they exhibit a regular alternation which occurs in parallel fashion for the three pairs of front vowels /āy/ ~ /ĭ/ (as in *divine* and *divinity*); /ēy/ ~ /ă/ (as in *profane* and *profanity*); and /īy/ ~ /ĕ/ (as in *serene* and *serenity*). In all of these examples, a stressed tense diphthongized vowel occurs in the isolated morpheme (*divine*) and a stressed lax vowel occurs in the derived word (*divinity*).

Further examination of words exhibiting front vowel alternations reveals that there are a number of items, unlike those of Table 1a, which do not involve the alternation of full vowels. The words instead exhibit a lax vowel in the stressed position of most of the underived morphemes. Consider, for example, the vowels in the stressed position of *mental* and *simple*. The [ɛ] of *mental* and the [ɪ] of *simple* are both lax vowels. A few words in this group occur with tense vowels in both members. See for instance *base* and *basic* and other examples noted in Table 1b.

Table 1b. Derived morphemes without alternations of full vowels (Moskowitz, 1973:227).

stupid-stupidity	total-totality	base-basic
rustic-rusticity	mental-mentality	scene-scenic
valid-validity	simple-simplicity	obese-obesity
liquid-liquidity	lax-laxity	phoneme-phonemic

The secondary alternating pattern involves a group of word pairs in which a nonlow vowel occurring in one member alternates with a reduced vowel in another member. Word pairs exemplifying this pattern are listed in Table 2.

Table 2 (Moskowitz, 1973:227).

īy - ɔ	ēy - ə
funereal-funeral	Canadian-Canada
managerial-manager	marginalia-marginal
	algebraic-algebra

The words containing the nonlow vowels are listed on the left while those containing the reduced vowel are listed on the right.

A third, but minor, alternating pattern produced by the GVS involves three sets of back vowel alternations occurring in a limited number of word pairs. The alternating vowels of these pairs are /ə/ and /ōw/ (as in *custody* and *custodian*); /ā/ and /ōw/ (as in *verbosity* and *verbose*); and /ʌ/ and /ǣw/ (as in *abundant* and *abound*).

Since the forms of Tables 1a and 1b are the most numerous, their pattern has served as the basis for constructing the IM RULES we will be concerned with in this paper.

2.3 Other consequences of the GVS

The effects of the GVS are generally discussed only in connection with vowel alternations. However, there are a number of word pairs in English exhibiting consonant alternations which were determined in part by their vocalic contexts. The effects of the GVS on the consonant system of English have resulted in forms exhibiting the following alternations:

Table 3. Word pairs exhibiting consonant alternations.

s ~ k	ǰ ~ g
criticism-critize-critical	allege-allegation
medicine-medical-medicate	rigid-rigor
	regal-regicide
	analogous-analougize

In the words involving the s ~ k alternation, the underlying /k/ of *criticism* and *medicine* is pronounced as /s/ before the non-low, non-back vowel [ɪ] in each of these words. Chomsky and Halle (1968) have referred to this process as velar softening. Velar softening can also be triggered by the non-low, non-back vowel [e] as evidenced by the example in Table 3 involving the /ǰ/ and /g/ alternation in *allege* and *allegation*. In this case, /g/ undergoes velar softening and is pronounced as /ǰ/ in *allege*. To represent the predictable nature of the consonant alternations exemplified in Table 3, Chomsky and Halle formulated the following phonological rule.[3]

$$\left\{ \begin{array}{c} g \longrightarrow ǰ \\ k \longrightarrow s \end{array} \right\} \Big/ \underline{\hspace{2cm}} \left[\begin{array}{c} \text{-low} \\ \text{-back} \end{array} \right]$$

The rule states that the segments /g/ and /k/ are pronounced as /ǰ/ and /s/ respectively when they follow a vowel that is non-low and non-back, e.g. [i] or [e]. More will be said about the formal representation of phonological rules when we discuss the form of the IM rules in section 3.

In summary, we have seen that the historical changes which occurred in English several centuries ago resulted in three recognizable patterns of vowel alternations. The patterns include a primary one involving alternation of front vowels; a secondary one involving the alternation of non-low vowels with reduced vowels; and a third, but minor, pattern involving the alternation of back vowels. We have also seen that the primary pattern has been the basis for constructing the IM rules also known as vowel shift rules in English. Another result of the GVS is the alternation of consonants in some English words.

The consequences of the GVS made it necessary for speakers of English to construct IM rules which would generate the correct pronunciations for the word pairs in their language. At this point we will examine the formal representation of these rules.

3. THE FORM OF INTERNAL MORPHOPHONEMIC RULES

When we examine the form of the IM rules which account for the vowel alternations in word pairs like *divine* and *divinity*, it becomes apparent that such rules are more complex; that is, they involve more oper-

---

[3]Schane (1974) has proposed an alternative formulation for the rule of velar and velar softening. See page 310 for a discussion of the formulation.

ations than segment and sequence redundancy rules discussed in 1.1 and 1.2 above. Consider, for example, that in order to account for a speaker's knowledge of the alternate forms of the word pair above, Chomsky and Halle posit four major rules. The rules are vowel shift, tensing, laxing, and diphthongization.[4] Before demonstrating how these rules would change the underlying vowels of *divine* and *divinity* to their surface representations, it will be helpful to summarize Wolfram's discussion of the operation of phonological rules.

In Wolfram's discussion of the form of phonological rules, he pointed out that "there are several essential aspects which must be captured in any phonological rule...." First, these aspects include the input to the rule, which in the case of a lexical item is one of its units. Second, the unit must undergo certain specific changes in order to emerge in an alternate form. The alternate form is called the output of the phonological rule. Finally, there must be a specified environment within which the change can take place. Wolfram presented the following simple convention to capture the relevant aspects of phonological rules.

$$X \longrightarrow Y \quad / \quad A \underline{\hspace{1cm}} B$$

The following interpretation of the above convention was also presented:

> ...X is the input for the rule and the arrow indicates that it is changed to or "becomes" Y, the output of the rule. The slant line / indicates that anything beyond that point is relevant environment for the rule to operate. If the relevant environment precedes the sound, then it is placed before the "environmental bar" (i.e. the line_____) and if the following environment is relevant, then it is placed following the bar. In other words, the convention captures a change of AXB $\longrightarrow$ AYB.

In regard to our example of the change from the underlying tense /ī/ in divine and divinity to their specific surface forms, we stated earlier that Chomsky and Halle proposed four major rules. Recall that the rules were tensing, laxing, diphthongization, and vowel shift. Consider the lexical item *divine* first. In order for a speaker to arrive at its correct pronunciation, he will need first to apply the rule of diphthongization. The input to the rule in this case would be the tense vowel of the underlying form /divīn/. (Note, in this case, the rule of tensing does not apply since the input vowel is already tense.) The output of the rule is the diphthongized vowel /īy/.

Below is a highly simplified version of the diphthongization rule which is needed to accomplish the change.

1. $\emptyset \rightarrow y \quad / \quad \bar{\imath} \underline{\hspace{1cm}}$

The rule states that $\emptyset$ (zero) becomes /y/ in the environment following a tense vowel that is non-back.

---

[4]For simplicity purposes the rules which account for backing adjustment and rounding adjustment have been omitted from the discussion.

The second rule the speaker needs to arrive at the correct pronunciation of *divine* is the vowel shift rule. Since the input to this rule, in the case of *divine* is the diphthong /īy/, its input is the output of the diphthongization rule. The vowel shift rule changes [+high] /ī/ to [-high] /ǣ/. The rule can be simply represented as follows:[5]

2. /ī/ → /ǣ/   / _____ y

The rule states that /ī/ is lowered to /ǣ/ in the environment preceding /y/.

So far we have seen that two rules are needed in order to derive *divine*, the surface form, from its underlying form /divīn/. In order to derive *divinity*, the other member of the pair, from the underlying form, /divīn/, a speaker will need to apply the laxing rule which will change the tense /i/ of the underlying form to the lax /i/ of the surface form. The tense /i/, of course, is the input to the laxing rule and the lax /i/ is the output.

The preceding discussion of the form of phonological rules was presented for two reasons. First, we wanted to show that the notion of a rule as discussed and formulated by linguists is an attempt to represent formally the speaker's knowledge of the sound system of his language. In this framework the job of the rule, as we stated in the introduction, is to account for the predictable aspects of a speaker's pronunciations, whether they relate to alternate pronunciations of the same basic morpheme (as in *divine* and *divinity*) or the different phonetic forms the phoneme /p/ takes in the lexical items *pit* and *spit*.

The second reason for discussing the form of phonological rules was to emphasize the relative complexity of the rule schema utilized by speakers for the purpose of arriving at the correct pronunciations of word pairs in their language, specifically those involving alternating morphemes. We pointed out that for such items, the speaker must first hypothesize an abstract underlying form and then apply the appropriate rules of the phonological component to derive the alternate surface representations.[6] The important question regarding the subset of rules (IM RULES) under discussion is, Do the rules reflect psychologically real constructs; that is, do speakers really have knowledge of such rules as we have proposed or are the rules merely artifacts of the grammars constructed by linguists?

According to Ohala (1974:225) one way to determine whether IM RULES are psychologically real for speakers is to devise experiments which will provide the necessary psycholinguistic evidence. Ohala states (225):

---

[5] The vowel shift rule as formulated by Chomsky and Halle is much more complicated than the one presented here. However, for our purposes, this simplified version is sufficient.

[6] When we compare morphemes which participate in alternations with those that do not (e.g. *pit*) we find that for the latter we do not need to posit abstract underlying forms and the associated morphophonemic rules. Morphemes which do not participate in alternations simply have phonemic representations and are exempt from the morphophonemic rules.

> If the [rules] which linguists write are to reflect psychologically real constructs, then purely structural evidence is not sufficient proof of them; some form of psychological evidence is required.

The question regarding the psychological reality of the rules accounting for consonant and vowel alternations is of particular importance here since we proposed in section 6 that knowledge of such rules can be exploited during the reading process. In the next section we will examine some experimental studies, the results of which suggest that IM RULES are indeed psychologically real for some speakers.

4. EXPERIMENTAL STUDIES

We will first examine Moskowitz' study since it not only provides evidence which supports the claim that speakers have knowledge of IM RULES but it also provides information regarding the age of acquisition and the source from which such rules are acquired.

4.1 The Moskowitz study

For her experiment, Moskowitz first developed two sets of nonsense word pairs that contained vowel alternations like those in a number of morphophologically related real words in English. The underived member (the member without a suffix) of a nonsense pair was presented to the subjects who were instructed to add the -*ity* suffix. The instructions, however, included no mention of the vocalic difference between the underlined member which exhibited a tense vowel and the derived member which exhibited a lax vowel. The stimuli included, for instance, pairs like /kliyǰ/* -/klɛjity/* and /pāyp/* - /pĭpity/*. An example of the instructions presented to the subjects was as follows: "My word will be shorter than yours. I want you to say a word that is almost the same as mine but has the suffix -*ity* at the end. So if I say /kliyj/ you say /klɛjity/. If I say /pāyp/ you say /pĭpity/" (1973:234).

The experiment included a total of 39 subjects: 9 seven-year-olds, 4 five-year-olds, and 25 subjects between the ages of nine and twelve. All subjects were from middle-class homes in the San Francisco Bay area and all were native speakers of Standard English.

One goal of the experiment was to determine the number of trials it would take a child to notice and correctly produce the vowel alternations. For example, Part A (Condition I) included 72 nonsense word pairs exhibiting front vowel alternations like those on Table 1a in section 2.1. The subjects were required to produce ten correct responses in a row as an indication that they had learned to criterion the internal morphophonemic rules which generated the vowel alternations.[7]

---

[7]For convenience, only Condition I, Part A will be discussed and related to the central issue of this paper. Altogether, however, the experiment included three conditions which employed different types of stimuli. The stimuli were presented in three parts: A, B, and C (A and B included pairs exhibiting front vowel alternations while C included pairs exhibiting back vowel alternations). Condition I stimuli differed from that of Conditions II and III in that the former employed a larger subset of the rules of the phonological com-

Moskowitz hypothesized that the natural acquisition of the rules controlling the vowel alternations could be accounted for by one of the following proposals.

> (i) The vowel alternations are phonetically paired as alternate surface pronunciations, e.g. [āy] and [ĭ] simply alternate under specified surface conditions, as do [īy] and [ĕ].

> (ii) There is a single underlying representation for a given morpheme, and a particular subset of the rules of the phonological component are utilized in arriving at appropriate surface forms. In other words, the child must hypothesize an underlying vowel, such as ī, and employ the rules of laxing, diphthongization and vowel shift to derive from ī the surface forms āy and ĭ under specific conditions stated in the rule (1973: 235).

The results of the experiment revealed that children who knew the IM RULES accounting for vowel alternations adopted strategy (ii) of the second proposal. We propose that if children, when confronted with word pairs in their reading texts involving alternations, also adopt strategy (ii) they will be able to arrive at the correct pronunciations of such pairs.

At this point we will turn our attention to the more detailed results of the experiment. On Part A, which involved the ability to correctly shift front vowel pairs, the nine- to twelve-year-olds did not exhibit any difficulty in applying the appropriate IM RULES. All subjects learned the task to criterion (that is, they were able to produce ten correct responses in a row), and three subjects made no errors at all. Four of the seven-year-olds learned the rules to criterion while the other three did not. The five-year-olds were only able to add the appropriate suffix. It appeared that the control of vowel alternations was beyond their knowledge. Based on the performance of the subjects, Moskowitz was able to draw several conclusions.

First, the experimenter concluded that children do have knowledge of vowel shift rules as evidenced by the ability of the nine- to twelve-year-olds and four of the seven-year-olds to correctly apply IM RULES; second, the experimenter concluded that knowledge of these rules seems to be acquired by some children as early as age seven and by others at age nine; and third, she concluded that the source of the knowledge of IM RULES is the spelling system of English.

---

ponent. Correct responses to Condition I stimuli required knowledge of three rules (diphthongization, laxing, and vowel shift), while correct responses to Condition II stimuli required knowledge of only two rules (laxing and diphthongization). In addition to requiring knowledge of the rules for Condition II stimuli, Condition III also required the postulation of a new "incorrect" vowel shift rule for English: /īy/ would shift to /ēy/ and /āy/ would shift to /īy/. It was hypothesized that Condition II would be simpler than I since it involved fewer rules. The data did not support this hypothesis. It was further hypothesized that of the three conditions, III would be the most difficult to learn. This was not supported by the data either. See Moskowitz (236-247) for further details of the experiment.

The second and third conclusions warrant further discussion. Conclusion two is a step toward answering the question raised by Carol Chomsky (1970:327) regarding the age of acquisition of IM Rules. She stated:

> An interesting and important question...is...the age at which the child achieves a mature command of the phonological structure of his language. It is quite possible, perhaps most likely, that full knowledge of the sound system that corresponds to the orthography is not yet possessed by the child of six or seven, and may indeed be acquired fairly late.

The age of acquisition of IM Rules, as indicated by the findings of Moskowitz' experiment, can be used as a guideline for teachers who are in a position to determine when a child is ready to be exposed to vocabulary items that exhibit vowel and consonant alternations. Without access to the crucial information concerning the age at which children acquire these particular phonological rules, textbook writers and reading teachers might be forced to decide arbitrarily when a child is ready to be exposed to vocabulary items like *electric* and *electricity*. Moskowitz' findings imply that the age of seven is not too early to begin exposing children to the more familiar vocabulary items that require the application of IM Rules. More will be said about this point in Section 7.

Moskowitz' third conclusion (that the source of the subjects' knowledge of IM Rules is the spelling system of English) warrants examination since it was not drawn directly from the results of the experiment but rather from a comparison of the educational exposures of the five- and seven-year-olds.

In reference to the performance of the seven-year-olds, the experimenter pointed out that at first it seemed mysterious for a seven-year-old, relatively unfamiliar with much of the relevant vocabulary of his language, to be able to manipulate the necessary vowel shift patterns needed to produce the correct alternations exhibited in his responses to the nonsense stimuli. However, Moskowitz noted that the facts appeared less mysterious after considering that a substantial amount of time is spent on spelling during the early years of education. Unlike the five-year-olds, the seven-year-olds had been exposed to at least one year of reading and spelling instruction. As a result, they had acquired enough information about the standard spelling system to begin construction of the IM Rules which account for the word pairs in the language involving alternating vowels and consonants. Moskowitz claims that the source of this knowledge of underlying phonology is available only to those speakers who are exposed to the spelling system of English. The fact that the five-year-olds had no knowledge of the appropriate IM Rules seems to support the experimenter's claim.

Read's examination (1971) of the invented spellings of preschoolers provides further evidence that children who have not been exposed to the standard spellings have no knowledge of the underlying relationship between the alternating surface vowels of word pairs and the appropriate

IM Rules which generate such vowels. This lack of knowledge is exemplified by the phonetic spelling for the vowels of the word pairs in Table 4.

Table 4.

Phonetic Pair	Examples	Adult Spelling*	Child Spelling
1. [āy-i]	divine-divinity	I	Different: I-E
2. [īy-e]	serene-serenity	E	Different: E-A
3. [ēy-æ]	nation-national	A	Same: A
4. [ōw-a]	tone-tonic	O	Different: O (W)-I
5. [āw-ʌ]	abound-abundant	(O) U	Different: O (W)-I
			O-U later
6. [uw-ʌ]	reduce-reduction	U	Different: OW-I
			O-U later

*Comparison of adult and child spellings for word pairs exhibiting vowel alternations (Read, 1970:112).

In general, the children do not use abstract spellings (one letter to represent two different but related sounds, e.g., the underlined vowels of divine and divinity) to represent the pairs in Table 4.[8] The preschoolers' spellings strongly imply that they have not posited abstract vowels in their sound system for the pairs in the table above. Read pointed out that above type spellings persisted well into the first grade, but they gradually gave way to standard spellings as instruction in reading and writing became more rigorous and influential.

We have seen that both Read's and Moskowitz' findings imply that the source from which IM Rules are acquired is the spelling system of English. To ultimately determine the real source of IM Rules, one might consider conducting a Moskowitz-type experiment with illiterate speakers of English. The source of their knowledge or lack of knowledge of IM Rules could then be more clearly determined.

We will examine two other experimental studies which provide some evidence for the psychological reality of IM Rules. The following studies, however, do not propose any answers to the questions regarding the age or source of acquisition of such rules.

4.2 The Sherzer study

Sherzer (1970) examined a word game played by the Cuna Indians of Panama. The results of his investigation showed that some speakers do

[8]Note that first vowels in *nation* and *national* are represented by the same letter. This would be the correct representation for these vowels in the orthography. Read (1971:13) did not provide an explanation for this correct representation. He suggested the empirical hypothesis "that children find it easier to learn the relationship and the first vowel spelling of *nation/national* and similar forms than that of the derived forms in 1 and 2." At this point we can only ask the question: Why?

posit abstract forms for certain lexical items. Within the framework of phonology we have been discussing, these speakers must then apply the appropriate ɪᴍ ʀᴜles in order to arrive at the correct pronunciation of such items. At this point, it will be helpful to examine some of the details of Sherzer's study.

His analysis of Sorsik Sunmakke[9] (talking backwards) revealed the rule for playing the game. It consisted simply of moving the first syllable of a word to the end of the word, for example, the input [obsa] (bathed) gives the output [saob].

The lexical items to which Cuna speakers applied the syllable movement rule provided a view of the underlying forms the speakers had posited for that item. Consider the following lexical items from the Cuna language which served as inputs to the Sorsik Sunmakke syllable movement rule.

A. [gammai] (from [gab-mai]) sleeping
B. [baysa] (from [bag-sa]) bought

In Cuna phonology, the surface forms [gammai] and [baysa] are derived from their underlying forms ([gab-mai] and [bag-sa], respectively) by consonantal assimilation rules like the following

3. [b] → [m] / _____ m
4. [g] → [y] / _____ -$\overset{c}{g}$

Rule 3 states that /b/ is pronounced like /m/ when it is followed by /m/. Rule 4 states that /g/ is pronounced as /y/ when it is followed by a consonant other than /g/.

Referring back to the syllable movement rule, Sherzer found that for some speakers the surface forms served as the input while for other speakers, the underlying forms served as the input to the rule. The different inputs yielded the outputs exemplified in the table below.

Table 5. Variable inputs and outputs of the syllable movement rule.

Input	Output
a. [gab-mai]	[maigab]
[bag-sa]	[sabag]
b. [gammai]	[maigam]
[baysa]	[sabay]

Output *a* in Table 5 provides evidence that for *a* speakers the input to the syllable rule was [gab-mai], the underlying form, while for *b* speakers

---

[9] According to Sherzer, "Sorsik Sunmakke is one of at least four linguistic games found among the Cuna Indians of San Blas, Panama. The game is played mainly by children."

PHONOLOGY

the input was [gammai], the surface form.[10] It would be interesting to know if there were any significant differences between *a* and *b* speakers— that is, if the *a* speakers were literate and the *b* speakers illiterate. The important point here is that *a* speakers' choice of the underlying forms strongly indicates that IM RULES are psychologically real for them.

4.3. The Ohala study

The final study which supports the notion that IM RULES are psychologically real was conducted by Ohala (1974). The purpose of her experiment was to determine if [ghō:sla:] type words in Hindi (words pronounced with clusters at the phonetic level) have an underlying form with an abstract [ə], i.e., [gʰa:səla:]. According to the experimenter, there are few forms in Hindi which are pronounced with clusters at the phonetic level but have no alternating forms with [ə].

The following are some examples of these forms.

[gʰō̃:sla:] nest	[čutki:] snap of a finger
[jʰɔ̃:pri:] hut	[sɛ̃:kra:] 100

In addition to the forms above, Hindi also has a large number of related forms like the following:

[pəkər] catch	[pəkra:] caught
[pʰisəl] slip	[pʰisla:] slipped
[sərək] road	[sərkē:] roads
[hičək] hesitate	[hički:] hiccough
[sisək] sob (verb)	[siski:] sob (noun)

Ohala points out that alternations of the above type are fully productive in Hindi; for example, [pəkər] - [pəkra:] and [phisəl] - [phislə] are part of a common verbal inflection. For the [pəkra:] type words she posited an underlying form with the vowel [ə], e.g. /pəkar/. The surface forms are then derived by an ə-deletion rule. To determine experimentally whether /ə/ should be posited in the underlying forms of the [ghō:sla:] type words, 27 native speakers of Hindi were asked to add the -*iya* suffix (which blocks the application of the ə-deletion rule) to 30 common Hindi words.[11] An analysis of the results revealed the following:

---

[10]Sherzer explained the different outputs of speakers *a* and *b* by saying that different models of linguistic structure were being employed. Regarding the employment of different models, one could ask: Why were different models employed? Possibly the literacy status of the speakers could shed some light on this question. Determining whether the orthographic representation of a form resembles more its underlying form or its surface form might also shed some light on the question.

[11]After addition of the -*iya* suffix, some of the [ghō:sla:] type words yielded outputs unattested by semantically reasonable forms. Nine of the 30 words were of no interest to the experimenter but were put in so that the subjects would not answer automatically according to a certain pattern. See Ohala (p. 228) for a complete list of the words.

Three speakers gave predominantly [ə] responses (when presented with the stimulus [gʰō:sla:] + -iya, their response was [gʰō:sə liya:]); another three speakers gave predominantly zero responses ([gʰō:sliya:] as the response to the stimulus [gʰō:sla:]). The remaining 21 subjects showed some variation.

Ohala's study, like Sherzer's study, is relevant to our question regarding the psychological reality of IM RULES because it also has provided evidence that such rules *are* real for some speakers. For example, in order for a speaker to derive [gʰō:sla:] from the underlying form [gʰō:səla:], he must apply the IM RULES which will delete [ə] and yield the surface form. We pointed out earlier in this paper that speakers who posit underlying forms for phonologically related lexical items employ a strategy for arriving at the correct pronunciation of such forms that can be utilized during the reading process. This potential application of IM RULES during reading, particularly the more advanced stages of reading, is due mainly to the way in which a great many words are represented in the English spelling system. It will be instructive to examine their representation.

5. THE REPRESENTATION OF WORDS IN THE ORTHOGRAPHY

Carol Chomsky (1970) has pointed out that words are represented two ways in the orthography: lexically and phonetically. Examples of phonetically spelled pairs are words like *kill* and *sill* in which the phonetic difference between [k] and [s] is represented by different letters. Examples of lexically spelled words are pairs like *divine* and *divinity* in which the phonetic difference between the second vowel in each word is *not* represented by a different letter; the vowel segments of each member are represented in the same way in the conventional orthography.

There are two advantages of representing words lexically in the spelling system. The first is that a person learning to read will be aided by lexical spellings because words in the lexicon that are similar in meaning will look alike in the orthography. The second advantage is that a speaker can exploit his knowledge of IM RULES and systematically arrive at the correct pronunciation.

6. A STRATEGY FOR PRONOUNCING LEXICALLY SPELLED WORDS

Our purpose for focusing on word pairs involving vowel and consonant alternations is to point out that a reader will need to abandon the strategy he used to arrive at the correct production of phonetically spelled items in favor of a strategy (involving knowledge of IM RULES) that will enable him to correctly pronounce lexically spelled items. The reasons you will recall is that the graphemic difference between the *k* and *s* of phonetically spelled *kill* and *sill* is a signal to the reader to match the difference with a phonetic change. However, in lexically spelled *medicine* and *medicate* (to use an example involving a consonant alternation) there is no such signal, but in order to pronounce these words correctly a phonetic change is required. The underlying /k/ in *medicine* must be pronounced as [s], while in *medicate* it must be pronounced as [k]. The new strategy requires the application of IM RULES like those discussed in section 3. If speakers have IM RULES in their phonological component (the experimental studies have provided evidence that some speakers do have such rules), then they are in a position to utilize these rules during the reading process. We hypothesize that mature readers are able to arrive at the correct pronunciations of lexically spelled words because they have learned how to use their knowledge of IM RULES as a strategy for approaching these kinds of words.

This view of the reading process implies that a speaker will not need to exploit his knowledge of IM RULES until he reaches the more advanced stages of reading. However, examination of some of the introductory reading texts revealed that a speaker might need to utilize his knowledge of such rules long before he becomes a mature reader. For example, consider the following passage from *Uptown, Downtown*, the first reader in the Bank Street Basal Reading Series.

> "You are silly!" said Johnny.
> It isn't magic.
> "The new doors work by *electricity*."

If the correct pronunciation of words like *electric* and *electricity*, in which the consonants /k/ and /s/ alternate, is contingent upon the speaker's knowledge of IM RULES, and if a speaker is required to utilize his knowledge of these rules at an early age, then he needs to be systematically introduced to the examples (data) that will allow him to construct such rules. More than likely the reading teacher will be faced with the task of introducing the child to the relevant examples. Below we will make some recommendations based on our discussion of IM RULES that might be helpful to the teacher faced with the task of introducing lexically spelled words (that is, presenting for the first time a text that contains such words) to readers.

7. RECOMMENDATIONS FOR READING TEACHERS

At this point we can make several recommendations to the reading teacher based on the findings from the experimental studies discussed in Section 4. Before making the recommendations, we will briefly summarize the relevant findings. First, the findings of the studies done by Moskowitz, Sherzer, and Ohala support the notion that IM RULES are psychologically real for some speakers, that is, that they have knowledge of such rules; second, Moskowitz' findings indicate that knowledge of IM RULES is acquired, for some children, by the time they are seven years old; and third, her findings indicate that the spelling system of English is a possible source from which IM RULES are acquired. We can now return to the matter of what the reading teacher can do with respect to teaching the child how to exploit his knowledge of IM RULES.

7.1. Strategies for exploiting knowledge of IM Rules

First of all, it would seem that the age of seven is not too early to start presenting some of the relevant vocabulary the child will need to know in order to begin constructing the IM RULES like those accounting for vowel and consonant alternations in so many words of Romance origin in the English language. For example, recall that the word *electricity* appears in the text of the very first reader of the Bank Street Series now being used in some Washington, D. C. schools. Even though *electricity* is a derived word, it is quite common in the spoken language; therefore, some children will know how to pronounce this word before they learn to read. When they come across *electricity* in the textbook, the teacher could mention other members of this lexical family and point out why the family exhibits predictable consonant alternations. For example, the teacher could point out that *electricity* is related semantically to *electric, electrical,* and *electrician*. At the same time, the teacher could explain that when the suffix *-ity* is added to electric the [k] is pronounced like [s]. In her discussion of the pronunciation of *electrician* and *electrical* she could point out that when the suffix *-ian* is added to *electric* the [k] is pronounced like [s]; but when the *-al* suffix is added to *electric* the underlying final consonant, /k/, is still pronounced [k]. Other lexical word families that exhibit the pattern found in the *electric* family could be mentioned in order to show that the pattern is a general rather than a specific one. For example, the teacher could discuss the *magic* family, which includes *magic, magical,* and *magician*. The principle underlying the production of the members of the *magic* family is the same as the one underlying the production of the *electric* family. We hypothesize that the child's exposure to word families such as these under disucssion will enable him to construct the IM RULES which can account for the predictable phonetic realizations of the members of each lexical family. Once the child has constructed the relevant IM RULES, he will be in a position to exploit his knowledge of such rules when he comes across new words that operate like the members of the *electric* and the *magic* families; for example, he should be able to use his knowledge of the rules to arrive at the correct production of *optic, optical,* and *optician*. This ability to exploit his knowledge of IM RULES will enable the reader to attack lexically spelled words independently. As a result he will be in a position to move on to more advanced levels of reading without the constant guidance of the teacher.

We are not recommending that the teacher should encourage the child to incorporate all of the members of the lexical families into his speaking vocabulary, but rather we are recommending that the reader should be encouraged to note: first, that members of the lexical families are semantically related; and second, that he can use his knowledge of IM RULES to pronounce the members of such families. We are not implying in our recommendation that the child should be told that he has in his brain a thing called an IM RULE. All he needs to know is that the last sound of *optic, electric,* and *magic* is pronounced like [š] when the suffix *-ian* is added. The point we are trying to make is that it will be necessary for the reading teacher to first expose the child to the relevant vocabulary in a systematic way so that he can construct the IM rules needed to arrive at the correct pronunciation of lexically spelled words like *electric* and *electricity*.

When introducing lexical families it is important for the reading teacher to start with families containing members that are relatively familiar to the child. For example, the two members of the *sign* family, *sign* and *signature*, occur frequently in the spoken language, and as a result, some children will have no difficulty with the semantic content being expressed by these items. The same can be said for pairs like *resign* and *resignation* and *design* and *designation*. The first member of these pairs is likely to be the more common one, and if it occurs in the text and the second member does not, the reading teacher could mention the less common members for the purpose of pointing out the pattern underlying the phonological relationship between the two words. In some instances, the derived members of a word pair might occur without the underived member first occurring. For example, the word *implicit* occurs in Book Two of the Bank Street Series but *imply* does not. When discussing the meaning of a new word like *implicit*, the teacher could mention its root word and discuss how the two words are related phonologically and semantically.

Many lexically spelled items, however, are not frequently used in the spoken language but are often found in books for mature readers. Unfamiliar words that pattern phonologically like ones already known should not pose a problem for the reader if he has been shown how to exploit his knowledge of IM rules.

In deciding when to discuss the phonological patterns of lexical families, the teacher should keep in mind that age is not the most crucial factor but, rather, the reading level of the child, adolescent, or adult. If the reader doesn't know the members of phonetically spelled families like the *-at* family which is composed of words like *cat, rat, bat, sat*, etc., and the *-it* family, composed of *sit, bit, hit, fit*, etc., then one would assume that he is not ready to be exposed to lexically spelled items like *sign* and *signature*. We are following Carol Chomsky and proposing here that it's probably best for the reader to start with phonetically spelled words first, and later progress to the lexically spelled items. However, when it is time to make the transition from phonetically spelled words to lexically spelled words, the reader will need to adopt a new strategy for arriving at the pronunciation and the semantic content being expressed by the lexically spelled items. We have suggested here that the reader can begin learning the new strategy by first learning and later exploiting his knowledge of the relevant IM rules.

A strategy for pronouncing lexically spelled words, which involves knowledge and application of IM rules, immediately raises a question with regard to speakers of lects other than Standard English. How will speakers of other lects use IM rules that are not part of the phonological component of their lect? Obviously they will not be able to exploit rules which are not part of their phonological system. This does not present a problem for the strategy we have suggested because, as we have already pointed out, once the speaker is exposed to the relevant examples he will be able to construct the necessary IM RULES.

7.2 The necessity of a strategy involving IM Rules

In this paper we have proposed a strategy for arriving at the correct pronunciation of lexically spelled words. The strategy involves exploitation of the speaker's knowledge of IM RULES. One could question the necessity of our proposed strategy on four conditions. First, one could ask why a reader would need to adopt the strategy we are proposing if he can learn the semantic content and the pronunciation of lexically spelled words without our specific strategy? We realize that there are thousands of mature readers who have developed strategies for deriving the semantic content and the correct pronunciation of the words under discussion without ever hearing of the strategy we have proposed. However, we are not concerned with the readers who successfully develop their own strategies; we are concerned with the many readers who never do. Readers who never develop a method independently might profit from one in which they can draw upon their knowledge of IM RULES.

It would be much more economical for a reader to learn the IM RULES that will generate the correct output (pronunciation) for a whole class of words than for him to approach each word in the class as if it were unrelated phonologically to the other words. For example, *electricity, elasticity*, and *stoicity* are all related by a general rule which changes the final consonant, /k/, to /s/ when the *-ity* suffix is added. If a reader is made aware of this pattern he should be able to independently arrive at the correct production of *rubricity* by applying the appropriate IM RULE.

Second, the necessity of our strategy can be questioned on the grounds that few words requiring knowledge of IM RULES occur in texts other than highly advanced ones. One could ask why a reader would need a special strategy for dealing with such a small number of words. We are not sure what percentage of the words in reading texts are represented by lexical spellings, but even if they represent a small percentage, a reader will need to know how to approach such words if he is to become a successful reader.

Third, the necessity of such a strategy can be questioned regarding its usefulness for beginning readers. Wardhaugh (1970) has stated that a beginning reader neither knows nor needs to know vocabulary of Romance origin. However, we have observed that the item *electricity* occurs in the first reader of the Bank Street Series. A child confronted with words like *electric* and *electricity* must use some kind of strategy for arriving at the correct pronunciations of these words. If he adopts a strategy which can be used for other words exhibiting a pattern like *electric* and *electricity* (*elastic* and *elasticity*), he will have adopted a method that will allow him to proceed independently to other lexically spelled words exhibiting such a pattern. It is likely that a beginning reader would have fewer occasions on which to employ the strategy we are proposing than a more advanced reader, but as soon as lexically spelled words appear in the reading text the reader should be equipped with a strategy for approaching them.

Fourth, the necessity of the strategy being proposed can be questioned regarding the implied importance of the ability to correctly pronounce words during the process of reading. While a reader may very well reach a level on which it is not necessary to pronounce the words he is reading, one must bear in mind that such a level is an advanced one, and that it is probably attained only after the reader passes the stage during which it *is* necessary for him to pronounce words. For example, some kind of strategy will be most definitely necessary for the level one reader using the Bank Street reader.

Also part of the strategy we are proposing is a method by which a speaker can sharpen his comprehension skills. By recognizing that members of a family of lexically spelled words are semantically related, one can add an entire family of words to his reading vocabulary. If a reader knows the meaning of the root word *optic*, for example, then he should be able to arrive at the general semantic content of *optician* and *optical*. Once noting that most lexically spelled words are semantically related, a reader exposed to an individual member of a particular lexical family will only need to isolate the underlying root word in order to arrive at the general semantic content of the new family member.

To summarize, the model constructed by theoretical phonologists which represents a speaker's knowledge of the sound system of his language credits speakers with a complex set of rules that make up their phonological component. We have proposed that the speaker's knowledge of certain phonological rules (IM RULES) can be exploited for the purpose of improving reading skills. A method by which such knowledge can be exploited has been suggested.

REFERENCES

Black, I. S. *Uptown, Downtown: The Bankstreet Readers Series.* New York: Macmillan, 1965, 184.

Chomsky, C. 1970. "Reading, Writing and Phonology," in M. Lester (Ed.), *Readings in Applied Transformational Grammar.* New York: Holt, Rinehart and Winston, 211-236.

Chomsky, N., and M. Halle. *The Sound Pattern of English.* New York: Harper and Row, 1968.

Darden, W. "Introduction," in A. Bruck, R. Fox, and M. W. LaGaly (Eds.), *Papers from the Parasession on Natural Phonology.* Chicago: Chicago Linguistic Society, 1974.

Jesperson, O. *A Modern English Grammar on Historical Principles. Part I, Sounds and Spellings.* Heidelberg, 1907.

Krohn, Robert. "How Abstract is English Vowel Phonology?" in R. Shuy and C. J. N. Bailey (Eds.), *Toward Tomorrow's Linguistics*. Washington, D.C.: Georgetown University Press, 1974, 220-226.

Leopold, W. F. "Speech Development of a Bilingual Child: A Linguist's Record," *Sound—Learning in the First Two Years*, Volume 2. Chicago: Northwestern University Press, 1947.

Moskowitz, A. "On the Status of Vowel Shift in English," in T. E. Moore (Ed.), *Cognitive Development and the Acquisition of Language*. New York: Academic Press, 1973, 215-260.

Moskowitz, A. "The Two-year-old Stage in the Acquisition of English Phonology," *Language*, 46 (1970), 426-441.

Nichols, B. "A Rationale for Vowel Shift," in R. Shuy and C. J. N. Bailey (Eds.), *Toward Tomorrow's Linguistics*. Washington, D.C.: Georgetown University Press, 1974, 226-239.

Ohala, M. "The Abstractness Controversy: Experimental Input from Hindi," *Language*, 50 (1974), 225-235.

Preston, M. S. "Some Comments on the Developmental Aspects of Voicing in Stop Consonants," in D. L. Horton and J. J. Jenkins (Eds.), *Perception of Language*. Ohio: Merrill, 1971, 236-246.

Read, C. "Preschool English Phonology," *Harvard Educational Review*, 41.1 (1971), 1-34.

Schane, S. "How Abstract is Abstract?" in A. Bruck, R. Fox, and M. W. LaGaly (Eds.), *Papers from the Parasession of Natural Phonology*. Chicago: Chicago Linguistic Society, 1974, 297-318.

Sherzer, J. "Talking Backwards in Cuna: The Sociological Reality of Phonological Descriptions," *Southwestern Journal of Anthropology*, 26 (1970) 343-353.

Smith, N. *The Acquisition of Phonology: A Case Study*. New York: Cambridge University Press, 1973.

Wang, W. S. Y. "Vowel Features, Paired Variables, and the English Vowel Shift," *Language*, 44 (1968), 695-708.

Wardhaugh, R. "Linguistic Insights in the Reading Process", in Mark Lester (Ed.), *Reading in Applied Transformational Grammar*. New York: Holt, Rinehart and Winston, 1970, 236-257.

SOCIOLINGUISTICS

Sociolinguistics

Roger W. Shuy
Georgetown University

WHAT IS SOCIOLINGUISTICS?

Although any effort to define a new and broad field of study such as sociolinguistics is subject to question and criticism by some of its practitioners, it will be useful to attempt at least a broad definition of the term here. Three major characteristics tend to characterize the field:

1. A concern for viewing language *variation* rather than the sort of universals upon which grammars are usually based.
2. A concern for seeing language in real *social contexts* rather than as abstract representations.
3. A high potential for relationship and application to other fields such as education, sociology, anthropology, and psychology.

In a sense, the third characteristic is really an outgrowth of the first two, but, for our purposes, these three aspects will be treated equally.

At the present time, a sociolinguist may be defined as a person who studies variation within a language or across languages with a view toward describing that variation or toward writing rules which incorporate it (rather than, as in the past, ignoring it); relating such variation to some aspects of the cultures which use it; doing large scale language surveys (macroanalysis); doing intensive studies of discourse (microanalysis); studying language function (as opposed to language forms); discovering the comparative values of different varieties of language or of different languages for the benefit of political or educational planning and decision making; studying language attitudes, values, and beliefs; and relating all the above to other fields (including education).

Although there has been a recent flurry of interest in language in real social settings, it would be foolish to claim that sociolinguistics is a new concept. It is quite likely, in fact, that man has been interested in the sorts of variation by which people set themselves off from each other since the very beginnings of speech. Humans have always lived with the cultural and linguistic paradox of needing to be like one another while, at the same time, needing to establish individuality. These needs, coupled with the multitude of complexities involved in cultural and linguistic change, motivations, attitudes, values, and physiological and psychological differences, present a vast laboratory for sociolinguistic investigation.

WHERE DID SOCIOLINGUISTICS COME FROM?

In many ways, sociolinguistics involves a putting back together, within the field of linguistics, a number of separations that have taken place over the years. For one thing, the separation of language from the realistic context in which it is used has proved very troublesome in recent years. The more traditional view of linguistics (common in the sixties), which excludes the variational and functional aspects of language from formal linguistic analysis and describes such characteristics as mere trivial performance, is finding disfavor at a rapid pace. The term *static* may be used to refer to the frameworks of both structural and transformational linguistics. A static grammar is one which excludes variation of any sort, including time, function, socioeconomic status, sex, and ethnicity, from the purview of formal linguistic analysis. Thus, when Noam Chomsky (1965:4) states, "Linguistic theory is concerned primarily with an ideal speaker/listener, in a completely homogeneous speech-community, who knows its language perfectly and is unaffected by performance variations," he is illustrating the static view of language quite succinctly. Thus linguists more or less abdicated any responsibility for studying many of the interesting, dynamic aspects of language in a vain effort to be "purely linguistic," whatever that might mean.

Another clear separation, which has been vigorously maintained in linguistics over the years, is the separation between synchronic and diachronic studies. That is, the separation of the study of language change from the analysis of a language at a given point in time. Such a notion dates back many years in the field but is perhaps most notably stated by Bernard Bloch (1948:7) when he attempted to define the goal of phonological analysis as the study of "...the totality of the possible utterances of one speaker at one time in using a language to interact with one other speaker...." Such a theory would seem to imply that a speaker's phonological system is somehow cut off from the developments which gave it life. If, on the other hand, one were to view life as constant movement, one might also hypothesize that language is in equally constant movement in its futile effort to catch up with life. That is, life keeps moving away from the attempts of language at freezing it long enough to interact with it.

Thus, the period of linguistics called the structuralist period (the forties and fifties) was actually no different from the following transformationalist era with respect to the adherence to the study of static rather than dynamic language. But by the late sixties some fascinating new developments were taking place in several fields at the same time.

Led by William Labov, a group of scholars interested in variation in American English began to discover some new dimensions of systematic variation.[1] Past studies in American dialectology had described wide-meshed variation but had not accounted for it systematically. Using techniques borrowed largely from sociology, anthropology, and psychology, Labov clearly demonstrated that the study of a speech community was more revealing and systematic than the study of individual speakers and that instead of studying presence or absence of given features in the speech community, a great deal could be learned by seeing such features on a continuum. Such analysis began to be called gradient analysis. Thus it became important to know not just whether or not a speaker produced a given sound or grammatical structure but also the circumstances under which that form was produced (linguistic and psychosociological) as well as the frequency of occurrence of that form in relationship to consistent, comparable measures. Not all such scholars agreed with one another on the exact nature of this gradience, but the excitement generated by the notion quickly led to an alignment with linguists who had been studying creole languages such as William Stewart, who in 1964 presented his formulation of a continuum with what he called an acrolect at one end and a basilect at the other (1964:10-18). By this Stewart meant to indicate that speech communities could be plotted on a broad continuum rather than at artificial polarities such as standard or nonstandard per se. Acrolect was a person's most standard form. Basilect was his least standard. Creolists had long argued that pidgins and creoles, languages which are under construction and are therefore dynamic, offer the best opportunities to see how languages actually are developed.

At about the same time, the variationists and creolists were joined by a group of transformational linguists who were becoming disenchanted, among other things, by the static nature of their premises. James McCawley, Paul Postal, Robin and George Lakoff, Charles Fillmore, John Ross, and others began to raise objections against transformational syntax, noting its inability to accommodate real language, its failure to take into account that language is used by human beings to communicate in a social context, and its claim that syntax can be separated from semantics.[2] These scholars, currently called generative semanticists, see variation as heavily involved in grammar whenever the social context of a discourse changes. For example, one might dismiss the sentence, "Ernie thinks with

---

[1]See William Labov (1963).

[2]For an account of the effects of social situation on formal grammar, see Charles Fillmore (1973).

a fork," as ungrammatical unless one knew that such a sentence is a response to the question, "How do you eat potatoes?" In her work on politeness, Robin Lakoff demonstrates the importance of context when she notes that when addressing a child, "You may do so-and-so" is politer than "You must do so-and-so." But in addressing a dignitary at a party, the hostess who says "You must have a piece of cake" is politer than one who says, "You may have a piece of cake" (Lakoff 1972:907-927).

All of this recent emphasis on social context by linguists was old hat to anthropologists, especially ethnographers of communication. Dell Hymes has been arguing many years for a realistic description of language, observing that institutions, settings, scenes, activities, and various sociocultural realities give order to such analysis.[3] An ethnographic approach to speech requires that the analyst have information about the relative statuses of the interlocutors, the setting of the speech act, the message, the code (including gestures), the situation, the topic, the focus, and the presuppositions that are paired with the sentences. At long last, the ethnographers of communication are beginning to get some help from linguists with other primary specializations. The upshot of all this ferment within the past few years has been an almost entirely new set of attitudes within the field of linguistics. It is difficult to describe linguistics at any point in its history as being settled with an orthodoxy; but some broad, general movements can be discerned with hindsight. In the forties and fifties we saw a structuralist emphasis, with a focus on phonology, a concern for the word, and a philosophical framework which was positivistic and empirical. In the sixties we witnessed the transformationalist era, with a focus on syntax, a concern for the sentence, and a philosophical framework which was rationalistic or idealistic, with innate knowledge and intuition playing a prominent role in analysis.

As C.-J. Bailey (1973) points out, in the seventies we are entering a new period with an emphasis on discourse and a philosophical framework which is dynamic rather than individualistic or static. It is characterized by the concerns noted above by the variationists, ethnographers, generative semanticists, and creolists. Of particular concern to the interests of education is the underlying principle of the continuum. Like many such principles, it is patently obvious when noticed yet conspicuously absent from the history of language teaching.

It should be apparent, therefore, that sociolinguistics arose from a number of factors within the field of linguistics itself. A convergence of different avenues away from orthodox generative theory took place among dialectologists, creolists, semanticians, and anthropologists. Although the avenues were different, each shared a concern for variation, social reality, larger units of analysis (discourse), and a sense of continuum.

_____

[3]One might cite many references over a period of time. For a recent overview, see Dell Hymes (1973).

In addition, two factors outside the proper domain of linguistics also contributed heavily to the development of sociolinguistics. One was the general broadening of interests which began to develop in the sixties, leading to new kinds of interdisciplinary studies. The second was the development of interest in problems faced by minority peoples, especially in the schools. Linguists began to take an interest in urban language variation and to understand that past research methodologies were not viable for such investigation. New data-gathering techniques were required and new modes of analysis were needed. Meanwhile, linguists who had been interested in language variation as it is found in the creolization and pidginization of language also began to apply their knowledge to urban social dialect, particularly the urban, northern black, often providing important historical backgrounds for language change and offering analytical insights brought about by their perspectives. The general focus, of course, was on variability, not abstract uniformity and the critical measurement point was provided by the variability offered by Vernacular Black English. It was thought of as an area worthy of educational attention. Everything seemed ripe for this focus on Black English except for one thing—nobody in the academic world knew very much about it.

Seminal studies were done in New York by William Labov, Paul Cohen, Clarence Robbins, and K. C. Lewis; in Detroit by Roger Shuy, Walt Wolfram, and William Riley; in Washington by Ralph Fasold; and in Los Angeles by Stanley Legum. Generalizations about the findings of these studies have been made by Fasold and Wolfram in relatively nontechnical language (1970). Today variability in language analysis has become a crucial issue thanks, at least partially, to the influence brought about by the study of Vernacular Black English.

WHAT ARE SOME IDENTIFIABLE CHARACTERISTICS OF SOCIOLINGUISTIC WORK?

A focus of study which has developed out of a diversity of interests is likely to have an equally diverse literature. Yet there are some common threads which seem to help hold sociolinguistics together. One such characteristic is the concept of gradience mentioned earlier.

Gradience

As is often the case, personal experience provides a good first example. When I was in college I had a part-time job in a wholesale grocery warehouse loading and unloading trucks and boxcars. My fellow teamsters knew that I was a college kid but also expected me to be one of them in some sense of the word. As a native speaker of their local version of nonstandard English, I found it possible to use the locally acceptable "I seen him when he done it" forms; but their linguistic expectations of a college kid made them suspicious of me every time I tried. Years ago the novelist Thomas Wolfe wrote a novel called *You Can't Go Home Again.* His thesis was that people are the products of their changing environment and that this changing environment includes the changing expectations of others. Translated to our situation this means that no matter how uneducated a person's parents may be, they expect their child to speak something other than the nonstandard English they grew up with. The child who is sensitive to his parents' wishes may respond by rattling off a locution that appears to be within the range of his parents' expectations. On the other hand, some situations may require him to not deny his heritage but to not appear uppity either. Precious few linguistic situations will require him to preserve his nonstandard dialect exactly the way it was before he was educated and elevated to some other level of expectation by those who love him. The following sentences may serve as illustrations of some of the points on such a continuum.

1. Hey! Don't bring no more a dem crates over here!
2. Hey! Don't bring no more a dose crates over here!
3. Hey! Don't bring no more a those crates over here!
4. Hey! Don't bring any more of those crates over here!
5. Please don't bring any more of those crates over here.
6. Gentlemen, will you kindly desist in your conveying those containers in this general direction?

Number 6 is surely undesirable in most communications and it is included only to extend the limits of the continuum as far as can be imagined. Most of the adjustments that an educated speaker makes to his audience are found in various modifications of numbers 4 and 5. Most certainly, there are few opportunities for him to go home to the nonstandardness of numbers 1 or 2. Those who know him will think he is patronizing them or, worse yet, making fun of them. Consequently, what the speaker does is to make subtle adjustments in his vocabulary, grammar, and phonology depending on the informality of the situation, the audience, and the topic. One safe move is to standardize the grammar, since grammar is the most stigmatizing aspect of American social dialects, while occasionally preserving a few of the lesss stigmatizing pronunciations and leaving in some flavor of the lexicon. This is a highly subtle and complicated linguistic maneuver which can hardly be oversimplified or underestimated.

In no way should it be implied that the specific continuum given as an example above is meant to be a right to wrong slide. Each item of the continuum has the potential for appropriateness and accuracy if the proper setting, topic, and person is discovered. But the schools would be likely to take it as a right-wrong series with a sharp line between numbers 3 and 4 with *wrong* facing one direction and *right* facing the other. Similarly, all of the *rights* would be considered good and all of the *wrongs* would be thought bad. What such an oversimplification denies are the following things:

1. That language use is more complex than any presupposed context or psuedomoral code will permit.

2. That users of language may intentionally select so-called stigmatized constructions.
3. That users of language may unintentionally select so-called constructions which, having been used, provide clear evidence of their having learned part, though not all, of the pattern.

It has been argued by linguists that people tend to be unable to perceive the fact that they are using language as they use it. One might ask, for example, if the fish see the water in which they are swimming. Much rather clear evidence seems to indicate that users of language are fairly unaware of how it is that they are giving themselves away as they speak. Studies of social stratification using only language data may well be the most accurate indices of socioeconomic status yet devised. Since people have such a hard time seeing the language they and others use (for they are after all, concentrating on understanding it, not analyzing it), they remain relatively naive about the subtle complexities they are able to engineer in using it. Contrastive norms in language production and in subjective reactions to language are a clear case in point. Many new Yorkers and Detroiters, for example, will utilize a high frequency of a stigmatized feature in their own speech despite the fact that they can clearly recognize the same features as stigmatized in the speech of others.[4]

Frequency of occurrence

In addition to the complexities growing out of gradience and general variability, another area of complexity to which linguists have only recently attended is quantitative variability. As odd as it now may sound, it has not been the practice of linguists to note the frequency of occurrence of a given variable feature until very recently. An amusing internal argument is still going on between linguists who understand this principle and those who do not. It is said, for example, that copula deletion is a characteristic of Vernacular Black English as it is spoken in New York, Washington, D.C., and Detroit. Certain linguists violently object to this idea, noting that southern whites also say "he here" or "you gonna do it." And, of course, they are quite correct. What they fail to see, however, is that those who posit copula deletion as a characteristic of Vernacular Black English are not comparing southern whites to northern blacks but, quite the contrary, are concerned about what is considered Vernacular Black English in those specific northern contexts. But even there, we find that speakers of that dialect do not delete every copula. In fact, the frequency of occurrence of that deletion stratifies quite nicely according to socioeconomic status. Similarly, not every standard English speaker produces a copula every time it might be expected in his speech, although the frequency of occurrence is probably very high. An even clearer case is that of multiple negation which is also said to characterize Vernacular

---

[4]See William Labov (1966).

Black English, even though it is quite clear that many whites also use the form regularly. What, then, can it mean to call it Vernacular Black English? Simply that it is consistently found to occur in the continuous, natural speech of blacks at a much higher frequency than it occurs in the speech of whites from the same communities and of the same socioeconomic status (SES). Strangely enough, this sort of finding is still rather new in linguistics and, to some linguists, is quite heretical.

An example of a display of such data on the frequency of occurrence of a linguistic feature which is shared by all social groups (most of them *are* shared) is shown in Figure 1.

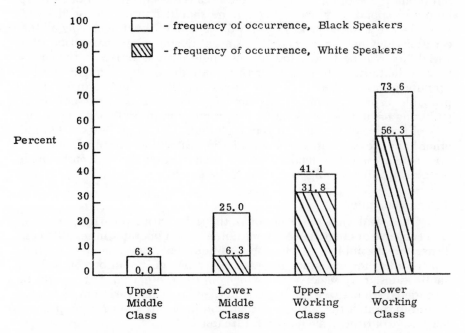

Figure 1. Multiple negation: frequency of occurrence in Detroit, by SES group.

Note that the frequency of occurrence of the use of multiple negation across four SES groups in Detroit is maintained regardless of the race of the speakers, but that blacks use multiple negation at a higher frequency than do whites. Further information reveals that men use them at a rate higher than women. Such data cannot tell us that blacks use multiple negatives and that whites do not. Nor could it say that men use them and women do not. But it does offer richer information about the tendencies toward higher or lower variability usage than we could ever obtain from a methodology which offered only a single instance of such usage as evidence of its use or nonuse. The figures represent a number of informants in each of the four SES groups and a large quantity of occurrences of the feature for each informant represented in the group. In the case of multiple negation, in addition to tabulating the occurrences, it was necessary to see them in relationship to a meaningful touchstone. Thus every single negative and every multiple negative in each speaker's speech sample were added together to form a universe of potential multiple negatives. The tabulated figures display the relationship of the occurrence of multiple negatives in relationship to all potential multiple negatives.

It is reasonably safe to assume that the extent of language variation is much broader than previous research methodologies ever revealed. If an informant is asked, for example, what he calls the stuff in the London air, he may respond only once /fag/. If he should happen to use the /a/ vowel before a voiced velar stop only 50 percent of the time during all the occasions in which he refers to this concept during a ten-year period, this variability will be totally lost in this single representation in the interview. If he talks continuously for thirty minutes or so, he might use this pronunciation a dozen or more times, giving an increasingly more probable representation of his actual usage. Of course, such data gathering techniques work better for pronunciations in which the inventory of possible occurrences is very high than they do for lexicon. On the other hand, research in sociolinguistics indicates that pronunciation and grammar are more crucial indicators than vocabulary, a factor which certainly justifies highlighting them for research.

Selectional options

Once we dispose of the notion of the right-wrong polarity evaluation and conceive of language as a continuum which operates in realistic contexts, the possibility of selectional options becomes meaningful. It is conceivable, for example, that a speaker out of a number of possible motivations, may select forms which, in some other context, would be considered stigmatized. Detailed studies of language variation have only begun to scratch the surface of such continua but several examples are suggestive of fruitful avenues of future research.

For example, I can clearly remember that as a child in a blue-collar industrial community, certain language restrictions were operational among preadolescent boys. To be an acceptable member of the peer group, it was necessary to learn and to execute appropriate rules for marking masculinity. If a boy happened to be the toughest boy in the class, he had few worries for whatever else he did would be offset by this fact. Those of us who were not the toughest could establish our masculinity in a number of ways, many of which are well recognized. Tough language (especially swearing) and adult vices (such as smoking) were sometimes effective means of obtaining such status. Likewise, if a boy were a good athlete, he could easily establish himself as masculine (in our society this was true only for football, basketball, and baseball and not for swimming, soccer, or tennis). On the other hand, a boy could clearly obtain negative points by having a nonsex-object relationship with a girl, by liking his sister, by playing certain musical instruments (especially piano and violin), and by outwardly appearing to be intelligent in the classroom. It is the latter avenue which is of interest to us here since the major instrument for adjusting one's outward appearance of intelligence was his use of oral language. Interestingly enough, what one did with written language seemed less crucial, as long as it remained a private communication between teacher and student. That is, a boy could be as smart as he wanted to on a test or an essay as long as the written document did not become public (displayed on the bulletin board).

Thus two strategies for reasonably intelligent males in this society were as follows:

a. *Keep your mouth shut in class.* If the male is white, this might be interpreted as shyness. If he is black, it usually is read as nonverbality. The strategy of keeping one's mouth shut in school is employed for different reasons at different times. In early elementary school, the child soon learns that the name of the game is to be right as often as possible and wrong as seldom as possible. One way to prevent being criticized by the teacher is to keep one's mouth shut. By preadolescence, the male's strategy for keeping his mouth shut grows out of a complex set of pressures stemming from stereotyped expectations of masculine behavior (boys are less articulate than girls and less interested in school) and the inherent dangers of appearing unmasculine to one's peers.

b. *If you give the right answer, counteract the "fink effect" by sprinkling your response with stigmatized language.* It is this strategy which boys must certainly master if they are to survive the education process in certain speech communities. Those who only keep their mouths shut tend to drop out ultimately for whatever reasons. But males who learn to adjust to the conflicting pressures of school and peer pressure are those who have learned to handle effectively the sociolinguistic continuum. In the proper context, and with the proper timing, an intelligent male can learn how to give the answer that the teacher wants in such a way that his peers will not think him a sissy. In English class he will learn how to produce the accepted forms with the subtle nuances of intonation and kinesics which signal to his peers that rather than copping out, he is merely playing the game, humoring the English teacher along. If he appears to be sufficiently bored, he can be allowed to utter the correct response. If he stresses the sentence improperly, he can be spared the criticism of selecting the accurate verb form. The six stage continuum noted earlier in this paper is a gross example of several choices available in such a situation. It is tempting to postulate that the male's need to counteract the "fink effect" by deliberately selecting stigmatized language forms is merely a working class phenomenon. Recent personal observations, however, have led me to question such a notion. My teenage son has lived his entire life in a middle-class, standard English speaking environment, but it is only since he began playing on a football team that he has developed a small number of nonstandard English features. The production of these features, which include multiple negation and *d* for *th* in words like *these* and *them*, is situationally confined to the present or abstract condition of football. He appears to use the standard English equivalents in all nonfootball contexts. Closer observation seems to indicate that not all members of the football team feel the same requirement. It would seem, in fact, that there are different pressures for different roles. My son is a defensive tackle, a position which seems to require the characteristics of an aggressive ape. Thus, apprentice apes must do everything possible to establish this condition. It is interesting to observe that pressure to select nonstandard forms seems less evident among quarterbacks and flankers.

A second recent observation has to do with the diagnosis of reading problems in an affluent Washington, D.C. suburb. A well meaning third grade teacher had diagnosed one boy's reading problem as one of "small muscle motor coordination," and she suggested that the parents send him to a neurologist. His father, a physician, objected strenuously, muttering something about teachers practicing medicine without a license. Since I knew the family, I was asked to help discover the child's real problem. After a quick examination, in which the boy evidenced little or no problem with decoding or comprehending material which was unknown to him, the only problem I discovered was that his reading was monotonous and mechanical. In the school's terminology, he did not read with "expression." A hasty survey of teachers revealed that boys tend to not read with expression, a fact which is generally accepted along with their nonverbality and dirty fingernails. Why didn't this boy read with expression? My hypothesis is that he considers it sissy. This boy is the smallest male in his class and he is using every means possible to establish his masculinity. What he lacks in athletic skill he more than makes up for with careless abandon. His voice is coarse. His demeanor is tough. He swears regularly. And so on. It would behoove the schools to do several things here. One might question the usefulness of reading with expression at all, but teachers should certainly be able to distinguish this presumed problem from other types of reading problems, particularly neurological ones. But this seems to be evidence of the same sort of pressure, this time in a middle-class community, which pits school norms against peer norms to the extent that the child is willing to deliberately select the nonstandard forms.

In addition to intentional selection of linguistic options, speakers also make unintentional selection of stigmatized language. One such selection involves the use of hypercorrections, a term which linguists use to refer to incorrect overgeneralization from already learned forms. Several years ago I noticed such a pattern in the development of my younger son's use of *-en* participles. Suddenly he seemed to be using the inflectional *-en* in all participle slots such as "have taughten," "have senden," and "have playen." My first reaction was to drill Joel on the proper form but I soon realized that he was actually evidencing awareness of a newly acquired pattern. What he had not yet learned was how to sort the participles out into -*en* and non-*en* forms. That would take time, but it would come. Hypercorrection is perhaps more readily recognized by English teachers in the form of the malapropism, a vocabulary item which comes close to the sound of the word intended but which clearly misses, yielding a humorous combination such as "prosecuting eternity." Grammatical hypercorrection yields equally psuedo-elegances such as "between you and I." In terms of selectional options, hypercorrections in vocabulary, pronunciation, and grammar pose an interesting problem which illustrates clearly the need to see language in a realistic social and psychological context. Hypercorrections, when detected, can count double or more in degree of stigmatization. If undetected, they are unlikely to be favored more than neutral. Thus, when people make judgments about the language used by a speaker, there are at least three areas of judgment involved: stigmatization, favoring, and hypercorrection. Detected hypercorrection probably runs the greatest risk of negative social stigmatization. Oddly enough, vocabulary hypercorrection (malapropism) is probably the most highly stigmatized, followed by pronunciation hypercorrection (the pseudo-elegance of *vahz* for *vase*, for example) and last by grammatical hypercorrection (such as "between you and I"). Stigmatization reverses this procedure, with grammatical features most stigmatized (at least in America), followed by phonological and lastly by vocabulary. This process of favoring is still relatively unknown, and it is difficult to tell whether vocabulary or grammar is the most favored condition. Within each linguistic category (pronunciation, grammar, and vocabulary), individual features can be placed and rank ordered, although the exact nature of this ordering is not totally known at this time.

Perceptual viewpoint of the whole

Still another characteristic of sociolinguistics is involved in the very viewpoint from which language phenomena are perceived. It is logical to believe that once the basics of language are understood, other less central features will fall into place. It has been traditional in linguistics to follow this logic. Thus linguists of various theoretical persuasions have searched for the core, the basics, and the universals of language and have paid little attention to the peripheral, the surface, or the variables. Sociolinguists do not decry an interest in universals or basics, but they feel that the peripheral variables are much more important than have ever been imagined. In fact, sociolinguists tend to treat peripheral and basic componets on a par, and they believe that to understand one, they must also know a great deal about the other. Sociolinguists, therefore, stress variation, especially as it is related to sex, age, race, socioeconomic status, and stylistic varieties. They feel that by paying attention to such variables, they can better understand the exciting dynamics of language and see it as a whole.

Subjective reactions

The development of sociolinguistics has also been paralleled by an interest in the subjective reactions of speakers to language. If speakers produce linguistic features with varying frequencies, if they make use of complex selectional options, and if they shift back and forth along a base line continuum, they most certainly also react to language produced by others. In recent years, sociolinguists have become interested in three types of subjective reactions to variation in spoken and written language:

1. Studies which compare subjective reactions to more than one language.
2. Studies which compare subjective reactions to variation within the same language.
3. Studies which compare accented speech, the production of a language by nonnative speakers.

It is felt that such studies will enable linguists to get at the threshold, if not at the heart, of language values, beliefs, and attitudes. From there it is a relatively short step to relating such attitudes to actual language teaching and planning. For example, research by Wallace Lambert and his associates (1960) attempted to determine how bilingual Canadians really felt about both English and French in that area. Therefore several bilinguals were tape recorded speaking first one language, then the other. The segments were scrambled and a group of bilingual Canadians were asked to listen to the tape and rate the speakers on fourteen traits such as height, leadership ability, ambition, sociability, and character. The listeners were not told that they were actually rating people twice, once in French and once in English. It was somewhat surprising to the researchers that the speakers were generally stigmatized when they spoke French and favored when they spoke English. This was interpreted as evidence of a communitywide stereotype of English speaking Canadians as more powerful economically and socially.

An example of a study which compares listener reactions to variation within the same language was done in Detroit (Shuy, Baratz, and Wolfram, 1969). An equal number of black and white, male, adult Detroiters from four known socioeconomic groups were tape recorded in a relatively free-conversation mode. These tapes were played to Detroiters of three age groups (sixth grade, eleventh grade, and adult). An equal number of males and females, blacks and whites listened to the tape. These judges represented the same four socioeconomic groups as the speakers. The purpose of the study was to determine the effects which the race, sex, socioeconomic status, and age of the listener have on identifying the race and socioeconomic status of the speaker. The results of the study showed that racial identity is quite accurate for every cell except for the upper middle-class black speakers, who were judged as white by 90 percent of the listeners, regardless of their race, age, or sex. It also showed that the lower the class of the speaker, the more accurately he was identified by listeners, regardless of all other variables. The significance of this lies in the fact that listeners apparently react negatively to language more than favorably to it. That is, stigmatizing features tend to count against a speaker more than favoring features tend to help him. Such information is, of course, useful in determining how to plan a language learning curriculum, among other things.

A recent study of accented speech was done by A. Rey (1974) and contrasted the subjective reactions of Miami teachers, employers, and random adults to the accented speech of Cuban born and native white and black Miamians. Rey's interest was in the extent to which accent played a role in both employability and school evaluation. He played tape recordings of various speakers to groups of listeners and concluded that the lower status Cuban born Miamians have the least chance for success, even if the employer or teacher is also Cuban born.

WHAT ARE THE PROSPECTS FOR SOCIOLINGUISTICS IN THE FUTURE?

To date, the study of sociolinguistics can be said to have hardly begun. Variation is a vast expanse of possibilities which should keep linguists busy for years to come. A very small dent has been made in the study of variation among certain minority groups. Through an accident of history, a great deal has been learned about Vernacular Black English but very little is known about the variation used by standard English speakers, regardless of race. Little is known about the sort of variation which establishes a speaker as a solid citizen, a good guy, or an insider. Despite some intensive research in the area, little is known about how people shift from one register to another or, for that matter, from one dialect or language to another. Only the barest beginnings have been made in the study of special group characteristics related to language (language and religion, law, medicine). A great deal of research needs to be done on language attitudes, values, and beliefs. Although language change has received attention in a number of recent studies, sociolinguistic research still lacks knowledge of a number of aspects of the exciting dynamics of language.

In short, the social contexts in which language can be studied have almost as many variations as there are people to vary them. In some fields of study, graduate students writing theses or dissertations often become discouraged over the fact that all the good topics for research have already been used up. This dilemma is far from a reality in sociolinguistics, where topics abound and where we are only at the beginning.

REFERENCES

Bailey, Charles-James N. "Contributions of the Study of Variation to the Framework of the New Linguistics," paper presented at the International Linguistic Association, Arequipa, Peru, 1973.

Bloch, Bernard. "A Set of Postulates for Phonemic Analysis," *Language*, 24, 3 (1948).

Chomsky, Noam. *Aspects of the Theory of Syntax*. Cambridge: M.I.T. Press, 1965.

Fasold, Ralph W., and W. A. Wolfram. "Some Linguistic Features of Negro Dialect," in Ralph W. Fasold and Roger W. Shuy (Eds.), *Teaching Standard English in the Inner City*. Washington, D.C.: Center for Applied Linguistics, 1970.

Fillmore, Charles. "A Grammarian Looks to Sociolinguistics," in R. Shuy (Ed.), *Sociolinguistics: Current Trends and Prospects*. Washington, D.C.: Georgetown University Press, 1973.

Hymes, Dell. "The Scope of Sociolinguistics," in R. Shuy (Ed.), *Sociolinguistics: Current Trends and Prospects*. Washington, D.C.: Georgetown University Press, 1973.

Labov, William. "The Social Motivation of a Sound Change," *Word*, 19 (1963), 273-309.

Labov, William. *The Social Stratification of English in New York City*. Washington, D.C.: Center for Applied Linguistics, 1966.

Lakoff, Robin. "Language in Context," *Language*, 48 (1972), 907-927.

Lambert, W. E., and others. "Evaluational Reactions to Spoken Language," *Journal of Abnormal and Social Psychology*, 60 (1960), 44-51.

Rey, Alberto. "A Study of the Attitudinal Effect of a Spanish Accent on Blacks and Whites in South Florida," unpublished doctoral dissertation, School of Languages and Linguistics, Georgetown University, 1974.

Shuy, Roger W., J. C. Baratz, and W. A. Wolfram. "Sociolinguistic Factors in Speech Identification," National Institute of Mental Health Research Project No. MH-15048-01, 1969.

Stewart, William A. "Urban Negro Speech: Sociolinguistic Factors Affecting English Teaching," in R. Shuy (Ed.), *Social Dialects and Language Learning*. Champaign, Illinois: National Council of Teachers of English, 1964.

Sociolinguistics and Reading

Barbara M. Horvath
University of Sydney

Many of the insights gained in sociolinguistics studies over the past several years have implications for the field of education in general and for the teaching of reading skills in particular. As sociolinguists, our task has been to describe geographic and social dialects, with an emphasis in the past few years on social dialects. That is, we are interested in how the speech of people from different social classes varies; how the speech of young people is different from that of old people; how women's speech differs from men's speech; or how social setting affects speech. Using these descriptions, we construct grammatical theories to explain language variation. /But we are also interested in the ways that these various dialectal differences are significant in everyday life.⌉ We want to know what role these differences play in school performance, in performance on standardized tests, in cognitive ability, or in getting a job.

Because of interest in describing through direct observation the language the child brings to school with him, sociolinguistics complements the current educational philosophy of meeting the individual needs of the child by starting where the child is. As is well-known, it is our firm belief that no child comes to school without language. No child comes to school as an empty vessel waiting to be filled by the school system.

Five areas that have interested sociolinguists are pertinent for educators: the language deficiency notion; the difference among the various dialects of American English; attitudes people have toward dialects and their speakers; standardized testing, including reading tests; and, finally, approaches to the teaching of reading to nonstandard dialect speakers.

THE LANGUAGE DEFICIT NOTION

The first, and by far the most important, question we have dealt with is whether language or dialect differences can be viewed as deficiencies. There has been a widespread feeling (based on the notions of naive observers of language) that some lower socioeconomic class children, particularly black and Chicano children, are deficient in terms of language development and that this deficiency, in turn, affects their cognitive development (Bereiter and Engelmann, 1967). Another related issue has to do with whether this deficiency is genetically based (Jensen, 1969).

These positions have been attacked by many sociolinguists, probably most effectively by Labov in his article, "The Logic of Nonstandard English." Very often the child is judged deficient in language development as a result of his performance in an interview situation. Many children have been assessed as nonverbal or completely lacking in language development because when faced by white, middle-class observers in fairly formal settings, they respond in one or two word sentences. It so happens that, at about the same time psychologists were making these observations, sociolinguists also were faced with situations in which they were using interviews for collecting data.

The primary methodology of sociolinguistics is direct observation of language in its social setting. In this way, we differ from traditional linguists of the transformational school who, by and large, limit themselves to the study of the standard English of college professors and graduate students (the English they speak themselves). Because we are interested in social dialects, it has been necessary for us to develop techniques for collecting speech samples in natural situations. Early studies in New York (Labov, 1966) and Detroit (Shuy, Wolfram, and Riley, 1967) had shown that social context could affect the speech characteristics of an individual. Social context includes such things as the topic being discussed; the physical situation (the principal's office vs. the playground); and the socioeconomic class, age, sex, and race or ethnic backgrounds of the conversants. Knowledge that social context affects speech characteristics has been an important consideration in the collection of speech samples for inclusion in descriptive studies.

Labov (1969) in his studies—and his findings have often been replicated—found that an interview situation can be a threatening event for children, especially in a very formal setting and when the interviewer is from a higher class or different racial or ethnic background than the child. The same children who replied to his questions in monosyllables during a formal interview became very verbal in a less structured situation, sitting on the floor and eating potato chips with friends.

This kind of information is of use to educators. For instance, many children are interviewed as part of the initial school registration process or during individualized testing situations. It has often been the case that children on these occasions do not talk much and are described as nonverbal. We have learned that the kinds of questions asked during an interview elicit more or less speech; for example, if you ask a child to descibe a particular object or to tell you a story about a picture—a technique often used in language and IQ tests—you are not likely to get much of a response. People seem to respond best when an interviewer, after establishing some rapport, discusses topics of personal interest to the one being interviewed.

Much of the evidence used to argue for genetic deficiency comes from standardized tests of intelligence. Most of these tests are biased so that middle-class white children do best because the dialect they learn at home and the kinds of experiences they have had are just those which are equated with success in school and, therefore, are used as test items to predict success. A child with nonstandard English and nonstandard experiences may not succeed in school and on tests. But, is the deficiency in the child or in the school? Do kids fail school or do schools fail to educate kids? There is no reason to believe that multiple negatives, copula deletion, consonant cluster simplification, or any other linguistic feature should interfere with an individual's being able to think creatively. Speakers of dialects other than the standard are no more logical or illogical, verbal or nonverbal, than speakers of the standard dialect. All dialects, standard or nonstandard, are acquired in much the same way; the acquisition of language is a natural, developmental process.

Too often, nonstandardisms are interpreted as "nonlanguage." Different phonological or grammatical systems are heard as mumbles or as garbled speech. Because the middle-class observer does not understand what is being said, he jumps to the conclusion that nothing is being said.

It is a mistake to assume that, because a particular surface form is not present, the process also is lacking. When a child is asked, "Where is the squirrel?" and then replies, "In the tree." it cannot be said that the child cannot construct complete sentences. This is a normal response in a conversational setting. Because a child does not use "if" or "whether" in surface level sentences does not imply that he is illogical. A Standard English sentence like "I asked John if he knew where the ball was." is said in Black Vernacular English as "I ax John did he know where the ball was." The underlying question in this sentence is signaled by the "if" complementizer in the Standard English sentence and by inverted subject/verb order in the Black Vernacular English sentence.

Most insidious of all, of course, is to jump to the conclusion that speaking a different dialect implies a cognitive deficit. Again, Labov has demonstrated what most of us have personally experienced: that profound notions can be expressed in nonstandard dialects and fairly unprofound ideas can be expressed in elaborate standard dialect.

MAJOR DIFFERENCES AMONG DIALECTS OF
AMERICAN ENGLISH

What differences have we come up with between standard and nonstandard dialects? Excluding Standard English (SE), Black Vernacular English (BVE) is one of the most intensively studied American dialects. Some of the major differences between BVE and SE that have been reported include those in the following list.[1]

1. The absence of -s in the third person singular (he go)
2. Multiple negation (didn't do nothing)
3. Absence of -s possessive (man hat)
4. Invariant be (he be home)
5. Absence of copula in certain constructions (he nice)
6. Been auxiliary in active sentence (he been ate the food)
7. Existential it (it is a whole lot of people)
8. Word-medial and final ð and ɵ(/tuf/ *tooth*)
9. Word-final consonant clusters (/gɛs/ *guest* and *guessed*)
10. Word-initial ð (/den/ *then*)

Preliminary studies have also been made of English as spoken by Puerto Ricans (Wolfram, 1974) and by Chicanos (Horvath, ms) and research is now being done on other dialects of English including Appalachian English, southern white English, Italian-English, and others.

What do all of these add up to? In other words, how different are these dialects from Standard English? The majority of rules used to generate sentences in Standard English and these nonstandard dialects are the same. The bulk of the differences are what linguists call low-level, primarily phonological, differences. For example, let us take copula (to be) deletion in BVE in such sentences as:

> It mine.
> He gonna go home.
> He good.

If we were limited to sentences like this, we might conclude that speakers of BVE do not have the copula in their grammars. However, by examining different kinds of sentences, we can demonstrate that BVE speakers do indeed have the copula in their grammar. For instance, the copula is present in cases like the following:

> It mine, I know it is.
> He good, I know he is.

What Labov (1969) was able to demonstrate was that in sentences of the "It mine." type, BVE speakers carry the process of contraction one step further than speakers of Standard English, so that wherever SE speakers

---

[1] This is a partial list taken from Wolfram (1970a: 105-119).

can contract, BVE speakers can delete. Copula deletion, then, is a low-level phonological process, meaning that in the generation of the sentence, at a given abstract level, the grammar is the same in both dialects. At the risk of oversimplification, we can say that the rules for pronunciation differ but the basic elements of the sentence are the same.

These phonological processes often eliminate grammatical categories on the surface. That is, consonant cluster simplification can make it appear that such grammatical features as past tense are not used or understood by a given speaker. This can be disproven easily by demonstrating that the person knows the event took place in the past or by looking at the irregular verbs, where the present/past tense distinctions are usually kept.

A number of grammatical differences also have been found. (See 1-7 on the preceding list.) Wolfram (1969) found in his Detroit study that these grammatical features were more highly stigmatized than the phonological features. He reported sharp, qualitative differences between social classes on grammatical features, whereas phonological features showed gradient, quantitative differentiation. This led him to suggest that in teaching SE, it is important to teach grammatical features before phonological ones.

THE STUDY OF LANGUAGE ATTITUDES

What does it mean when you say that linguistic features are stigmatized? Another area that sociolinguists have addressed is social evaluation of particular linguistic forms. Although we can say scientifically that no one dialect or language is any better or worse than another or that any idea can be expressed in any dialect or language, we must report that speakers *evaluate* dialects as better or worse and associate stereotypes with these dialects. Comedians and playwrights often make use of our evaluations of certain dialects to create effects.

We have come to find out in sociolinguistic studies that attitudes toward a dialect are focused on a number of linguistic features. In other words there are certain linguistic features that are marked, either as prestige features or as stigmatized ones. Of course, the majority of language is not socially marked, but several recurrent features are picked out as markers.

A number of studies have been done on attitudes people have toward a dialect and toward the speakers of that dialect. Normally, a segment of taped speech is played for an audience and they are asked to make judgments about whether the language is pleasing or not pleasing and are asked to speculate about the educational level, class background, race, or job held by the speaker (Shuy, Baratz, and Wolfram, 1969). Shuy (1973) did a study in Washington, D. C., asking employers for what positions they might hire various speakers. The telephone company simply would not have hired some of the people for any job based on samples of their speech alone.

Williams and Whitehead did an interesting experiment with teachers, essentially finding out that teachers—like the rest of humankind—formed stereotypes of children based on speech patterns.

We can accept that an employer's attitude toward nonstandard speech may keep a prospective employee from obtaining a job. But how do teacher's attitudes toward a child affect the child's performance in school? An experiment reported by Rosenthal and Jacobson indicates that when the teacher is told that the children in her class are bright, even though they have been tested as dull, the children perform better than would normally be expected. In other words, children reflect in their performance what their teachers think about them. Rosenthal and Jacobson have termed this the Pygmalion effect.

A teacher's attitude toward a dialect probably comes from two sources: the first is the socialization process and involves the racial, class, and regional background he or she may have; then, depending upon the kind of educational background or inservice training the teacher has had, so-called scientific theories may reinforce those attitudes. For instance, if one came to the university with negative feelings toward the speech of lower-class, urban blacks and took a course on early childhood intervention strategies, many of which are essentially based on the notion that black children have no language, the original attitude becomes reinforced and is justified through "objective science."

There are many approaches that can be taken toward bringing about change in attitudes toward nonstandard dialects and their speakers. One suggestion is to find out about regional and social dialects, particularly through careful observation of the speech of others and of oneself. The important thing is to be aware of the social evaluations made of linguistic features and not to confuse these evaluations with the child's real abilities, assuming that a child cannot do well in school because he speaks a nonstandard dialect.

TESTING

The field of testing is another area in which sociolinguists have done some work. We are particularly interested in pointing out standardized and other tests which are biased against speakers of nonstandard dialects or people with nonstandard experiences. Of special interest are tests purporting to measure intelligence, which make the claim that they are measuring some innate ability of the individual. The Peabody Picture Vocabulary Test (PPVT) is an example of the approach taken by sociolinguists to the criticism of standardized tests.

The PPVT consists of 150 words; the child is presented with the stimulus word and asked to indicate which of four pictures represents the meaning of that word. The PPVT claims to estimate verbal intelligence through the measurement of hearing vocabulary.

This test can be criticized from a number of points of view, which can be exemplified by the following.

1. The test is given on a one-to-one basis and, as has already been discussed, this kind of interview setting can be threatening to some children.

2. The examiner is asked to pronounce the words "correctly." Aside from the fact that this rule probably causes little harm because people look it up in Webster's and then pronounce it according to their own dialect, the real danger comes when the author indicates that where both a "local" and "correct" form are used, the examiner should use both. Knowing how insecure many people are about their language, some examiners may be tempted to do just that! Imagine the child's confusion at being presented with two forms. More importantly, in many cases the examiner does not speak the dialect of the child taking the test.

3. The pictures used in the PPVT depict no blacks, Chicanos, Indians, Orientals, men without ties, or women doing interesting things. Class bias is obvious on every page, in just the pictures alone.

4. The basic content of the test is words. The unsophisticated view of language is that it is basically a list of words; therefore, if you want to measure verbal intelligence, you devise a test that shows how many words a person knows. Throw in some esoteric words and you separate those who *really* know language from those who do not. The next jump is impossible for linguists to take. That is, if you know the meanings of "osculation," "humunculus," "cryptogram," and "pensile," you are very intelligent. Whether a child knows what these words mean has more to do with exposure to situations in which these words are used (probably very stuffy writing) than to any inherent intellectual capacity.

5. A cursory examination of the 150 words shows that the majority of them come out of a middle-class experience. The black ghetto child, the migrant Chicano child, the lower-class white child all are put at a disadvantage by this test.

6. The norming population consisted of white children from Nashville, Tennessee. The author does not make any note of the socioeconomic class of these students. This hardly seems a representative sample.

Sociolinguists are also critical of test directions which state that the child should mark the "best" answer when the best answer is obviously what the test designer expects. If the test taker is from the same background as the test designer, it probably will be easier to come up with the right answer because the expectations match. However, if the social and linguistic background of the child is not that of the test giver, the chances are fewer that he will come up with the best answer.

It seems to me that reading tests are particularly vulnerable to criticism from this point of view, particularly when comprehension tasks are being tested. Such tasks as getting the main idea, problem solving, drawing inferences, separating fact from opinion, or evaluating the author's purpose depend heavily on one's socialization. A few examples from a series of reading tests used in a large, urban school system can illustrate this idea.

By answering the following test item correctly, the student is said to be demonstrating that he/she can predict or anticipate what is to follow a specific situation in a story.

> Yellow Cat had something to eat in her dish. Just then her kitten, Jumper, walked by. "What is in your dish?" asked Jumper.
> What will Yellow Cat probably do next?
> 1. Run away from Jumper.
> 2. Let Jumper see the dish.
> 3. Have a party for Jumper.

What is the "best" answer—that is, what does the test designer think ought to be the outcome here? "Let Jumper see the dish" of course, reflecting his strong belief in "being nice." But what about the child who says that (1) is the right answer "because Yellow Cat doesn't want Jumper to have any of the food." Now running away does not mean that Jumper will not get the food, but it is the only answer that in any way allows a child to express the negative feeling that Yellow Cat does not want to be nice to Jumper. We certainly cannot say that is not a possible outcome in the real world, although in the world of children's stories where everyone is always nice, it may not be the usual outcome.

In another item, the student is asked to identify the author's purpose.

> Mr. Brown liked animals. He had a duck, a pig, and a bear. They liked Mr. Brown. He was kind to them.
> Why was this story written?
> 1. To tell about someone.
> 2. To tell something funny.
> 3. To tell how to do something.

The "best" answer is (1), but the child answered (3), explaining that the point of the story was that if you had one of those pets, he told you how to take care of it, to be kind to it and not to be mean. There are many different reasons why an author writes a piece; quite often the reason is to point up some moral, perhaps more often than not in children's stories. It is true that at one level this story tells about someone, but it seems to me that this child is demonstrating a deeper level of understanding of the author's purpose. But he's called wrong because it is not the "best" answer.

At a more advanced level of the reading test series, the student is asked to demonstrate that he can separate fact from opinion.

> Tony: The Center is great on Friday nights!
> Jenna: I like to go after school, too.
> Hoyt: Everything the Center offers is fun and well planned.
> Lew: But sometimes it's too noisy!
> Donald: Well, there will be only twenty people in each class next month.
> In the conversation you have just read, who told a *fact* about the Center?

The "best" answer is *Donald*. However, if we examine this set of sentences more closely, we can see that the last sentence can be used to express the opinion that, if only twenty people were present, it would no longer be too noisy. That is, the noise was caused by the quantity present, not the quality. Beginning the sentence with "well" is a good indicator that a simple fact is not to be presented but that a fact is being used to express an opinion.

Linguists have recently become interested in looking at different ways of doing things with sentences. Take, for instance, making requests. Normally a request is thought to have a form like:

> Shut the window, please.

But, requests can also be expressed as:

> Can you shut the window?
> Will you shut the window?
> Would you mind shutting the window?

Or even, given the right context:

> It's very cold in here, Jeeves.

A child who intuitively recognizes that Donald is expressing as much of an opinion as the others then becomes confused about what task he is being asked to perform.

For those of us who are adept at taking tests (and if we were not, we would not occupy the positions we do), the answers on these items seem obvious. I have recently begun a project in which I administer reading tests to children and tape record their responses, having them read and work out the answers aloud. Often I question them about why they have made a particular choice. Some interesting things have turned up.

1. A child can make mush out of the reading passage and still get the correct answer. How such a test can then be a test of reading becomes difficult to understand.

2. On some items, children are asked to override their own intuitions. For example, on items where the child is given a word and asked to identify another word that has the same vowel sound, pronunciation rules can get in the way. Take, for instance,

> big / find   ride   give.

The child immediately hears that the vowels in "give" and "big" sound alike, but he hesitates to put down the correct answer, saying "even though it says [sic] an *e* at the end of it, they sound alike." In another instance he insisted upon pronouncing "shoes" as "shows," even though it made no sense in the story and when questioned, he quoted again the rule for long vowels. I asked him if it made any sense to him and he rather matter-of-factly said, "no." He has almost come to the point where reading does not really have to make sense; the important thing is to apply the pronunciation rules.[2]

3. If we are willing to believe Frank Smith that the techniques used by beginning readers differ from those used by accomplished readers, then we should expect reading tests to reflect this fact. We would not expect word attack skills (rules for pronunciation) to be as important to the more mature reader as they are to the beginning reader. In fact, as we have already seen, they may even get in the way of good reading. The tests I have been working with do not at all reflect this distinction. In fact, as the reading level increases, the word attack skills become very complex—reminding me of reading Chomsky and Halle's *The Sound Patterns of English*. Many of these rules relate to recently formulated rules of stress and vowel quality that transformational grammarians have tried to make explicit but of which speakers of English already have subconscious knowledge. It does not seem necessary to have students make these rules explicit in order to read. Surely, if a student did not know the word "propeller," knowing the following rule would not help much.

> The primary accent in words with double consonants before an inflectional ending or a derived form suffix is just before the suffixal ending and the vowel is usually short in that accented syllable.

The student would be better off if he figured out that the subject matter was airplanes and guessed that the funny word with the *p*'s, *l*'s, and *-er* was propeller. Even if he said propeeler or pro-peller as a wild guess, he would soon realize what it was—if his intuitions had not been totally stamped out of him—and then pronounce it correctly, using his innate linguistic competence.

THE TEACHING OF READING

Before discussing the teaching of reading, I must make it clear that we offer no "sociolinguistic" method that will one day replace the "linguistic" method of teaching reading. As a matter of fact, most linguists have failed to understand what is linguistic about the so-called linguistic method. Any teaching method can contain a sociolinguistic perspective if it embodies an understanding of and an allowance for dialect variation. We do, however, have some opinions on approaches that have been suggested.

In the past few years, five different approaches have been considered as alternatives for teaching nonstandard speakers to read (Shuy, 1973). Starting from the realization that some change is necessary because Johnny is not learning to read, these approaches differ in which aspect of

---

[2]Goodman has been saying for some time that the rules can get in the way of learning to read. That was certainly demonstrated by this child who is classified as a poor reader. On numerous occasions, he intuitively knew the right answer but ended up, instead, trying to force pronunciation rules in places where they did not work.

the learning system is asked to do the changing: the child, the teacher, or the reading materials.

We can change the child by teaching him Standard English first and then teaching him to read. This would put off reading for some time and probably would not be well received by many parents, teachers, and administrators. But, more importantly, we cannot in any way guarantee that we know how to accomplish the task of teaching Standard English as a second dialect (Fasold, in press). Even if possible, it would take hours and hours of drill and, as Wolfram (1970) has noted, "the sociocultural facts which inhibit the widespread acquisition of Standard English as a second dialect do not suggest this alternative as a reasonable solution."

Another approach has been suggested involving change on the part of the teacher (Labov, 1967; Goodman, 1967). This approach would instruct teachers about particular nonstandard dialects so they would not confuse the use of the dialect with reading problems. For example, if the test read,

"Joe goes to the store for his mother after school."

and the child read,

"Joe he go to the store for his mother after school."

the teacher would know that the child knows how to read, even though he may not know Standard English.

Two more suggested approaches involve changing the reading materials. The first suggestion is to develop dialect materials; the idea behind this approach is that the child can begin to read in his own dialect and gradually can be brought to Standard English texts. Another approach along this line is to develop beginning materials that avoid the grammatical mismatches between the dialect and the standard.

Language experience is the approach that seems to embody the ideal of starting where the child is. There are evidently a number of different techniques that go under this rubric. It can entail having the teacher write down a story composed by a group or an individual or it can mean taping a fairly spontaneous oral story told by an individual. The latter would seem to be the best initial approach because it involves only the individual child's ideas expressed in his own way. The major problem with this approach would be to train teachers to be careful observers of the way children speak so that they accurately record the story. If the teacher translates a story into Standard English, the point of using the language experience approach will have been missed.

All of the approaches lead eventually to teaching reading in Standard English; they are offered as ways to begin the teaching of reading, emphasizing that learning to read and learning to speak Standard English should not be confused.

SUMMARY

It would be ideal if, in a summary statement, a plan could be formulated that would bring about an end to educational problems arising from dialect differences. Regretfully, that cannot be done. What we are able to do is describe the variety of ways in which people speak and to demonstrate that these various ways are equally systematic and equally capable of expressing the finest thoughts of humankind. We can expose stereotyping based on language attitudes and we can expose bias in standardized tests and suggest appropriate techniques for teaching reading. The final decision on which actions to take relating to these matters must rest ultimately with the people about whose language we are talking. What we have been able to prove is that there is no problem internal to any language or dialect that affects intellectual development. The variation within a language and the ways people evaluate this variation reflect the organization of the language community, geographically and socially. A change in that organization is, without a doubt, the most effective way to bring about linguistic change.

REFERENCES

Bereiter, C., and S. Engelmann. *Teaching Disadvantaged Children in the Preschool.* Englewood Cliffs: Prentice-Hall, 1967.

Fasold, Ralph W. "What Can an English Teacher Do about Nonstandard Dialect?" in Rodolfo Jacobson (Ed.), *English to Speakers of Other Languages, Standard English to Speakers of Nonstandard Dialect*, special anthology issue of *The English Record*, in press.

Goodman, Kenneth. "Reading: A Psycholinguistic Guessing Game," *Journal of the Reading Specialist*, 4 (1967), 126-135.

Horvath, Barbara. "Aspects of the English Syntax of Chicano School Children," unpublished masters thesis, Michigan State University, 1971.

Jensen, Arthur R. "How Much Can We Boost IQ and Scholastic Achievement?" *Harvard Education Review*, 39 (1969), 1.

Labov, William. *The Social Stratification of English in New York City.* Washington, D. C.: Center for Applied Linguistics, 1966.

Labov, William. "Some Sources of Reading Problems for Negro Speakers of Nonstandard English," in A. Fraizier (Ed.), *New Directions in Elementary English*. Champaign, Illinois: National Council of the Teachers of English, 1967.

Labov, William. "The Logic of Nonstandard English," in J. Alatis (Ed.), Georgetown Monograph No. 22, *Languages and Linguistics*, 1969.

Labov, William. "Contraction, Deletion, and Inherent Variability of the English Copula," *Language*, 45 (1969), 715-762.

Rosenthal, Robert, and Lenore Jacobson. *Pygmalion in the Classroom.* New York: Holt, Rinehart and Winston, 1968.

Shuy, Roger W., Walter A. Wolfram, and William K. Riley. *Field Techniques in an Urban Language Study.* Washington, D. C.: Center for Applied Linguistics, 1968.

Shuy, Roger W., Joan C. Baratz, and Walter A. Wolfram. "Sociolinguistic Factors in Speech Identification," Final Report, Research Project No. MH 15048-01, National Institute of Mental Health, 1969.

Shuy, Roger W. "Nonstandard Dialect Problems: An Overview," in James L. Laffey and Roger Shuy (Eds.), *Language Differences: Do They Interfere?* Newark, Delaware: International Reading Association, 1973.

Shuy, Roger W. "Language and Success: Who Are the Judges?" in Richard W. Bailey and Jay L. Robinson (Eds.), *Varieties of Present Day English.* New York: Macmillan, 1973.

Smith, Frank. *Understanding Reading.* New York: Holt, Rinehart and Winston, 1971.

William, Frederick, and Jack L. Whitehead. "Language in the Classroom: Studies of the Pygmalion Effect," *English Record,* 21.

Wolfram, Walt. *A Sociolinguistic Description of Detroit Negro Speech.* Washington, D. C.: Center for Applied Linguistics, 1969.

Wolfram, Walt. "Sociolinguistic Implications for Educational Sequencing," in Ralph W. Fasold and Roger W. Shuy (Eds.), *Teaching Standard English in the Inner City.* Washington, D. C.: Center for Applied Linguistics, 1970a.

Wolfram, Walt. "Sociolinguistic Alternatives in Teaching Reading to Nonstandard Speakers," *Reading Research Quarterly,* 6 (1970b), 15-16.

Wolfram, Walt. *Sociolinguistic Aspects of Assimilation.* Washington, D. C.: Center for Applied Linguistics, 1974.

PRAGMATICS

Pragmatics:
On Conversational Competence

Bruce Fraser
Boston University

There is little argument that there is an important difference between knowing a language and knowing how to use it. This point is particularly well made in *Stranger in a Strange Land* by Robert Heinlein. Mike Smith, a Martian, has learned English through a grammar book but is without any cultural context or experience. Smith is suspected of being able to levitate objects, and is put to the test by Jubal and Jill, two Americans. The dialogue runs (with slight modifications) as follows:

> Jubal: "Mike, sit at my desk. Now, can you pick up that ash tray? Show me."
>
> Mike: "Yes, Jubal." Smith reached out and took it in his hand.
>
> Jubal: "No, no!"
>
> Mike: "I did it wrong?"
>
> Jubal: "No it was my mistake. I want to know if you can lift it *without* touching it?"
>
> Mike: "Yes, Jubal."
>
> Jubal: "Well, are you tired?"
>
> Mike: "No, Jubal."
>
> Jill: "Jubal, you haven't *told* him to—you just asked if he could."
>
> Jubal: (looking sheepish) "Mike, will you please, without touching it, lift that ash tray a foot above the desk."
>
> Mike: "Yes, Jubal." (The ash tray raised, floated above the desk.)

Few adults familiar with the rules for using English in everyday conversational situations would have misunderstood what Jubal meant when he uttered the sentence "Can you pick up that ash tray?" But children often take the meaning of an utterance literally, rather than with the meaning intended by the speaker (or at least they conveniently *act* as if they perceive only the literal meaning—for those in doubt, spend a few hours with a group of five-year-olds), and those learning a second language often respond with "I know what he said, but what did he mean?"

The present paper is intended as an attempt to clarify, in part, the nature of our ability to use a language. The knowledge underlying this ability is usually termed *communicative competence* (Hymes, Gumperz, 1971), parallel to the term *linguistic competence* (or *grammatical competence*). Communicative competence, however, covers both verbal and nonverbal aspects of communicating between persons and, as such, is too broad a term for the present purposes. I will use the term *conversational competence* to refer to only the verbal aspects of an interchange, leaving the nonverbal features aside. (One might use the term *phone booth competence* to keep clear the domain of ability.)

To begin, I want to make clear that my use of the term conversational competence should not be taken as a renaming of Chomsky's term *performance* when he speaks of the competence/performance distinction. The notion of linguistic competence in the sense in which Chomsky has characteristically used the term refers to what a speaker knows about his language as a formal system which relates an indefinite number of phonetic strings to semantic interpretations, independent of any particular context in which one such string might be uttered. A grammar is simply a statement of the systematic and nonsystematic relationships between these strings of sounds and meanings. Because the relationships are usually found to be highly complex, linguists have found it useful to analyze sentences on at least the phonological, morphological, syntactic and semantic level of representation, with the grammar capturing what counts as being well-formed on each level and how the representations of a sentence on one level can be related to its representation on another. A grammar of English, for example, must capture the fact that *blick* is an acceptable though uncoined English word, while *ftick* is not even acceptable; that "I hope I to leave on time" is ill-formed syntactically; that there is no existing word for dead plants analogous to *corpse*, though there well might be; and a word for "a left-handed short-order cook" is highly unlikely. Performance, in Chomsky's sense, is a psychological notion involving what a speaker does when he utters (or tries to understand) a well-formed sentence of the language; he might stumble over his words, forget what he was saying, or stop in the middle of the sentence. But none of this need bear directly on his knowing or not knowing the language.

Quite analogously, we can speak of conversational competence as opposed to performance. But now, rather than talking about *sentences* (what they are, how they are formed, and what they mean), we must talk about *utterances*, the speaking of sentences to do things. In particular, we ask the following question. What are the principles which relate 1) a sentence with a particular meaning uttered on a particular occasion by a particular person to the meaning of the utterance; and 2) the utterance meaning with the effect of the utterance on the hearer? By the effect of the utterance we mean whether it convinces the hearer, embarasses him, causes him to reconsider his former position, and the like; what Austin called the "perlocutionary effect" of an utterance. Important as this second part is to the total theory of conversational competence, we will not deal with it further and will focus on the relationship between sentence-meaning and utterance-meaning or, stated in the form of a question: What are the principles that relate what we say to what we mean?

What, then, do we mean by the meaning of an utterance? Although I realize that what I am about to suggest will ultimately be shown to be inadequate, I propose we begin by distinguishing among speaker-meaning (the meaning that the speaker intends to convey); hearer-meaning (the meaning that the hearer understands the speaker to be conveying); and utterance-meaning (that part of speaker-meaning shared by the hearer-meaning). For our purposes, we will assume that hearers always understand what speakers intend; that speaker = hearer = utterance-meaning. We can divide utterance-meaning into two parts: utterance-force and utterance-affect. By *force* we mean how the utterance is to be taken: as a promise, a request, a claim, a suggestion, or an act of congratulation—what Austin called an "illocutionary act," an act one performs in the utterance of a sentence. By *affect* we mean what personal opinion of the speaker is conveyed either about the hearer (a sense of disrespect, scorn, contempt, friendship, dismay, or pride), or about the illocutionary act being performed (reluctance at having to refuse to do something, pleased at being able to thank someone, indifference in diagnosing an ailment). If our efforts in this area are ultimately successful, we will have a theory which can predict, for a normal conversational interaction (where no special codes have been established) that utterance-meaning of a given sentence can be such-and-such, only if certain assumptions are made about the speaker, the hearer, and the conversational context (the past conversational history, and shared knowledge of the world). Or equivalently, for a normal conversational action, if we know the speaker, the hearer, and context, we can predict the utterance-meaning (or class of utterance-meanings).

Utterance-meaning will depend on a variety of things. Obviously, sentence-meaning will play a significant role: the more directly the sentence-meaning specifies the intended force and attitude, the less reliance must be placed on conversational principles. For example, the utterance of "It gives me great pleasure to declare you the winner, Mr. Jones" directly conveys the force of a declaration and the attitude of speaker-favor towards both the act and the person: all this by virtue of the sentence-meaning. The speaker of "Here is the first prize award, Mr. Jones" makes his intentions and attitude less clear.

Position in the conversation will also play an important role in determining utterance-meaning. One cannot ordinarily intend the first sentence of a conversation to count as a reply or an answer, though the force of a claim, report, or request is quite appropriate.

The roles of the speaker and hearer in the conversation will play a role as well. Anyone can request something of another; but only, if the hearer perceives the speaker as holding some power over him, can the speaker successfully issue a command. And it is the situation very often which determines who holds the power position. For example, it is itself perfectly consistent for teacher A to issue orders to student B, and then for B, in the course of administering first aid at an accident, to order A who comes upon the scene. In a similar sense, one cannot seriously intend an utterance to count as a diagnosis unless he has the requisite credentials; or as the granting of permission unless there is the appropriate authority; or the making of a motion at a meeting without prior recognition by the chair. In short, who you are and how you are perceived by your hearers will determine to some extent the force of your utterance.

Leaving aside that part of utterance-meaning concerning speaker attitude, we turn to the question of how we capture the relationship between sentence-meaning and utterance-force. There are three positions in the current literature; we will refer to them as the *performative approach*, the *prescriptive approach*, and the *pragmatic approach*, and consider them in turn.

The performative approach takes the position that a part of the deep structure (or remote structure, or semantic representation) of each sentence is a precise specification of the force of the sentence when uttered. Since the sentence "I will be there" can be used as a warning, a promise, and a prediction (to name but three of its possible uses), the performative approach requires that there be three underlying sources for the sentence, one corresponding to each use. In the presentation of this approach (Ross, 1971), the specification takes the form of a highest clause consisting of "I-performative verb-*you*"-S, with the example sentence being embedded into the S. The deep structure for the promise case under discussion would be "I promise you that I will be there." The highest performative clause is to be deleted by an optional, though sometimes obligatory, rule.

There are many objections to the technical details of this approach which render its statement questionable, at best (Fraser, 1974; Anderson, 1971). However, the more serious objection is that it simply denies the distinction between language as a system relating sound and meaning, and the use of language as a means of communication. There do, indeed, seem to be significant differences (some of which we have alluded to) between the kinds of rules to account for the well-formedness of a sentence at its various levels of analysis and the rules to account for how it can be used (some of which we will allude to shortly). Consider, for example, the fact that the simple example used ("I will be there") can be used for perhaps twenty different illocutionary acts of which we mentioned but three. The performative approach demands that there be one deep structure for each use. Hardly a desirable conclusion. And more discomforting for me is the fact that the sentence "It's getting late" can be used to perform some of the same acts as "Could we go home now, please?" neither of which seems related grammatically in any way to its putative underlying sources, "I request that it is getting late" and "I request that could you take me home now please," respectively.

The second type of effort to relate sentences to their utterance-meaning is what we call the prescriptive approach. The papers of Gordon and Lakoff (1971), Heringer (1971), and Forman (1974) best illustrate this approach wherein the goal is to state rules which specify how the speaker might perform a particular speech act. Since Forman's paper is the latest, and presents its conclusions on a revision of the first two papers, we will confine our remarks to this work.

The main thrust of his paper can be captured by the following material (Forman's numbering):

(9) a. A speaker-proposition is a proposition about which the speaker has more direct knowledge than the addressee.

b. A hearer-proposition is a proposition about which the addressee has more direct knowledge than the speaker.

(10) The Speaker Knows Best Principle, SKB (disguised version)

One can indirectly perform a speech act by

i) asserting a relevant condition which is a speaker-proposition; or

ii) questioning a relevant condition which is a hearer-proposition.

(11) The All Else Being Equal Clausula (first version)

All else being equal, if P is a proposition about a person X, then X is assumed to have more direct knowledge than anyone else about P.

Examples which fit under these three rules and which count as the indirect performance of speech acts are easy to find. Consider requesting which has among its conditions: 1) that the speaker wants the action being requested to be done, 2) that the hearer is able to carry out the action, and 3) that the hearer is not expected to carry out the action in the normal course of events. In uttering "I want you to stand over there," I am asserting a requesting condition which is surely speaker-based, given (9)-(11); the three principles predict that in doing so I can indirectly make a request, a prediction that is surely borne out. Similarly, in uttering

"Can you move that for me?" I am questioning a hearer-based proposition dealing with the condition on the hearer's ability to act. And in uttering "Will you do that for me?" I am questioning another hearer-based proposition dealing with the obviousness condition on request. Forman's principles predict that these will count as requests, predictions once again borne out. Indeed, it is easy to find examples which fit under the domain of these three principles.

My main objection to this approach does not rest with the vagueness of terms such as *relevant condition, addressee, hearer,* or what it means for a proposition to be about something or someone. Forman, in particular, acknowledges that these difficulties exist in his work; were they the only problems, the task would be to tighten the framework. I think that this approach, like the performative one, fails in two important ways: it does not account for many of the relevant examples of indirect performance in a particular illocutionary act; and, more importantly, it does not provide an explanation for *why* the utterance of one particular sentence or class of sentences should characteristically count as the performance of an act, while so many others fall short.

The sense of the first criticism is that the prescriptive rules—at least as stated—fail to account for all of the facts. Consider the following taxonomy for strategies by which the speaker can make a simple request.

> *Strategies for Requesting*
>
> 1. Performative sentence
>   "I request that you answer me."
> 2. Imperative sentence
>   "Please sit down."
> 3. Interrogative sentence
>   "What is your name?"
> 4. Declaration of the speaker's desire for some action
>   "I want you to bring that over to me."
> 5. Speech act idioms
>   "How about doing that for me?"
> 6. Via acts of suggesting
>   "I suggest that you come another time."
> 7. Via acts of requesting permission
>   "May I take a look at that vase over there?"
> 8. Via acts of declaring the speaker's
>   > 8.1 obligation to request
>   >   "I must request that you sit over here."
>   > 8.2 desire to request
>   >   "I would like to request that you stay longer."
>   > 8.3 intent to request
>   >   "I intend to ask you whether you were here before."

9. Via acts of declaring the hearer's
   9.1 obligation to act
       "You have to turn that second one over."
   9.2 appropriateness of acting
       "You should do that now."
   9.3 ability to act
       "You can help me by unlocking the door."
10. Via acts of questioning the hearer's
   10.1 reason for acting
        "Why are you playing the radio so loudly?"
   10.2 obligation to act
        "Do you have to keep the light on?"
   10.3 appropriateness of acting
        "Should you be erasing that tape?"
   10.4 desire to act
        "Would you like to uncover the statue now?"
   10.5 ability to act
        "Can you pass me the salt?"
   10.6 future action
        "Will you take him that envelope?"
11. Via acts declaring a reason for why the act should be done
    "It's cold in here."

To be sure, I have selected examples which make it easy to agree that each strategy for requesting is available to the speaker (see Fraser, 1974 for a detailed discussion of strategies for requesting). At issue, however, is the fact that Forman's principles for indirectly requesting account for only a few of the twenty strategies presented above. Within Forman's approach, the suggestion, "You might bring over some of that cheese," can count as a request (which it does) only if the possibility of acting is a condition on requesting (which it isn't) and, moreover, if it is a speaker-proposition (which it isn't). Similarly, for "Should you be banging on that pan?" to count as a request would entail that "It is appropriate that the hearer be banging on the pan" is a condition (the opposite polarity holds for this case), and that this be a hearer-proposition, meaning that the hearer knows more than the speaker about the appropriateness (a doubtful conclusion in this case). Extending the principles to other acts meets with equal lack of success. Looking elsewhere, a condition on promising, for example, is that the speaker be able to do the action promised, but "I can do X" is the assertion of a relevant condition, which is a speaker-proposition, but the utterance doesn't characteristically count as a promise. And "I have the power to grant you your freedom" meets the criteria (according to Forman's principles) to count as an authorization, but it doesn't. But even should the proponents of the prescriptive approach patch up these sorts of difficulties, the result will still fail to provide an explanation for *why* the utterance of a given sentence in a particular context characteristically has a certain force.

The pragmatic approach attempts to meet the types of objectives raised for the performative and prescriptive approaches. Central to this approach in accounting for the relationship between a sentence and its potential use is the assumption that utterance-force is a function of 1) the sentence-meaning (not part of it), 2) the identity of the speaker and hearer, and 3) the shared knowledge of the world; and that these factors are related to the utterance-force by principles of conversation.

Like most nascent theories, the pragmatic approach is more promise than proof, at present. It is possible, however, to show for the various cases presented in the taxonomy of requesting strategies above how each might be accounted for, though not how these strategies for requesting relate to one another, nor what structure the overall theory might take. Let us consider one of the most quoted and often discussed strategies for requesting: asking a *why* question of the hearer. In the following example,

> Why are you sitting there?
> Why don't you resign from office now?
> Why aren't you leaving town?
> Why do you talk like that?

the literal interpretation of each sentence is that of a direct question: asking for a reason for why the hearer is or is not doing something. Each, however, also may count as a request to not take the action specified (to not sit there, to resign from office, etc.). At issue is an explanation for why a *why* question can function as a request.

I will first discuss the various stages of the analysis and then summarize them. Several preliminary points are relevant. First, as we have indicated in the taxonomy for strategies for requesting, speech act idioms do exist. The phrase "how about," in "How about helping me today?" is one such idiom: part of the meaning of the phrase involves the semantic information that the speaker intends the utterance to count as a request. *Why* questions are not such speech act idioms. There is no reason to treat *why* as ambiguous, one reading containing this "performative" information.

Second, certain sentences are semantically ambiguous, with a semantic interpretation corresponding to each of its uses. The utterance of "The grass is green" might be used as a report in referring to a pastoral situation, while more likely as a warning in referring to the quality of some questionable marijuana. There is no convincing evidence that leads one to the conclusion that *why* questions are semantically ambiguous: that such sentences have one semantic reading corresponding to the use as a request, another reading corresponding to the use as a question. For our purposes, *why* questions are unambiguous (ignoring possible irrelevant ambiguities). Third, we must recognize that certain strategies have a great currency of use and, for the *why* question case, we might want to conclude that this has become a conventional, accepted strategy for making a request. But because people often request by asking *why* questions or, in fact, nearly always intend *why* questions to count as requests, it does not follow that the high frequency use is associated necessarily with a separate semantic reading.

Finally, our account of relating a sentence to its potential use will take the form of a sequence of steps: the starting point will be the literal meaning of the sentence, the end point the conveyed force, and the intermediate points will be utterance-interpretations as seen from the hearer's (or equivalently the speaker's) point of view, and determined by general rules of conversation of the sort we will suggest. Just as no one contends seriously that to determine the meaning of the sentence, "John was believed to have been shot," the hearer must "undo" two passive transformations, two agent deletions, and so forth, so we are not claiming that the hearer consciously performs the analysis we present. What we are suggesting is that these levels of our account appear to reflect generalizations.

Our account of *why* questions rests, in part, on the realization that the asking of questions in general sets up an implicature: that the speaker actually believes what would be conveyed by an assertion of the same proposition as that expressed in the sentence but with a reversed polarity. In short, all questions are potentially rhetorical questions. The following pairs illustrate a question and the corresponding implicated assertion.

> Why are they doing that?—They are doing that for no reason.
> Should he leave now?—He should not leave now.
> Must she come?—She must not (doesn't have to) come.
> Will we arrive on time?—We won't arrive on time.
> Are we going to accept this?—We aren't going to accept this.
> Can he succeed in that?—He can't succeed in that.

The reason why a question should establish such an implicature is obvious: If the question is worth asking, it is reasonable to infer that there is some doubt in the mind of the speaker about the accuracy of the underlying proposition. That is, the speaker might just believe that the negated version is actually the state of affairs. Grice (1967) provides an example where one person utters "Your wife is faithful" to a colleague on the street —to have raised the issue at all is to suggest that there might be some reason to question her fidelity.

But the fact that the implicated assertion is present doesn't assure that it will be attended to. What is required is that the question be asked in the context in which the hearer realizes that the speaker does not believe there to be an adequate justification for the action which he is questioning (and analogously for the other types of questions). Thus, if I were to ask my biweekly trash collector, "Why are you dumping those broken bags of garbage in my back yard?" he can reasonably infer from the situation that I don't find any justification for this action and that I am allowing him to focus on my implicated utterance: "You are doing that for no good reason."

The next step in the analysis rests on what I take to be a basic tenet of human action: if you don't have an adequate reason for doing something, then you shouldn't do it. Applying this to the example at hand, the hearer can reason further: since the speaker is "telling" me that he thinks I am doing this dumping for no good reason, than I can infer that he thinks that I should not do it. In short, his opinion, albeit one inferred from the sentence uttered and the processes outlined, is that he thinks I should stop the dumping. In some (left undefined) sense, it is as if the speaker had uttered "Hey, I don't think you should be dumping those bags in my yard."

At this point, we have moved from the speaker, *saying* that he wants to know the reason for some action, to the hearer *interpreting* the speaker to be conveying his opinion that the action should not be done. Such interpretation, whether directly or indirectly conveyed (as in this illustration), can be reinterpreted as a suggestion: an illocutionary act in which the speaker indicates to the hearer that the speaker believes that the hearer should consider the merits of undertaking or ceasing some action. So we might, at this point, summarize by saying that the hearer has interpreted the speaker as making a suggestion to him.

Suggestions, however, are different from requests. Suggestions are more like statements of beliefs, while requests are statements of desires. One can thank the speaker for a suggestion, and ignore it; but the same luxury does not reside with a request. How, then, is it that a suggestion, whether direct or inferred, can be a request?

The answer to this lies, I think, on an additional condition on the context: suggestions become requests only if the action indicated bears directly on the speaker. The utterance, "I suggest you try it again," could be interpreted as a request (perhaps even an order); for example, if the speaker were in a position of authority (the boss), and the "it" were a crucial report due from the hearer; but not if the "it" were an attempt at a reconciliation between the hearer and his wife (unless, of course, the speaker—the boss—felt directly involved with the situation). Given that the hearer in our example has inferred that the speaker believes he should stop throwing trash into his yard, and the assumption on the hearer's part that this action directly affects the speaker, the hearer can now infer that, unless the action ceases, the speaker will do something to bring about the cessation. We might term this a principle of self-preservation. That something in this case could consist of a request. (It could, of course, also consist of the speaker hitting the trash collector over the head with a trash can, but we can assume nonviolent action for the moment.) And, moreover, the hearer knows exactly what will be the content of the request: "Stop throwing the trash in my yard." At this point, the hearer is fully justified in invoking a basic principle of conversation which underlies many cases of indirect speech acts, the Principle of Efficiency:

> Given nothing to suggest the contrary, whenever a further utterance would be redundant, one can infer that the speaker

need not make the utterance, that he will operate as if he had made it, and will expect the hearer to operate similarly.

When applied, this principle leads the hearer to conclude (infer) that the speaker and he share the knowledge that the speaker probably will ask him to stop dumping the trash, unless he voluntarily ceases, and that there is really no need to go through the actual asking. And, of course, if the nature of the action touches on the speaker in terms of some authority power-relationship he holds over the hearer (e.g., a boss asking "Why don't you try it again?"), the inference can be fairly made that the implicated act is not just a simple request but, rather, an order.

A summary of the analysis for why *why*-questions can count as requests is the following:

1. Speaker asks hearer for reason for doing A (literal interpretation)
2. Hearer recognizes that speaker probably doesn't believe that there is adequate justification for doing A (shared knowledge of the world)
3. Hearer concludes that speaker believes that hearer should not do A (application of principle of justification)
4. Hearer recognizes that the speaker believes that A directly affects his well-being (shared knowledge of the world)
5. Hearer concludes that because speaker believes that A should not be done and because he believes it directly affects his well-being, that the speaker will act to bring about the cessation of A (principle of self-preservation)
6. Hearer concludes that he should operate as if speaker had requested him to cease A (application of principle of efficiency)
7. Hearer concludes that the intent of the speaker in uttering S was to convey a request to stop A.

Such an analysis is highly speculative, particularly since each of the principles appear to be contrived for just this illustration. The fact that they have a broad range of application in accounting for many of the indirect strategies for requesting specified in the taxonomy above, as well as accounting for nonverbal action, may not placate the ardent critic. My response at this point must take the following form. First, unless we want to subscribe to the view that one use-one meaning (that *why*-questions have at least two separate readings, a position for which there is no evidence), we must provide some systematic account for the consistent pairing of certain sentence-forms (with associated semantic interpretation) with characteristic utterance-force. *Why*-questions just are not used to make promises, give evaluations, or even make reports, except in highly contrived circumstances. Second, when we examine the strategies for requesting, to take one example, across a wide variety of languages, we found that with only a few exceptions, the strategies used in English are used in languages such as Thai, Japanese, Chinese, French, Arabic, Finnish, and German. This certainly suggests, though doesn't prove, that there are some general principles of conversation that underlie at least requesting in language. If the principles along the lines I have suggested turn out to be speech-act specific, then they are no better than a listing of rules for each illocutionary act. Our preliminary work points to the very opposite conclusion.

Turning now to the other part of the utterance-meaning—the attitudes of the speaker which are conveyed—the example provides us with some information. The *why*-question of the example is surely a polite way of requesting. I suspect the reason lies with the fact that the speaker has not said to stop throwing trash, nor even suggested directly that the hearer stop throwing trash, but he *has* asked for a reason for the action. By doing this, he has presumably given the hearer an opportunity to legitimately reject the implication and the request force without taking on a defensive posture: the hearer need only answer the question directly and thereby deny the implicature which was raised. By offering such a face-saving device to the hearer, whether or not he accepts it, the speaker reflects an intent to show respect for the hearer, which is the essence of what it is to be polite. By asking "Could you stop throwing trash in my yard?" the speaker could convey the same force, but with a good deal less finesse. And by asking "Just why are you throwing trash in my yard?" he has quite impolitely conveyed a request to stop the action. And, by asking "Why don't you try to stop throwing trash in my yard?" (if asked without a sarcastic intonational pattern) he might be interpreted as making a very polite, almost reluctant request for the action to stop.

The fact that our preliminary examination of the strategies for requesting does indicate that these strategies for requesting are not language-specific suggests, I hope, some implication for second language acquisition. For if it is the case that the strategies for how we use language are in a sense part of the principles for human interaction, rising above cultural and language differences, then the task of learning a second language might be viewed as the task of learning how to fulfill strategies in L_2 which they already have mastered in L_1. We might, then, view the problem of second language acquisition from the perspective of asking: what are the strategies which the learner brings to learning how to do things with words?

We might, in fact, find that some of the errors in L_2 acquisition arise not from what usually has been called "language interference" in terms of syntactic, morphological, and phonological differences, but because the speaker is trying to use a coding for a strategy in his native language into the one he is learning. The English speaker can, for example, use the abbreviated form "Why not stop here" to convey a request; the German speaker cannot use the equivalent coding: "Warum nicht hier halten." And finally, we might want to consider developing text materials which more closely mirror the acquisition of the ability to communicate effectively rather than "correctly." Why not encourage the student to learn effective though incorrect forms such as "Why do you there?" Since students are going to make mistakes anyway, why not encourage them to be "effective" ones.

I want to conclude by acknowledging my lack of experience in language teaching (though not in language learning) and with this lack, I am sure a lack of appreciation of the difficulties and impracticalities. The reader will notice that each of the suggestions above has been presented in a very hesitant way, because I have little confidence in their relevance. If they appear to be way out of bounds, and if the study and application of the system of conversational competence appear to be irrelevant to the study of second language acquisition (from either the research or teaching perspective), then the research presented herein is only a linguistic curiosity. However, if this type of research is, or at least can be made, relevant to the field of second language learning, then now is the time to begin a joint venture. Both the linguists and second languagers (if these are really two different groups) can stand around and wait for a visit from the other, much the same way as the Israelis and Arabs have discussed the Mideast situation. On the other hand, the two groups can engage in meaningful discussion and reach a constructive settlement. My only question, though, is "Where is Henry?"

In actual conversation, this idealization is far from the norm. Hearers often misunderstand speakers. Examples abound. The budding artist who utters to his female companion "Would you like to come up and see my paintings?" may intend the utterance as a serious invitation to another striving artist with a common interest, but may be interpreted as a much different invitation. Or "It's getting late," spoken to a hostess, may reflect the speaker's concern over the tardiness of a certain guest, but may be taken by the hostess as a complaint about the absence of dinner. And so on. There is no absolute guarantee that on any given occasion the speaker's intention and hearer's understanding will coincide.

Reading and Pragmatics: Symbiosis

Peg Griffin
University of Southern California

1.0 Facts about the real world, including facts about how language is used in that world, stand in some obvious, but relatively unstudied, relation to reading. This paper tries to shed some light on that relation, and to describe its operation within a particular model of reading.[1]

The relation is particularly important for "middle range readers," i.e., people who have been students in reading classes; people who may have been exposed to many different approaches to reading teaching; people who can read signs, menus, driving license tests, and some applications, but who can't "read." They don't like to read. To hear them read orally is distressing and depressing. The enjoyment and information they get from reading is nonexistent or minimal. Middle rangers are identifiable in public schools, universities, and in community education programs. There are special series of books designed for them. They know a few things about the activity called reading and they can perform some code-breaking tasks. They know many facts about the real world and how language is used in it. But they act as if the two kinds of knowing are not related. This paper makes more specific the kinds of problems a middle ranger encounters in reading, but extensions to other types of readers should not be impossible.

---

[1]There are two pieces of background information needed for the reading of this paper. First, in conversation about the pragmatics of natural language, fellow linguistic students and teachers have been responsible for the thoughts expressed here more than is evident from the citations. Second, the paper was prepared several years ago and the understanding of pragmatics has advanced considerably but, as far as I can see, not in directions that would appreciably change the argumentation in this paper.

These remarks should not be considered as a set of the only and all conditions for successful reading programs. That is, insights from linguistics or the pragmatics of natural language are not the light, the truth, and the only way to solve the problems of a reading teacher. Some children begin reading without instruction at all (Torrey, 1969). Seldom are we able to claim a genuine causal relation between a particular innovation in a program of reading instruction and the emergence of a good reader.

Correlations will not guarantee such causality. There is a case demonstrating this that involves a little boy, Harry. He was enrolled in a school that used a strictly controlled phonics approach. He didn't read at all when he entered the program, he was the "star" performer of his group in the phonics exercises and tests. He was also the "star" reader by the end of the first grade. The correlation between success at phonics and success at reading seemed perfect. The performance of other children in the class established a high group correlation between success in the phonics tasks and being good readers. However, a chance event revealed that, in Harry's case, the correlation was not the product of a causative relation between reading and phonics. It happened that Harry's little sister Edna was refused a library card because she couldn't read. Harry, being a kindhearted soul, immediately offered to teach her. He found a book, opened it and found a word which he pointed to. "G," he said, making the first sound in the word "general." Then, "O," he said. Then, he repeated "G.O." and then he said the word that was printed on the page, "go." He continued to do this. He gave sound correspondences for the printed letters. Although many of the sounds were not the correct ones for the word the letter appeared in, he immediately read the word correctly, with no hesitation. He did this very quickly, in an almost ritualistic way. Harry demonstrated knowledge of sound-letter correspondences, he demonstrated that he knew how to read; and he demonstrated that, for him, the two kinds of knowledge had no necessary relation to each other.[2]

With these kinds of experiences in mind and with a healthy respect for variation in learning styles, we will not claim that insights into language and usage are the only way to do a better job teaching reading. Nor are we going to say this is all that is needed or all that linguistics has to offer to reading. The goal is modest: to offer some points worthy of further thought and to note some ways to use insights to modify programs of reading instruction.

2.0 *Specifying the relation.* A symbiotic (mutually benefiting) relation holds between accomplished reading and the pragmatic aspects of language. Loosely defined, pragmatics involves facts about the world existing independent of language structures per se but facts that are needed to encode and interpret language on any occasion of its use

---

[2]Harry is the code name for one of three children whose development of reading ability I have been following.

(Fraser, this volume).[3] Accomplished reading refers to what good, non-beginning readers do (Shuy, 1976; Smith, 1971). To display the relation as symbiotic, there follow two demonstrations and an extension of an argument made by Carol Chomsky.

2.1 The first demonstration depends upon the fact that many accomplished readers do not know the names of three towns in the province of Cebu in the Philippines. Anyone who does know the names of three such towns is not a proper subject for this task. The second step is for the subjects to read the following short passage.

> "Have you traveled much since you came to the Philippines?" Elsa asked Carol.
> "Well, just in Cebu Province. I went to Danao and Moalboal last month and last week I visited some friends in Talisay," Carol answered.

The third step is to test who now knows the names of three towns in Cebu. At the IRA workshop where this paper was presented, all but a handful of the subjects knew the names of the towns after reading the passage. The remaining subjects, being test wary, reasoned that all could be parts of one town. But if "visited many towns" is substituted for "traveled much" in the first line of the passage, all of the subjects indicate they are possessors of new information—some new facts about the world revealed through reading. The demonstration shows that reading can add to the store of facts about the world that can enter into language use, that accomplished reading can add to one's pragmatic resources.

Furthermore, the acquisition of this information by each subject displays that the benefit is mutual: knowledge of facts about language use in the real world is needed for good reading. Readers are able to connect the three towns with the Philippines and to connect the towns specifically with Cebu Province. Yet, nothing in the passage said outright that Moalboal, Talisay, and Danao are towns in Cebu Province. People know that answers are relevant to questions, and that the name *Cebu* in the first part of the answer and the names of the towns in the second part of the answer must be related. Language users do not have to depend on outright statement, they expect brevity. Brevity and relevance are two of the maxims that Grice (1967) has outlined in his investigation of the *Cooperative Principle* that governs language use. No one teaches these maxims, specifically, and no one teaches readers to use them while reading. However, if one does not use them (if one merely decodes or sight reads words or interprets grammatical structures without recourse to what one knows about language use), then one wouldn't be able to read with full understanding the passage about the Philippine towns.

---

[3]Fraser's view of pragmatics differs slightly from mine, but not in ways that are crucial to a discussion of pragmatics and reading.

2.2 The second demonstration shows that accomplished readers can fail to comprehend a passage if they do not have sufficient pragmatic information. Suitable subjects are accomplished readers who are not familiar with everyday life in the Philippines. The first step is to have the subjects read the following passage.

> The waiter brought the steaks. Nick and John cut into them.
>
> "This is just right," John said. "It's rare but not too rare."
>
> The waiter walked by. Nick got his attention and asked for a glass of water.
>
> "What's the matter, Nick? You can send it back, you know. Go ahead and order something else."
>
> "No."
>
> "Oh. Well, I don't have to finish this. You want to leave now, huh?"
>
> "Yeah, yeah, I do."

The second step is a question: Why do John's questions to Nick follow from Nick's request for a glass of water? (Assume that the subjects have all the information needed to interpret *this* and *it* and are able to process the question/answer sequences, and the use of quotation marks and paragraph conventions to indicate speaker's turn.) Why should a request for a glass of water indicate to John that something is wrong with Nick's food or that Nick wants to leave? The results for this demonstration are invariable: nobody knows the answer. For most people, more information is helpful: the passage was written by a Filipino and, in the Philippines, one does not have water before or during a meal. When you are finished eating you ask for a glass of water or someone brings a glass of water to you if there is no food left. Thus, in the social situation of a meal in the Philippines, a request for a glass of water (as opposed to tea or a soft drink) has come to conventionally implicate that the person doing the requesting is not going to eat any more. John's questions are predictable and make sense in this context. These are cultural facts about language usage in a real world situation and the reader must know them to fully comprehend the passage. Without this information, a reader would have to assume either that Nick grimaced or moved his plate away or, perhaps, that he spoke with curtness to the waiter. Some readers might even assume that John has ESP.

2.3 The first passage shows that reading can provide us with new facts about the world and that part of getting that information depends upon knowing facts about how language is used. The second passage shows that facts about the world and language use, if unavailable, can prevent a reader from getting the full sense of a passage. Chomsky (1972) published a relevant piece of research focusing on the relationship between language and reading. She investigated the different developmental stages in the acquisition of certain grammatical structures by elementary school children and the ability of the children at different stages to read passages with these structures in them. There is evidence that not knowing the structure hinders reading, especially for children whose developmental stage is far from that needed to fully acquire the structure. However, Chomsky found that meeting the structure in reading hastened the developmental process for children whose developmental stage was not far from the stage needed to fully acquire that structure. On the one hand, the children needed to know the structure in order to read; on the other hand, reading helped them to acquire the structure more quickly. This evidence for a symbiotic relation between grammatical structure and reading seems to lend credence to the symbiotic relation between pragmatics and reading which is claimed here and which the two demonstrations display. Accomplished readers acquire facts about the world from reading but, on the other hand, need to know about the world and language use in it in order to *be* accomplished readers.

3.0 *Integration with a reading model.* At this point, a teacher or researcher might accept the argument that pragmatics is important to reading but still be ready to reject any implicit claim that the skills to be mastered by a reading student must be drastically changed or increased in number and complexity. Anyone aware of the current information explosion in the field of reading and the frequent suggestions for radical (and often rash) program changes can empathize with the urge to reject any such claim. However, while the discussion above does involve a different focus, it is not necessarily a call to devise a totally new approach to teaching reading or to modelling accomplished reading. In Sections 5 and 6, general and specific implications of this focus for reading practicioners will be presented; in this section, the place of pragmatics in a model of the reading process is noted. It is probable that the skills and processes related to pragmatics could be accounted for in an extension or refinement of any model of reading that is justifiable on other grounds. For economy of space, comments here will be limited to the model developed by Goodman[4] and his colleagues which seems amenable to handling pragmatics with a maximum of ease.

Central to this model is the notion that, contrary to expectation, the reading activity is not precise, exact, or sequential. Reading is a process involving the partial use of available language cues selected from perceptual input on the basis of the readers' expectations. Being selective, rather than precise and complete, the reader does not pay attention to everything printed on the page. What is selected to be used varies from one reading occasion to another. Smith (1971) notes that the selection process operates even on the level of letter identification. For example, in the process of identifying *h*, the reader selects different features as cues depending on whether the reader sees the alternate possibility in the slot

---

[4]Goodman's model can be described briefly with the title of his article, "Reading: A Psycholinguistic Guessing Game" (1967).

being identified to be a *b* or an *h*. The alternate possibilities are suggested, defined, or limited by other aspects of the reading passages. The redundancy of language and of the writing system makes it the case that several different combinations of partial information are available and sufficient for successful reading of a particular passage. The combination selected by a reader is related to the expectations the reader has as he begins the reading task and to those expectations as they are refined and directed during the reading. Expectations can be seen as tentative decisions about the content of what is read—decisions which are confirmed, rejected, or refined as the reader continues reading. Evidence for this position can be found in the literature from miscue analysis, eye movement and other optic experiments, memory span data, and mental processing experiments (Holmes, 1973).

3.1 Once more, a demonstration. This time the demonstration relates cues and guessing and pragmatics in reading. Look at the following sentence.

> *It brought order into disorder.*

That sentence comes from an Agatha Christie novel. Looking at it alone, there's no way to tell whether things ended up in total chaos or if everything was made neat. If I were writing about a day when, by some chance, a strong wind came into my office after I had just carefully arranged ten separate piles of pages, ready to collate, then the sentence would mean disorder reigns. On the other hand, if a passage were written about a particularly mean teacher with a particularly unruly class who was given a cat-o'-nine-tails and who answered that sentence when someone asked how the whip had worked, then the sentence would mean that order has triumphed.

In these cases, knowing what the "it" refers to helps. Unfortunately, it can get more complicated; some possible referents for *it* don't suggest which result should be picked and some situations don't suggest which result is desired. In the spoken language, the intonation of the sentence sometimes helps, but the intonation difference here is not necessary nor required. In reading, you may intone to yourself if you have the meaning and you'll get along fine. But how do you get the meaning? In this guessing game model of reading, it is claimed that a reader picks up partial clues and confirms or rejects them.

In the following passage, the problematic sentence is presented as part of a larger discourse unit:

> When he was in the midst of a perplexing case, he would take time out to work on a jigsaw puzzle. It brought order into disorder. Once he had completed this ritual, he was able to conquer the similar lack of orderliness of the particular case he was working on.

It is only when the reader gets to "the similar lack of orderliness" in the sentence *after* the problem sentence that it becomes clear the result meant was the neat one. Most of us are predisposed to select that as soon as "jigsaw puzzle" is mentioned, but it is not actually necessarily clear. The third sentence *could* have read:

> Perplexing cases always showed too much orderliness that fogged up one's vision, pointing in a strict orderly fashion to a very wrong conclusion. To change the order, to see the pieces as separate and disorderly, was a necessary first step.

This demonstration shows that: skilled reading *is* a matter of selecting cues; these cues sometimes occur in sentences after the problem pieces; the same cues need not be used by everyone; and guessing on the basis of the cue can be right or wrong. If any of you know Agatha Christie's hero, Poirot, and guessed that these passages were based on a passage about him, then you wouldn't have needed any of the possible clues for interpreting the sentence. Your expectations based on his personality characteristics would have predicted the answer. The Goodman model, supported with the experiments described in Smith (1971), is neutral as to where the reader's expectations came from or which available cues you make use of to confirm or reject them. Most of the published work has involved phonological, grammatical, and some semantic cues and expectations. I am particularly interested in expectations and cues related to pragmatics (i.e., to real world facts), including facts about language use. The suggestion is that these kinds of expectations and cues are present in reading and are used by the skilled reader.

4.0 For the rest of this discussion I am going to point out some interactions between language use and reading and some ideas of what to do given this interaction. First, however, the notion context will have to be explicated. It seems there's a difference in the usage of this word depending on whether the speaker is a specialist in linguistics or in reading. Both fields use the words *meaning* and *context*. Reading specialists find articles and texts that talk about picking out the meaning of an unknown word by looking at the sentence in which it occurs. Sentences like the following are given as examples:

> We were *careening* down the highway barely a car length ahead of the thugs.

Although the italicized word may not be in a reader's vocabulary, the sentence can be understood because of various other words and the syntax (grammatical structure). This skill is often mentioned in teacher manuals and various exercises are offered in reading texts which are designed to develop this context skill.

Linguists use the word *context* in a way that is at once more broad and more narrow. It is more narrow in the sense that the basic meaning of words is assumed to be known. The breadth comes with the additional elements linguists consider as context: the beliefs and attitudes of the speaker/writer and the other participants, the social class and status relations of the participants, and the purpose and intent involved in the situation. The following is an example:

Can you pass the salt?

The context, in the linguistic usage of the term, determines whether this is a question aimed at reaping a certain piece of information or a request aimed at getting the salt moved toward the utterer. In the following, context means these facts that influence language use in particular situations, even where the understanding of the individual words and structures is obvious.

5.0 The examples of reading and pragmatics given below have been chosen specifically because of their relevance to the middle range readers who know about various decoding skills but who haven't gone beyond a plateau of patching together enough reading to get through the driver's exam. Something to keep in mind is that many of these middle rangers enjoy (and do well at) reading comic books and instructions for hair fixing preparations and carburetor rebuilding. In both the comics and the instructions, expectations and cues related to the context in which the language is set are available from other verbal sources. Pictorial representatives of the situations give a big boost to the expectations and cues needed in the reading guessing game. However, the kind of reading material usually encountered in the school situation doesn't have as much nonverbal information. There are four ways in which language in context can be particularly problematic for middle range readers. I have labeled them as follows:

1. The Gap
2. Static
3. Stalling
4. Conflicts

5.1 The Gap is an obvious outcome of the big difference in the way the middle rangers can talk and the way they read. As they read the few sight words they control and sound out amalgams for other words, a listener can transcribe sentences and paragraphs. Their talk can be recorded, transcribed, and then typed as sentences and paragraphs. The differences between the two types of transcriptions are painfully clear. The reading is slow, segmented, and filled with pauses and recasting of words and phrases. While the differences are clear to anyone listening to the two sets, the similarities between language used in real life and language as read may not be clear enough to middle range readers. That is, those facts about language use which they know and use in their speaking may be necessary for reading a passage but never recognized by the reader. This is the gap. If the middle rangers do not understand that there are certain similarities between language use in reading passages and language use in speech, they have a problem. How can they channel their expectations and efficiently choose the cues that will allow them to read?

This notion is not far removed from the notion of establishing letter-sound correspondences or sight word responses in beginning reading. It is also part of what is behind the oft-berated "reading with expression" criteria, still used (at least informally) as an evaluation of reading ability. One who reads with expression is behaving as if he knows that the language he is reading is, in fact, language.

Following are some examples of language use knowledge, commonly accessible in speech, that are at least helpful and perhaps necessary for reading. These are items that are probably well-known to all middle rangers but which one might not recognize in his reading. The examples are key lines from passages.

In the first example, the story has barely opened. A mother and her adolescent son are the only participants. The mother has just asked her son what happened to the missing morning newspaper. The son answers with:

(1) "You're always criticizing me. Suppose..."

A reader who is willing to apply his knowledge about the use of sentences with *criticize* will know that (2) below is more expected as a continuation of (1) than (3) is, and the selection of cues to confirm the expectation can be made on a more efficient basis.

(2) (Suppose) I took it so I could look for a job!

(3) (Suppose) Dante took it or George!

Sentence 3 would be more expected if the original statement by the son was a sentence like 4.

(4) "You're always accusing me. Suppose..."

Charles Fillmore studied words like *accuse* and *criticize*. Both words can occur in sentences of the type *Verb X Prep. Y*, where *X* is a person or thing which can take responsibility and *Y* is any event or act or state. *Criticize* correlates with situations where everyone just assumes that *X* did, or is responsible for, *Y* and the real point being made is that *Y*, the act is bad. Using this information in sentence (1) yields an expectation that the material following "Suppose" will be directed toward explaining why the act shouldn't be considered bad—to wit, sentence (2). *Accuse X of Y*, on the other hand, correlates with situations where everyone just assumes the act (*Y*) is bad but the real point being made is that *X* is the one responsible for it. Using this information in example (4) yields an expectation that the material following "Suppose" will focus on explaining the lack of responsibility, hence completion with sentence (3) which blames someone else.

Many middle range readers use *accuse* and *criticize* perfectly well in their conversations, but they let a gap form between conversational use knowledge and reading. They don't let their conversational use play a part in the expectations and cue selection so important in skilled reading. However, a teaching program that would get readers to focus on individual words like *accuse* and *criticize* and to dredge out all that can be dredged is not the answer. The *real* problem is this gap between conversational use and what one finds in a reading passage. Treating the symptom (these particular words) is only of marginal benefit. In some cases, the task is pretty much impossible, anyhow.

The next set of examples illustrates that the conversational use of a term is not discrete enough to isolate and treat. A *bet* is an action that is accomplished by using the word *bet*. It's one of a class of words whose utterace is the act (*christen, order, ask*) in certain situations. Middle range readers use *bet* in conversations, yet passages (5) and (6) below can be problematic when met in reading. In (5), the first use of *bet* can function as the making of a bet. But the response functions as the refusal of a bet or as an agreement.

> (5) "I bet you five dollars I can climb that pole."
> "I bet you can."

Putting a negative on *can* would have made the bet go through and both speakers would be committed to a bet. In (5), however, the bet isn't finished. A reader using his knowledge from conversation would look to see whether the bet was taken. Even though it turns out it wasn't, the conversational use knowledge about *bet* will cover the situation. Look at (6) where *bet* is used simply as an agreement, as Jerry Sadock has noticed.

> (6) "You just don't know. The homework this guy gives is just too much."
> "I bet it is!"

The middle range reader who is not applying conversational use knowledge to reading encounters problems in comprehending (5). As he painfully decodes two instances of "I bet" from two different speakers in the passage he may conclude that a bet has been made and expect to read something about the outcome. Dredging out the meaning of bet could lead the middle ranger down a blind alley. What is needed is the connection between what one does when talking and what one encounters when reading.

The last example about the gap problem comes from nonfiction, nondialogue materials.

> (7) The colonists in Massachusetts were angry to learn about the new tax on tea.

A comprehension question on this might be: "What made the citizens of Massachusetts angry?" The real answer has to be "The new tea tax." An answer from someone who had a gap between reading and conversational use might be: "To learn or learning about the new tea tax." Don Larkin has studied sentences like (7). There are a number of cases where infinitives appear in this way. For example, the sentence,

> I was sorry to hear you were sick.

can have two readings. One occurs where the speaker is sorry he heard about it because he is particularly parsimonious and hearing about it meant he was obligated to spend money and send flowers. The other reading accounts for the more usual reading, where the sorrow is about the sickness and the "to hear" functions differently. This last account is what is needed for (7). Middle rangers use this "skipped infinitive" in conversation, they even make jokes based on some inappropriate usages. Yet, once again, the gap produces answers that are wrong and that may indicate lack of comprehension.

5.2 The second kind of problem is one that I've called *static*. Even if you want to bridge the gap, there are elements in reading passages that cause interference. There are certain locutions that one never uses in speaking and never uses in writing for adults, that turn up in books for children. Early primers exhibit many such examples. And any teacher is able to supply more examples in this category.

Adults can recognize the oddity of these passages; they can recognize a strange kind of language that makes the book read like a child's book. Many of the examples seem to be cases of syntactic (grammatical) formality, for example:

1. No contractions:
    "He will" not "He'll"
    "She is not bad" for "She's not bad"
    or "She isn't bad."
2. Full clauses in comparatives:
    "Mary can drive as well as Peter can drive."
    "He is taller than any boy in the class is."
3. The use of "will" as future rather than "going to."
4. Full form sentences for conjunctions:
    "John wants to learn how to drive and Peter wants to learn how to drive also." for "John wants to learn how to drive and so does Peter."

Even these cases which seem to be syntactic in nature present a problem that has some pragmatic considerations. We could, perhaps, say that the books simply use a more formal style of language than is found in everyday conversation. But if we look closely at the facts, it turns out that this isn't really true. Different styles of language correlate with aspects of the situation: the characters, the topics, the settings. Many books for children purposefully use situations that mirror those that the children experience in their everyday lives—situations which do not call for this more formal style of language. The children are asked, on the one hand, to relate the language to a very rare and special style and, on the other hand, to relate the situation to common everyday events. The following passage taken from Charniak (1972) shows this quite well. In the story, a child named Jack has some paints and his sister Janet has some pencils. But Janet wants the paints.

Janet said to herself, "I want the paints."

Jack began to paint a picture of a red airplane.

Janet went to look at it.

"Those paints make your airplane look funny," she said.

"You could make a good picture of a red airplane with these pencils. I will let you have the pencils. I will take the paints."

The children who are reading are supposed to relate to the real life situation that wanting something triggers; that is, it triggers a strategy for getting what is wanted, showing that one of the possible ways to get something is to trade. Furthermore, they have to apply their real life knowledge that a trade can be made if the other person has a "wanting" for what you have to trade. I don't doubt that children know and use strategies for getting things and for trading. The problem is in the last two sentences which in normal conversation would probably be only one sentence with the "will" contracted; "I'll let you have the pencils and I'll take the paints." The children have to accept the situation as familiar and the language as strange. That is static.

A particular kind of reading material strategy accounts for another example of static. These reading materials use a controlled vocabulary and controlled sentence structure, but the most outstanding and noticeable feature is the repetitiveness and length. As mentioned above, brevity is an important principle of language use. When the principle is ignored, when you spend a long time saying something that could be said more briefly, then the person in conversation with you has two possible responses. Either you aren't following the rules at all (you aren't really using language) or you mean something special by this temporary breaking of one of the rules. For example, recall the passage in Shakespeare's Julius Caesar where Marc Anthony talks about honorable men. The violation of the brevity principle in this play is an artistic tour de force. The repetitiveness supports the ironical interpretation of the passage. Unfortunately, the repetitiveness found in those controlled reading texts isn't artistic. If the reader uses his conversational knowledge and searches for what could possibly be meant by this blatant disregard of the brevity principle, his search will be unrewarded. He has to take the first response—the book isn't following the rules at all, the book isn't really using language.

A final example of static concerns violating the language use principle of relevance. Consider sentences like the following:

Mary, who wears green and blue polka-dotted sweaters with orange and purple shoes, applied to the fashion design school today.

The relative (or adjective) clause about the sweaters and the shoes gives information that seems irrelevant to the idea that Mary applied to school. But this apparent violation of the relevance principle means something special—that the speaker is giving an opinion about the badness of Mary's taste and incongruity of such a person applying to a fashion design school. In reading passages in children's textbooks, irrelevancies tend to remain just that: violations of the principle of relevance. For example, look at this sentence:

> Sir Francis Drake, whom you might remember, became one of the first to adopt this new fashion.

Here the adjective clause violates the principle of relevance but, again, nothing is meant by it. In contrast to normal language use, it is simply a rule violation, empty of any deeper significance. (This and the last example of static were collected by Jerry Sadock.) Adult readers unused to dealing with static filled passages tend to misread the comma after remember and expect another verb after *fashion*.

The last example involves one irrelevant word whose irrelevance is emphasized because it is also stylistically discordant.

> Hakluyt made one of the most impressive journeys in the history of the whole world.

Unless we've been reading too much reading book material, we'll recognize the oddity of the word *whole* in that sentence.

Both the principle of brevity and the principle of relevance are included under the rubric of the Cooperative Principle.

It seems that some reading materials for children are uncooperative, not only in terms of the principles of language use but, also, in terms of allowing and encouraging the reader to use his knowledge of language use in his reading. This gives static to the reader, to say nothing of what it gives to the teacher encouraging the student to bridge the gap between what he does when reading and what he does when conversing.

5.3 The third way in which language use facts can affect middle range readers is to cause them to stall. Skilled readers can pick up facts that conform to language use and know, or at least suspect, some pieces of information before the information is stated outright in the text. Skilled readers can get a head start on the information. Readers who aren't relating the reading passage to facts they know about language use get left behind. Look again at the reading passage on Janet and Jack. Suppose the next paragraph was as follows:

> "Oh Janet. My airplane looks good. You're just saying that so I'll trade you my paints for your pencils!" Jack laughed.

Skilled readers will already know most of the information in that paragraph. They will have recognized before they get to it that a trade was being offered and that the description Janet gave of Jack's drawing was more a strategy for the trade than a truthful description. But some middle range readers who don't connect their knowledge from life with their reading will have missed it in the first passage and they'll have to treat Jack's answer as though many new pieces of information were being presented. The only really new information is that Jack is onto Janet's game.

Another example of hints being dropped before a middle ranger would pick them up comes from various investigations of how people get other people to do things. Suppose a character in a story says one of the following:

1. Open that door, right now.
2. Can you open that door, please?
3. Would you mind opening that door?
4. It's terribly warm in here with that door closed, isn't it?

The action of the story could move along in the same direction no matter which of these is used. But the reader who is using his language use knowledge gets more information than one who isn't using that knowledge: he has some idea about the power relation between the character saying the sentence and his addressee. The middle range reader stalls again.

Recently, a popular magazine had a story in which the status and familiarity relations between the two main characters were important. The author chose to use facts about language use to display these relations rather than use descriptive prose. The story was set in a Spanish speaking milieu and the main characters were an adolescent boy of the upper class and a grown man of a lower class. The plot concerned their familiarity and the loss of it. The Spanish language has a good way of projecting this: The personal pronoun system has markers not only for singular or plural; masculine, feminine, or neuter; and first, second, or third person (as English is limited to); but, also, for the relative power and familiarity of the speaker to the person referred to. Since the magazine that had the story is an English language one, it had to do the best it could with English. When the story opens and the boy is thought of as close and as just a boy by the grown man from the lower class, the man addresses the boy as "thou." At the story's end, with familiarity and childhood gone, the man addresses the boy as "you." It doesn't really work in English at this point in history, but the author and the magazine tried to force it to. Someone who knows about language usage in Spanish, or an earlier version of English, would have a head start; but middle range readers (even those who are native Spanish speakers but who don't relate reading and language use) may well miss this and stall again.

5.4 The fourth type of problem that not using pragmatic knowledge can cause for a reader is what I call *conflict*. There is conflict when facts about the world according to the book do not match facts about the world according to the reader. Skilled readers reading good writing will suspend their disbelief and get into the world of the author. But some writing in reading books isn't all that good. It doesn't deserve suspension of disbelief. In addition, that's just another task that middle range readers will have to accomplish while they haven't caught on to others. There are series of reading books specifically prepared to be closer to the world of adolescents—particularly urban, minority group adolescents. Many of the stories in these books are less of a problem for middle range readers. Few of them, however, contain articles that deal with the really heavy issues or with current styles of entertainment. There are some reasons for these omissions. Schools are traditionally charged with establishing and upholding the mores of the society, as well as with teaching reading, so a series of pro and con essays on drugs, abortion, or contraception would be hard to get past most school boards to say nothing of stories of the joys found in some of the less approved adolescent pursuits. Also, fads are transient while books are more permanent. Using magazines solves some but not all of the conflict problem.

A specific problem of conflict involves certain locutions called "indirect acts of assertion." To get a reader into the world of his story, an author often makes use of these devices. In dialogue or in descriptive passages, he uses a sentence which depends upon the reader believing something that hasn't been said outright. This device is also used in conversation, for example:

> The man who is standing behind you with a gun—don't look!— will shoot you if you turn around.

Under ordinary circumstances, information in these kinds of relative (or adjective) clauses is presumed to be known, to be old information. For example,

> The girl *that I met yesterday* speaks ten languages.

The relative clause is italicized. It is presumed the addressee knows the speaker met someone yesterday. However, in some cases, this structure is used to indirectly assert something. In the sentence about the man with the gun, the speaker is doing just that. Commercials on television do a similar thing: "Aren't you glad you use X? Don't you wish everybody did?" For that *glad* sentence to work, the speaker presumes that the addressee uses X. (For example, if I said to a person in Washington, D. C., "Aren't you glad you're in Alaska right now?" I would have to be kidding or speaking ironically because the question, if meant literally, presumes the addressee is in Alaska.) Certainly, middle range readers come across indirect assertions and they use them in their everyday life. Part of the problem may be the particular devices authors use to make such indirect assertions but the real problem is that getting into the author's world, resolving the conflict between the worlds, may be problem enough without having to deal with an indirect presentation of the world of the book.

As a final point about the degree of elaborate knowledge required to deal with a part of reality, I'd like to give an example from the research of Charniak (1972:96) who works in artificial intelligence. Charniak was investigating the comprehension of children's stories and he found you need quite a bit of knowledge to tie the parts of a story together. Here are some things you need to know if the story deals with a piggy bank. While you're reading, try to imagine what would happen if your real world was in conflict with the story's—if all you had to go on was a dictionary definition or a picture of a piggy bank.

> PBS come in all sizes and shapes, though a preferred shape is that of the pig. Generally, the size will range from larger than a doorknob to smaller than a bread box. Generally, money is kept in PBS, so when a child needs money he will often look for his PB. Usually, to get money out, you need to hold the bank and shake it up and down. Generally, holding it upside down makes things easier. There are lesser known techniques, like using a knife to help get the money out. If, when shaken, there is no sound from inside, it usually means there is no money in the bank. If there is a sound, it means that something is in there, presumably money. You shake it until the money comes out. We assume that after the money comes out it is held by the person shaking, unless we are told differently. If not enough comes out you keep shaking until you either have enough money, or no more sound is made by the shaking (the bank is empty). In general, the heavier the PB the more money in it. Some PBS have lids which can be removed easily to get the money out. Sometimes it is necessary to smash the PB to get the money out. To put money in, you need to have the money and the bank. The money is put into the slot in the bank, at which point you no longer are directly holding the money. Money is stored in PBS for safekeeping. Often the money is kept there during the process of saving in order to buy something someone wants. PBS are considered toys, and hence can be owned by children. This ownership extends to the money inside. So, it is considered bad form to use money in another child's PB. Also, a PB can be played with in the same way as toy soldiers, i.e., pushed around while pretending it is alive and doing something.

Getting this kind of information to someone who didn't have it would be hard, yet Charniak's work shows that you need all that information to deal fully with relatively simple children's stories. Detailed information is required to understand a story about a piggy bank and a reader who has none or only part of it will be in conflict with the world of the story. Remember, also, that a conflict involving a nice concrete piggy bank would be considerably easier to resolve than one involving an abstraction or an action or a politically loaded word.

6.0 *What to do, what to do.* Given these problems—gaps, static, stalling, and conflict—what can be done? Here are six and a half general suggestions. All flow from thinking about what it is that the skilled reader can do that the middle range reader cannot.

One note of caution (a not to do) is in order. The students already know about language use; they know it intuitively. They may not know labels or how to verbalize their knowledge but they know it the way they know the syntactic and phonological rules of their everyday speech. Evidence for this intuitive knowledge is in their ability to use the language instantly and effectively. It may seem fatuous to warn people not to teach what students already know but, as Shuy points out, this error (which he calls "aphasic teaching") has been noticed in programs of instruction concentrating on other elements of reading proficiency like in some phonics programs which spend much time and effort on teaching sounds rather than sound-letter correspondences.

6.1 The first suggestion involves adjusting the diagnostic technique involving comprehension questions. Ask comprehension questions too early; ask them before the passage is finished. Ask a question whose answer has been hinted at but not stated outright, yet. Then pay attention to the answer—not just attention to whether the answer is right or wrong, but the kind of detailed attention that allows you to understand what the student answers and figure out what led him to that answer. His answers may show he is missing some cues and that he does so consistently. If the student isn't picking up on language use cues, observe to see if he can pick them up when he hears a conversation that uses them. Further test to see if he picks them up in a conversation in which he is involved. Observe his normal interaction with peers and notice whether he uses the structure that carries the cue when he is trying to communicate.

If he never uses the relevant language use cue, you have a *conflict* problem; he needs some materials closer to him and/or some help in dealing with the world assumed by the story. If he uses the structure in oral language but not in reading then the problem is a gap, static, or stalling. If other comprehension questions show that he picks up the notion further along in the reading passages, then it's a *stall* problem. Encouraging wild guesses is a good ploy here. If the material being read involves unusual language that violates the principles of cooperative conversation, the problem may be *static* and having the student deal with more cooperative reading passages should show it. A suitable approach would be to grade the material the student is to read and let him gradually approach those with the most static. If your questioning and answer analyzing suggest that the student isn't getting any usage cues at all in any reading material, then the problem is a *gap*.

6.2 For a gap problem, you have to convince the middle range readers that reading passages are really language. The remaining five and a half what-to-do's are aids in convincing them, so the second suggestion is to read to them for forty-five minutes, three times a week. What is read should be something the reading teacher likes to read and particularly likes to read to this audience. This should not be characterized by stumbling, mumbling hesitations but should be a prepared oral reading. If the material and the presentation are good, it will be hard to ignore the fact that reading is language. If the students get tired of hearing the teacher read, ask a respected community member (who is a skilled reader) to read to them.

6.3 Suggestion three is to use comic books and other materials that support the verbal input with pictures and diagrams. A lot of the cues that language use gives are repeated in other aspects of the situation; facial expression, body posture, clothing, and background setting. These materials shouldn't be seen as gimmicks to be used once or twice, but as a planned and regular part of a long term program. You might be surprised to find out many things about comic criticism and comic history from the students. There is a case of a young man who was considered a poor reader but who could 1) look at a page of isolated frames from a variety of comic strips and compare and contrast them on several planes; 2) identify the inker, the drawer, the letterer, and the idea man; and 3) give a brief history of each person's contribution to comics, to this particular strip, and to the strips he had worked on before and after. His activities weren't much different from what other students did in a literary criticism course except, of course, the other students' skills had been taught and were academically valued, whereas his had been subject to squelching in school and had never before been presented in an academic setting.

6.4 Suggestion four is to use detective stories and mysteries and to see the movie, *The Sting*. (As a confessed addict, I'm biased about this.) The whole idea of reading a mystery is to beat the book to the solution. As your familiarity with this genre increases, so does your desire to pick up on the smallest suggestion of a clue in the context, in the language used, in the language avoided. All these cues become really important. Reading or watching mysteries in a group increases the desire and ability to get cues. Besides, physical education is now concentrating on "life-time" sports (tennis and golf instead of pyramid building and team sports), so why can't reading do some life-time sports? Again, mysteries shouldn't be used only as an occasional gimmick but should be used in a regular, systematic program.

6.5 Suggestion five is to do a good and thorough job of preparation for reading assignments. Remember the piggy bank! Discard the idea of a five or ten minute preparation at the end of the class. Consider carefully the reading passage to be assigned, become aware of the hidden assumptions it requires, and give your students enough information and time to mull it over so they will be prepared to read it.

6.6 Suggestion six is to consider some language experience based work. Most of the available information on this approach is for beginning reading and for very young students. For middle rangers, the concept needs some extension. There is a magazine called *Foxfire*, edited by Elliot Wigginton of Rabin Gap, Georgia. The idea behind it suggests a way to use the language experience approach profitably with middle rangers. Have the students talk to members of their communities; have them use tape recorders to interview people to find out about the history, culture, art, values, religion, superstitions, and commerce of the place. Have the interviews transcribed, preserving the language (not "fixing" the vocabulary or the grammar), then use typescripts of these transcripts for your reading material. The material will include fiction, critical essays, how-to essays, biographies, and everything your average anthology includes. As the work progresses, some of the students will be able to transcribe and typescript. The fallout value of this kind of project to the community is obvious. Less obvious, but equally valuable, are the changes in the attitudes and relations between the youth group and the older community members. Other kinds of materials that turn up on tape recorders—spontaneous playlets, original poems, etc.—are bonuses that add more variety to the reading program. Once again, the value of this is in a sustained program, not in use as an occasional gimmick.

6.7 The half suggestion is a half because I'm not at all convinced it will have a direct bearing on improving reading. But it may turn out to reveal to teachers and students that they all have a wealth of knowledge about language and that looking at language can be interesting. The suggestion is to consider a subject like getting someone to do something by using sentences. What are the alternative things that people could say? What is it about the people, or about the setting that makes one alternative better or worse than another? Add to the list under 5.3. Some of these are *indirect speech acts*. Besides indirectly ordering, can you indirectly ask questions; e.g., "I suppose you can't tell me what happened at the secret meeting, huh?" How, besides the example under 5.4, can you indirectly assert something? Basically, this suggestion is to play with the untaught but known part of language—the variety possible in its use.

A final note on gimmicks versus programs: gimmicks cannot be evaluated, improved, replicated, or discarded. If gimmicks fail, they fail just once. On the other hand, programs are evaluated, revised, revamped, and evaluated and tried again. They can be replicated or discarded with just cause. If they fail, it's a long failure but a failure which is understood; a failure which leads to progress.

To summarize, there has been a discussion on the symbiotic relation between facts about the world and language use in it and about reading. These pragmatic factors help establish the reader's expectations and guide his selection of cues in a model of reading. Four different types of problems can occur and some suggestions have been presented about how these types may be recognized and how some programs of instruction may afford solutions to the problem.

REFERENCES

Charniak, Eugene. "Towards the Comprehension of a Children's Story," doctoral dissertaion, Massachusetts Institute of Technology, MIT Artificial Intelligence Laboratory, 1972.

Chomsky, Carol. "Stages in Language Development and Reading Exposure," *Harvard Educational Review*, 42 (1972).

Goodman, Kenneth. "Reading: A Psycholinguistic Guessing Game," *Journal of the Reading Specialist*, 4 (1967).

Grice, H. Paul. *Logic and Conversation*, lecture notes from William James Lectures. Cambridge, Massachusetts: Harvard University, 1967.

Holmes, Debora Lott. "The Independence of Letter, Word, and Meaning Identification in Meaning," in F. Smith (Ed.), *Psycholinguistics and Reading*. New York: Holt, Rinehart and Winston, 1973.

Shuy, Roger W. "The Mismatch of Child Language and School Language: Implications for Beginning Reading Instruction," paper delivered at the Conference on Beginning Reading Instruction, University of Pittsburgh, 1976.

Smith, Frank. *Understanding Reading*. New York: Holt, Rinehart and Winston, 1971.

Torrey, Jane. "Learning to Read without a Teacher," *Elementary English*, 46 (1969).

ETHNOGRAPHY OF SPEAKING

The Ethnography of Speaking

Joel Sherzer
University of Texas

The first question we must face with regard to the ethnography of speaking is: What is it? What is the meaning of this somewhat strange and cumbersome title, ethnography of speaking?

The ethnography of speaking is an approach to language and speech which studies language use in cultural and social contexts. In order to place the ethnography of speaking within the context of anthropology and linguistics in general or, more specifically, within the context of this discussion, it is one approach within the field of sociolinguistics. One type of sociolinguistics, if you like, but I prefer to think of it as offering a particular perspective to the understanding of the general problem of language in context.

The basic input and motivation for the ethnography of speaking is ethnography. For this reason, I want to spend a little time discussing ethnography. Ethnography can be viewed both theoretically, as a concept within anthropology and methodologically, as a way of doing research. Ethnography is that branch of anthropology which has to do with the description of the way people live in particular communities. Thus, the ethnography of the Navajo; of the Sioux; of American Blacks; of Chicanos in Austin, Texas; or of high school teachers in Chicago. Traditionally, ethnographies describe general patterns in the way of life of a group of people: subsistence, dress, child-rearing, religions, and world views. Ironically, traditional ethnographies tended not to deal with language and speech.

In recent years, some anthropologists have tried to be more precise about the concept of ethnography. They have defined it as "what one needs to know in order to get along in a particular community." Methodologically, ethnography offers a way of doing research—participant-observation. This consists of living in a community as both participant and observer; discovering and describing by means of a careful, intense study of face to face interaction, just what one needs to know in order to get along. The societies studied by this method have usually been small, relatively homogeneous, and relatively simple from a technological point of view. But recently, ethnographic approaches have been used in large, urban communities, and there is no reason why they cannot be, thus complementing the large survey approach which is more characteristic of sociology.

Ethnography of speaking has to do with what one needs to know in order to get along linguistically (with regard to speech) in a particular community. This involves the rules of grammar (phonology, syntax, semantics) of whatever languages are used in the community. But grammar as usually conceived is but a small part of linguistic competence, especially if this competence is viewed as speaking competence or, to use an increasingly popular term, communicative competence. Thus one has to know when to talk, when to be silent, and how much to talk. One has to know when and how to be fluent, glib, or exaggerated in speech and when and how to be curt, abbreviated, to the point. Or how to talk to your parents, your boss, your closest friend, your lover, a baby, someone you've never seen before. Every community has rules for how to greet, take leave, converse, be polite, agree, disagree, show thanks, insult. And everyone learns attitudes toward languages: one's own, the standard of the community, and the ways of speaking of the less privileged members of the community.

These are some of the things with which the ethnography of speaking is concerned. I want to stress that none of these can be understood by looking at language alone, abstracted from any context. Rather, serious attention must be paid to social and cultural factors as they relate to speech. It is these (what I am calling here ethnographic) factors which underlie and provide the basis for an understanding of speaking patterns. Some of these patterns may be universal, especially if studied at a very abstract level; but, often, patterns of speaking vary from group to group and society to society. Perhaps the most important contribution the ethnography of speaking can make to educators is the fact of social and cultural diversity in patterns of speaking, diversity which often exists within a single society (especially a complex one such as ours). I will return to this question of diversity in patterns of speaking when I discuss specific examples.

Before presenting examples, however, I want to sketch briefly the basic principles of the ethnography of speaking as an approach within sociolinguistics.

1. GROUP OR COMMUNITY AS BASIC

The ethnography of speaking, like all sociolinguistics, assumes a heterogeneous speech community. That is, it assumes that within single communities, in which individuals interact and communicate with one another, there are different ways of speaking. It is the task of the ethnography of speaking to explain these different ways of speaking ethnographically; i.e., to explain what social and cultural meanings are involved in selecting one way of speaking rather than another. Another way of looking at this matter is by noting that any group of speakers— several individuals, a network of individuals, or an entire community— has at its disposal many ways of saying the same thing. Take the idea, "John was opening the door." It can be said in the active form, "John was opening the door." Or the passive form, "The door was being opened by John." In a loud voice, "JOHN WAS OPENING THE DOOR." or in a soft voice, "John was opening the door." In clearly enunciated speech, "John was opening the door." Or in fast speech with many pronunciation simplifications, "Johnwasopeninthedo." Or, perhaps, in English or in Spanish, "Juan abria la puerta." The choices here are not random; nor are they purely linguistic in the sense of referring to different things in the world (the difference between "John was opening the door" and "John was opening the window"). Rather they depend on such matters as: Where are the speakers? Who are they? What knowledge do they share? What is the purpose of the message? What came before it and what will come after it?

It is important to recognize that no amount of looking at linguistic forms in isolation from ethnographic context will explain their usage. One of the first insights a cross-cultural and ethnographic perspective provides is that the same sociocultural meaning is often expressed in a variety of ways, from seemingly large and overt linguistic forms to very slight and subtle forms. Thus the difference between formal and informal and the related out group/in group distinction is probably a sociolinguistic universal in that it is linguistically expressed in every community. Yet the way it is expressed varies greatly from place to place. In our society it often involves a slight pronunciation modification; for example, from *ing* to *in* in words like "working" and "running." But it might involve a whole language change, from English to Spanish, in communities which have both of these languages at their disposal. In France and other countries of Western Europe, it involves a switch from one second person pronoun to another—from *vous* to *tu*. It is only by looking at these linguistic forms in ethnographic context that we can understand them.

Now the formal/informal distinction is only one type of sociocultural meaning to look for. There are many others. Some, like this one, are perhaps universal. But there are many which are specific to particular groups of speakers, communities, or societies. Much more research is needed in order to determine the types of sociocultural meanings that are expressed in speech and how they are expressed.

Ethnography of speaking approaches the question of speech community in a way quite similar to the way anthropologists deal with ecology. For anthropologists, ecology is the study of the relationship between man and his environment, the study of the ways in which communities exploit the resources available to them for particular social and cultural purposes. In ethnography of speaking, the resources are linguistic —the ways of speaking available to members of the community. Speakers draw on these resources, exploit them, and adapt them to new situations. A speech community can be viewed as a group of individuals who share basic rules for production and interpretation of ways of speaking. Viewed this way, individuals typically live in and have to learn to orient themselves to several overlapping speech communities (i.e., the Harlem black speech community, the United States black speech community, the New York City speech community, the United States speech community). Conflicts can and of course do arise because of misunderstandings between interactants orienting themselves toward different speech communities. It is crucial that teachers of minority groups understand the potential for and the causes of such misunderstandings.

2. RULES FOR SPEAKING

One basic task of the ethnography of speaking, and one which recent research has focused on, is the description of rules for speaking. The units of description are those appropriate to the communicative activities of the community: *speech acts* such as greetings, leave-takings, signs of agreement or disagreement, promises, threats; *speech events* such as conversations, jokes, speeches; *speech situations* such as cocktail parties, church services, street corner gatherings. The important point is that the structure of these speech acts, events, and situations is usually extremely complicated. It cannot be assumed to be in any way simple. Research by ethnographers of speaking is just beginning to show how complicated such structure can be. It is, of course, important for educators of students belonging to communities with different patterns of speaking to have an understanding of the nature of these patterns.

In order to describe rules for speaking, ethnographers of speaking analyze speech in terms of a number of components.

Setting: Where and when does the speaking occur?

Participants: Who are the speaker, hearer, audience? How are they related? What is their social status—male, female, baby, superior, inferior?

Linguistic variety: What language and style is used? What non-verbal modes of communication are used?.

Purpose: What is the aim of the event—to convince, put down, cajole?

These are examples of the kinds of components that must be taken into consideration in the analysis of speaking rules. Others may be needed, depending on the event and the community.

3. CROSS-CULTURAL PERSPECTIVE

One of the major contributions of the ethnography of speaking, like all of anthropology, has been to stress cross-cultural differences. It is, of course, by looking at persons radically different from ourselves that we are struck most by the relevance of the ethnographic perspective I am advocating here. Thus, learning about the people of the Northwest Amazon, who speak nine, ten, or more languages well and who keep learning new ones (even as adults, apparently mainly in order to regulate marriages), forces us to rethink the nature of language learning and the functions of multilingualism. But cultural differences exist within our own society and these are perhaps the most relevant to our discussion. The uses and functions of silence among Apaches and other American Indian groups are quite different from those of white middle-class Anglos. Yet, there are certain similarities and overlaps and thus, potential for misunderstanding and conflict. With regard to reading and writing, ethnographers have traditionally studied preliterate societies. But there are relatively few such societies today. And one major contribution the ethnography of speaking can make in this area is to point out that the simple dichotomy, preliterate/literate, is a false one. There are many kinds of literacy. We want to know who writes and reads, to whom, in what languages and varieties of language, in what contexts, and for what purposes. When a teacher announces to a class "I want you to read pages 50 to 75 for tomorrow," does that utterance have the same meaning for an Apache in Arizona, for a young black student in a Harlem ghetto, for a Chicano in Denver, for a middle-class Jew in Chicago? I will return to this question of the ethnography of writing and reading.

I think I can best describe the ethnography of speaking by discussing several examples and how they have been or can be approached by ethnographers of speaking. I will present the examples in terms of a very simple model which summarizes the ethnography of speaking approach I have been discussing. This model has been used either implicitly or explicitly by researchers in the ethnography of speaking. The model states that any linguistic (or communicative) behavior can be understood only in terms of several interacting and related perspectives. These perspectives are *linguistic or (socio) linguistic resources:* a set of potentials for social meaning and use. The linguistic resources take on meaning and provide meaning as they are used in *social interaction* (in order to indicate such social interactional notions as respect, deference, agreement, disagreement, and condescension) and in *discourse* (such as greeting, leave-taking, conversation, and joking). The total organization of uses of language, together with societal and individual attitudes toward language and speech, is an *ethnography of speaking*. The ethnography of speaking can be understood only in terms of the larger context of the total ethnography of a society; in terms of the social, economic, and other types of structure and organization basic to the society. It is the ethnography of speaking and the ethnographic that I am stressing as organizing perspectives, in the sense of providing the reasons why certain linguistic features or speech patterns are felt to "belong together" (women's speech, baby talk, black speech, stuffy speech, formal speech, or aggressive speech.

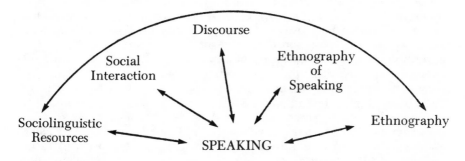

1. Let us begin with Black English, which has been described by various linguists, sociolinguists, and ethnographers of speaking. As a linguistic resource, Black English has certain properties which can be enumerated: intonation pattern, sound patterns, morphological and syntactic constructions such as double negatives and special uses of the verb *to be,* and particular vocabulary items. But what is interesting is that there is probably no one—black or white—who speaks Black English with the totality of its linguistic features, all of the time. Rather, features of Black English, expecially intonation patterns, certain syntactic constructions, and certain words are drawn on by both blacks and whites, in certain social contexts, for strategic, rhetorical purposes. The result is the well-known switching behavior from speaking more *black* to speaking more standard *white,* going back and forth, never totally in either direction. Using features of Black English signifies such notions as informality, emphasis, and in group solidarity. Using features of standard, White English signifies social distance, formality, and out group relations. The constant in group/out group patterning in the use of Black English makes sense only in the ethnographic context of black/white relations in the United States.

2. Similarly, Spanish/English switching in Chicano communities of the Southwest, while it draws on the linguistic resources of Spanish and English, can be understood only as a linguistic response; reflection; and, in part, definition of the particular relationship between Chicanos and Anglos. The rules for switching languages are complicated and involve linguistic as well as social considerations. But, as in the case of Black English, it is important to realize that members of the community, within single discourses, draw on both languages in a constant pattern of switching—Spanish indicating ethnic identity, emphasis, and in-group solidarity; English indicating social distance, formality, and identification with the dominant Anglo culture. The situation is quite analagous to that of

the black community, in that a serious understanding of the ethnography of the Chicano community is required in order to understand Chicano communicative behavior.

3. My next example has to do with a phenonemon not usually considered to be a part of linguistics, but one which clearly is part of communication, namely silence. An ethnographer of speaking, Keith Basso, has described various uses of silence among the Apache Indians of Arizona—between strangers until they get to know one another, between parents and children who have not seen one another for some time, between men and women while courting, by persons being "cussed out," by persons in the company of someone whose spouse or kinsman has recently died, by persons in the company of sick people. What is interesting here is not that silence is communicative for Apaches and not for us. We, too, have moments when silence is appropriate. Thus, for example, the term *silent communion.* But the contexts in which Apaches use and expect silence are different from those in which we do; in fact, they are often diametrically opposed. In the situations Basso describes, Anglo Americans will often use even more speech than normal. Anglo teachers in schools with Indian students should be especially sensitive to situations in which Indian children are likely to be silent and not take silence as a sign of stupidity, insolence, or lack of interest.

4. My next example has to do with the use of the pronoun *we,* a problem which at first glance may seem to be purely linguistic; yet it is one which is intimately tied up with the system of social groups and social relations in our society. *We* is one of the many and complexly interrelated ways of referring to persons in speech. As is typical of the elements in this complex, *we* is potentially ambiguous in many ways. It can refer to the speaker alone: "We'll deal with that later." The speaker and others with him: "May we come in?" The hearer alone: "How are we today?" The speaker and the hearer: "Don't you think we should leave now?"

These different uses of *we* can play an important role in the expression and definition of social relationships. The *we* of a single speaker (or writer) is the professional *we* of formal speech making and writing on specialized topics. The *we* of "How are we today?" is often the condescending *we* used toward social inferiors. It seems to be common in doctor-patient relationships, for example, especially if the patient is a child or a member of a minority group. It is also used by parents to children and teachers to students.

The use of these and many other types of *we* clearly depends on such ethnographically based factors as superior/inferior status or in group/out group relationship. Notice, for example, that were I to begin now to use *we* in such sentences as: "Well, you know, we linguists write transformations like this" or "We in the ethnography of speaking study many cultures," I would be setting up a we/you opposition in which *we* stood for me and the group of experts of which I am a member as distinct from *you,* the out group of persons who are not fortunate enough to be experts in this trade. Such use of *we* would be most unfortunate in that I would reinforce and exaggerate the distance between us, in a situation in which we are supposed to be interacting and cooperating. Yet, this use of *we* is typical of consultant interactions.*

I have chosen to discuss this particular example here because the problem of the expression of person in language is one that has attracted the attention of many sociolinguists and ethnographers of speaking precisely because it demonstrates so well the close relationship between language and its use in culture and society.

5. As a final example, I want to point out the possible relevance of the ethnography of speaking to the problem of reading and writing. As a start, there is the question of the ethnography of reading and writing. Do ethnographic differences in reading and writing make any difference in the reading process itself? This is part of a more general area in ethnography of speaking, namely the ethnography of learning and teaching. One finds various approaches to learning and teaching around the world. In some societies, learning is by observation and imitation. Very little teaching takes place. In others, verbal teaching is considered crucial. Many societies, especially those considered preliterate (for example the Cuna Indians of Panama among whom I have carried out research), have very rich oral traditions. Men achieve prestige and power by speaking well, knowing traditions, and performing them. What happens in such societies or groups when writing and reading are introduced? How do the traditional and the new interact within a single society? These are questions we might want to discuss together.

I would like to end with a comment about the current state of the ethnography of speaking and its relation to other approaches to language. There seems to be a tendency today for various researchers in language, who up to now have operated in isolation from one another, to work together on similar problems, problems which often have to do with the use of language in social context. I have in mind here linguists (most notably, semanticists), philosophers of language, sociologists, anthropologists, and educators. There are points of conflict and disagreeement, of course, but there is beginning to be mutual communication of an interdisciplinary kind. Too often linguists have considered the study of language in actual usage to be beneath them. Now they are slowly coming to the realization that such study is the only way to make theoretical progress. And, of course, such study also brings linguistics closer to the concerns of the ethnography of speaking and, hopefully, closer to the realization of being relevant to the practical problems of the users of language.

A bibliographic note. There is no textbook in the ethnography of speaking. The best way to get an introduction to the field is through such collections of

---

*I am grateful to Louise Bauman for pointing this out to me.

readings as J. J. Gumperz and D. Hymes (Eds.), *Directions in Sociolinguistics: The Ethnography of Speaking*, or P. P. Giglioli (Ed.) *Language and Social Context*. The field of the ethnography of speaking was originally called for by Dell Hymes, who has provided a basic framework for it in several articles. His articles in the Gumperz and Hymes and Giglioli books are most useful. My own understanding of the field has benefited greatly from having edited (with Richard Bauman) a collection of papers to be published late this year, entitled *Explorations in the Ethnography of Speaking*, Cambridge University Press. Keith Basso's paper on silence among the Apache appears in Giglioli.

The Ethnography of Speaking and Reading

Ray P. McDermott[1]
Rockefeller University

Today it is considered of primary importance to engage the interest of the pupil and to make sure that the reading situation is, from the beginning, a realistic and meaningful one for the child. Also, the child's total development is the objective, rather than one isolated aspect, such as reading. Reading, too, is treated within the overall framework of linguistic development—not as an isolated subject. The impatience with the search for "the correct method" of reading is shown in the title of a recent article, "How Long Will We Go on Waiting for 'the Great Pumpkin'?". In its place has come a realization that every effort must be made to consider the child's individual linguistic development in the context of all aspects of his growth.

—Mogens Jansen, 1973

INTRODUCTION

What works in classrooms and what does not? What kind of teacher talk leads to efficient, well organized classrooms, and what kind of talk leads to the opposite? Most importantly, what kind of teacher talk leads to children learning whatever it is they must learn to get by in the modern world and perhaps, to contribute to the quality of that world? These questions have been asked and answered many times, apparently to no avail as our educational system appears to be in considerable disarray. Most often, the questions are inappropriate, for buried in these "what works" questions are assumptions that good pedagogy is a bag of tricks: put the children into ability groups, cut class size, change the orthography, match the skin color of the child with the skin color of the teacher, etc. Each of these suggestions may have some validity; but, in the hands of a bad teacher, none of them will work and, in the hands of a good

---

[1]Much of what is clear and conceptually precise in this paper was achieved with the help of suggestions by Charles O. Frake. Many thanks to him and to Jeffrey Aron, Steve Langdon, and George D. Spindler with whom I have discussed these issues for the past three years.

teacher, none of them will be necessary. Apparently, there is more underlying good pedagogy, something which has not been available in teaching manuals—laymen call it love and concern and social scientists call it charisma and the ability to communicate.

It is the aim of ethnography, and particularly the ethnography of speaking, to detail the ability to communicate. The ethnography of speaking attempts to describe what a person needs to know in order to make sense as a talking and listening member of a particular community (Hymes, 1974; Sherzer, this volume). It follows, then, that an ethnography of speaking in classrooms is socially, as well as theoretically, important (Hymes, 1972). The effort is not only to enrich our conception of language and its role in the social world, but also to reach some conclusions about how best to talk in order to enrich the education of our children. The question of what is going on between children and their teachers that enables them to make sense of each other is no idle academic question. Actual lives, in the sense of social careers and social identities, are won and lost in the early years of grade school, depending upon whether teachers and children can make sense of one another. This paper is written in the hope that an ethnography of speaking can help us win more and lose fewer children in the process of learning to read.

It is not obvious that the ethnography of speaking can offer information relevant to researchers and teachers concerned with how children learn to read. As an inducement that you read this paper, I will present two possible points of mutual relevance. The first link has to do with ethnography as a set of methods for understanding behavior in a social context. Both speaking and reading are language behaviors learned and performed in social contexts. Students of language have only recently taken the social context of language behavior seriously, and their ethnographic efforts have added greatly to our understanding of language. Students of reading have virtually ignored the social context of reading activities. Although there are many correlation studies of the effects on reading test scores of decontextualized social variables such as race, social class, and personality, ethnographic descriptions of reading behavior are rare. Considering the powerful results of ethnographic approaches to spoken language, students of reading may want to take a cue from anthropologists and linguists and study written language in its social context. An ethnographic approach to studying reading may clarify greatly why and how some children learn to read and others do not.

There is a second and far more important linkage between the ethnography of speaking and the concerns of reading people. After a decade of intense work, the ethnography of speaking has documented two important patterns. One, people in different communities, particularly across cultures, appear to know quite different things about speaking. For example, the Japanese must know how to sprinkle tiny honorific particles throughout their speech in order to specify interpersonal relationships either unknown or handled in different ways by Americans (Miller, 1972; Passin, 1968). Two, in any given community, different people appear to know different things about how to get along linguistically, and they use these differences to negotiate statuses and roles. For example: doctors, lawyers, mechanics, cooks, cab drivers, and hustlers all appear to know some things that others do not know about how and when to talk, what to say, and how to say it; and, on the basis of their talk, people relate to them in different ways.

The same two patterns exist in the distribution of reading skills around the world. One, people in different communities appear to develop quite different ways of handling literacy. In particular, far fewer people in underdeveloped countries learn to read than in developed countries, at least to the extent that literacy is measured by standardized tests in school settings (Thorndike, 1973). Two, within any given community in developed countries, some people learn to do more with reading materials than do others, and they use these differences to negotiate statuses and roles with each other. In particular, fewer members of minority groups learn to read than members of more dominant groups (Downing, 1973). Just as it appears that the knowledge necessary to talk in certain ways in certain situations is unevenly distributed throughout a society, so is the knowledge necessary for learning to read certain kinds of texts in certain situations. What makes this inquiry into the ethnography of speaking and reading interesting is that there is increasing evidence that certain ways of speaking in certain situations are related to just what kind of literacy is achieved by particular people (Shuy, 1969). This is not to say that one way of speaking is cognitively more efficient for the child learning to read. Rather, different ways of speaking harbor different sets of social relationships, some of which may interfere with each other when a person talking one way tries to relate to a person talking another way. In the classroom, teachers and children who cannot relate do not produce successful readers. It appears that the same cultural context that frames a speech event also frames reading behavior. If the dynamics of the relational linkage between ways of talking and success in learning to read can be made explicit, we may know much better what does or does not work in classrooms. This knowledge will not equip us with more pedagogical gimmicks, but it may give each of us more insight into what we are doing right and what we are doing wrong.

The paper will proceed as follows. First, two examples of how teachers organize their talk in classrooms will be examined briefly. The point will be that both the authoritarian and guidance approaches to managing children are sometimes successful and sometimes unsuccessful, depending upon whether the social relations underlying the teacher's talk make sense to the children. The claim will be that any kind of classroom talk can do the instructional job as long as mutual trust and mutual accountability between the teacher and the children are achieved. Second, it will be suggested that ethnography is the ideal tool for both the professional and amateur student of classroom life to describe the interpersonal relations achieved in teacher-student communications, and a discussion of what an ethnography is and of its relevance to everyday life communication problems is offered. Third, recent developments in the ethnography of speaking are used to highlight the usefulness of ethnography, particularly for the study of the classroom. Fourth, and most important, the relevance of an ethnography of speaking to an understanding of how children learn to read is examined.

By way of conclusion, I will argue that if indeed the hypothesized relation between ways of talking and success in the teaching of reading can be upheld, then we are all potentially responsible, by virtue of the way we talk, for helping to produce the functional illiteracy we are all striving to eliminate. No one should feel guilty about this as we are all trapped in particular ways of knowing how to act by virtue of growing up in the way that we did. Nevertheless, we cannot absolve our responsibility in school failure simply because we are unaware of the consequences of our ways of talking, and a call is made for all of us to come to grips with ourselves as part of the school problem in order that we might discover how to do a better job in bringing equal education to all.

TEACHER-STUDENT RELATIONS:
THE SOCIAL CONTEXT OF SPEAKING AND READING

Successful communication is certainly the key ingredient in a successful classroom. If two or more people are able to construct a world with enough shared meaning, with enough common sense, then mutual definitions of a task to be done and mutual goals for doing it will be achieved easily, and the essential behavior will be performed. At their best, teachers and children work out ways of being with each other which simply coat all talk—requests, commands, instruction, whatever—with an aura of legitimacy and a call to activity. They make common sense with each other, and the children learn whatever is to be learned.

Underlying such a successful system are a set of relations rooted in mutual trust and mutual accountability. Good teachers will know how to draw on these relations and build them into their talk. Trust and accountability do not simply sit in the hearts of the children to be used whenever interaction with the teacher is at hand. Rather, trust and accountability are always on the spot accomplishments (McDermott and Church, in press).

In order to examine the role of trust and accountability in successful classroom conversation and learning, I want to consider two ways of teaching and show how either way can work, depending upon what is going on under the surface of the talk. Teaching is invariably a form of coercion. "Instruction is the occasion for adults to exercise their preference for making sense of the world for the child" (MacKay, 1973). Some teachers handle coercion directly; others are more guidance oriented. At the extreme of the guidance approach is the Montessori method. But even Montessori (1917) was well aware that there was much adult guidance built into a child's spontaneous activity. Ideally, the adult input comes in the form of a "prepared environment" (McDermott, 1965). Most often, however, even in Montessori schools, adult guidance is less subtle and involves much talk. The technology of the most enlightened teaching is still embodied in the vocal chords. Accordingly, all teachers—from the most authoritarian to the most freedom oriented—are faced with the task of using talk to get children's attentions, directing their attention to a problem or task, and leading them to some ways of handling it (Mishler, 1972). The specific strategies teachers use to get this job done have no effect on whether or not the children learn to read as long as the strategies make good sense to the children. The issue is not so much how a child is coerced, but whether the teacher is able to communicate that the child can trust the teacher's coercion to be in the child's best interests.

An important example of a pedagogically successful,[2] authoritarian strategy for handling classroom activities can be taken from the Hutterite schools of Canada and the Old Order Amish schools of Pennsylvania (Hostetler, 1974; Hostetler and Huntington 1967, 1971; Spindler, 1974b). Amish children did not do well academically when forced by local authorities into the public schools, and there was little reason to think they would perform more adequately in their own schools. Amish teachers seldom have more than eight years of academic training; they must teach children raised with a Germanic language to read English; and their classrooms are missing, indeed prohibit, competition—a key element of learning in groups. Nevertheless, Amish community schools are quite successful, not only by Amish standards but also by the standards of the larger American school community. Amish children from Amish schools score above the norms in standardized reading tests. The Amish teacher's way of handling talk flies in the face of much educational ideology in America. The teachers dominate their classrooms and an interaction analysis has shown a heavy use of imperatives and a high degree of direct instruction (Payne, 1971). What is the relation between this teaching style and pupil success in academic subjects?

To answer this question, we must look to the kinds of social relations which make sense to children raised in Amish culture. Socialization patterns among the Amish are quite different from those found elsewhere in America. Many aspects of an Amish identity are forged in antithesis to and in defense against other ways of being human, particularly ways of being human in a modern technological society. Such a defensive strategy, common among minority cultures, is marked by the merging of individual identities into a group life organized around a small number of unifying symbols manipulated and transmitted by a small number of authoritarian leaders (Siegel, 1970). The Amish educational system fits this model nicely. The symbols are religious, and people use them to communicate trust and accountability. The children are told what to do and when and how to do it. The teacher is in total control of the children's development. In terms of learning to read and in terms of enhancing an Amish identity, their system is most successful. The children and their

---

[2]The use of the term *ethnography* as developed in this paper is consistent with its use in mainstream anthropology. The ethnographic enterprise, however, is "critical, political, and personal" (Hymes, 1972b), and should never be restricted to mean only what academic anthropologists do.

teachers have been bathed in a closed community with highly specific routines for everyone to follow. In terms of these routines, everyone is accountable to everyone else. Common sense and mutual trust are strived for by community members according to a specific code. In this context, instructions are not blind imperatives, but rather sensible suggestions as to what to do next to further common cooperation. There is a warm relational fabric that underlies the instructions and transforms them from orders into sensible ways of routinizing everyday life. What to many appears an authoritarian and oppressive system for organizing a classroom may in fact make great sense to the children and, accordingly, allow them to feel good enough to learn whatever it is to which a teacher directs a class's attention. Outsiders simply miss the cues which ground teacher-student activities in trust and accountability.

No matter how successful authoritarian speech behavior is for the Amish, there is much evidence that the authoritarian teacher is running into increasing difficulties in contemporary America. Apparently, the trust which makes direct imperatives possible in the Amish classroom is not available in more open communities. In fact, in less conservative Amish communities, teachers use much less direct communication (Payne, 1972).

The failure of any attempt to teach with direct methods without a foundation of trust and accountability is well documented. In such situations, the children simply "don't listen," and the teacher winds up expending most of the day controlling the "behavior problems" or to borrow a phrase from a past principal of mine, "keeping the lid on." There appears to be a number of ways for teachers to get through such a bad year, and none of them are well designed for encouraging school learning. Most often, teachers will fall back into a formal definition of their role as teacher and expect the children to conduct themselves as if this role placed an exact set of rules on their behavior. In such a situation, the teacher often relies on institutional rewards and, more often, punishments. The effort is not to say "Do this, because it is a sensible thing to do," but "Do this, because, if you don't the principal will deal with you."

Intensive role definition work on the teacher's part creates some strange forms of behavior. For example, it is the teacher's role to teach relevant and motivating lessons to the class. Sometimes, we all fail at this task. The teacher trapped in role definition work can hardly admit to such a failure, however, and often camouflages an unresponsive class with a lesson directed to a phantom audience. Examples of this phenomenon are unfortunately legion in ethnographies of our urban schools (Roberts, 1970; Rosenfeld, 1971). Rist (1973) offers the following example of what he calls a "phantom performance":

> She asks the children to repeat the poem, and no child makes a sound. She asks the children to repeat the poem line by line after her, first with the words and then a second time through simply saying "lu, lu lu" in place of the words. The

children are completely baffled and say nothing. At the end of the second repetition she comments, "Okay, that was good. We will have to do that again next week."

The relational message underlying a phantom performance is not fertile soil for building a commonly sensible, trustful, and mutually accountable communication. Not attending to the class becomes part of the children's definition of the teacher's role, and they begin to dismiss teaching as an essentially insensitive task. As one sixth grader told me in one of my first classes, "You're not a real teacher. You listen to the children and expect them to learn anyway."

In addition to intensive role definition, direct control over a class can be built on insult and status degradation. Interpersonal warfare, rather than trust and accountability, is the result. Much of what I was offered as teaching and classroom control techniques, by a teacher trainer in the New York City schools, amounted to insults capable of binding a child into silence. Learning failures are encouraged in such classrooms. "Defensive blackboard boredom" is no more academically productive than the overt misbehavior of the less controlled blackboard jungle (Roberts, 1970; Rosenfeld, 1971). Even when the authoritarian approach to classroom management keeps the children under control, if it is not founded on more mutual understanding than the threat of detention or suspension, little learning will be accomplished. It is in the context of an authoritarian classroom without a grounding in trust and accountability that it is possible to talk of children achieving school failure (McDermott, 1974). In response to the teacher's authority, the children develop their own classroom organization in which not working and disrupting the teacher's procedures become a goal.

Less direct forms of coercing children into attending to classroom tasks are uniformly no better or worse than the authoritarian approach. Without a proper relational foundation, a child is no more likely to follow a gentle suggestion than a direct order. One classroom I observed produced the following episode: the Principal announces that the class is to proceed to a book fair in the gym. One particularly troublesome boy, Harold, stands up and yells, "We won't go!" The teacher reacts nervously to the challenge and says, rather hopefully, "Sure you will. You're only kidding." The relational message apparently was taken as something like, "You don't make any sense at all; you can't even be trusted to report on what it is that you are going to do next." Harold was apparently better at stating his future than this teacher had thought, or at least he felt compelled to prove that he was, for he did not attend the book fair and spent the rest of the day torturing this particular teacher. Another teacher in the room was much more successful with Harold, for relationally she was much more honest. In a similar situation, she asked Harold why he was not going to the book fair, accepted his reasoning, and then simply overruled it. Harold went to the book fair. The point of this is that children are not easily talked into activities. They respond most often, not to the activity, but to the feelings that the adult displays about them in the course of asking them to do whatever it is the adult has in mind. Whether direct or indirect forms of communication are used makes no uniform difference. The feelings communicated in the talk are the key to understanding children's attention patterns and learning abilities in the classroom.

Guidance approaches to teaching make much use of question imperatives rather than direct orders. The relational messages are often identical to those accomplished with direct orders. A teacher can say, "Close the door" or "Why don't you close the door?" In either case, the door must be closed by the student. The child would not be expected (nor permitted for that matter) to answer the Why? command with, "I am not closing the door because I don't feel like it." The question was not meant to be a question, but rather an imperative. Linguists have been studying such phenomena of late and have given them the delightful name of *whimperatives* (Sadock, 1969; Green, 1973). Literally, a whimperative stands for an imperative stated in a question form with a *wh-* word. But if *whim* or *whimper* are taken as roots, a whimperative can mean something quite different. And so it is with *wh-* imperatives in everyday conversation. They can be taken in so many ways depending on the context in which they are used and the relations which exist between the people in the conversation. Whether a whimperative is attended with an appropriate action response, an inappropriate verbal response, or no response at all depends upon how the whimperative is taken, and how it is taken is a function of the relation between the conversationalists at that time. An inappropriate whimperative, one which is framed as a whimper but in fact represents a command, can be as useless in a classroom as a direct command to a student who attends to teacher commands by doing the opposite of what they suggest; it will only further the decay of trust and accountability between the student and the teacher.

Guidance and negotiation approaches to communication in the classroom do not have to bring about relational disasters. In fact, Mishler (1972) has shown the superiority of the guidance approach. He examined the values the teachers displayed toward language, authority, and the classroom population as a group. The relative value put on each of the three were similar per teacher and different across teachers. The first teacher employed a guidance approach; accordingly, she used language as a resource in her dealings with the children, and the meanings of all words were up for constant negotiation; the teacher's authority was based on being a task leader, and she constantly attempted to share both the tasks and the authority with the children; finally, she defined herself as part of the group. A second teacher was more authority prone; she was the source of meaning in the class, and all language issues were directed to her for final evaluation; authority flowed from her lips in the form of directives; and finally, the class constituted a group quite apart from her. The guidance oriented teacher had quite successful lessons; the children showed great interest and appeared to follow the lesson as the teacher allowed it to unfold. The authoritarian teacher was having a much more difficult time. Without being able to draw on a shared reserve of communicative resources, of the type shared among Amish teachers and children, the teacher spent much of her time explicitly, and often unsuccessfully, calling for the children's undivided attention.

This section has explored the connections between ways of teaching and successful classrooms. The connections between the two are not obvious and an analysis of authoritarian and guidance approaches to teaching indicates that both can be successful or unsuccessful depending upon the interpersonal relations underlying a teacher's strategy. The point of this exploration has been to claim the primacy of teacher-student relations in the determination of a child's learning. Teaching involves more than a curriculum, a style or a way of talking. Most of all, it involves an achievement of mutual trust and accountability in terms of which teachers and pupils can open themselves to each other, care about each other, and learn from each other. This mutual trust and accountability must be communicated between teacher and students. Talk is a key element in the communication of trust and accountability, although there is no one way to talk that is inherently better than another. There is more to teaching than talk and there is more to talk than the transfer of information. In both cases, the missing ingredients are the relations achieved between people by virtue of their teaching or talking whatever they teach or talk, in the way they do at the time and the place they do. The most potent tool for the analysis of how people relate in the ways they do is ethnography. After an account of how and why ethnographic studies of ourselves are important, the paper will proceed to the interpersonal relations underlying mutually sensible talk, and, finally, the interpersonal relations underlying mutually sensible talk in classroom situations in which children are asked to learn to read.

THE ETHNOGRAPHY OF RELATIONS: WHAT AND WHY

At its best, an ethnography should account for the behavior of people by describing what it is they know that enables them to behave appropriately given the dictates of common sense in their community (Frake, 1964b).[3] Accordingly, ethnographies are an essential part of our everyday life. All people, especially people from different cultures, appear to behave differently, and we all do haphazard ethnographies when we

---

[3] The measure of pedagogical success used here is simply whether children learn how to read. There are various other criteria which could be applied: the children's abilities to function on their own, their desires for knowledge, or their politics. These are all important, but it is the point of this paper simply to show that children lean to read best in situations which make sense to them. There is no doubt that there are some relational contexts which will encourage the acquisition of literacy, but which are nonetheless pathological and, in the long run, degrading (Henry, 1973; Spindler 1974a).

struggle to decipher their ways of thinking so that we can understand, or at least anticipate, their behavior. We acknowledge this in everyday talk by saying that successful social relations depend on knowing "where a person is coming from" or "where a person's head is at." Successful psychiatry certainly demands an ethnographic approach (Sapir 1932; Shands and Meltzer 1974). So does successful teaching. Note that the first principle of good pedagogy, namely, starting at a student's present skill level, calls for good ethnography. Most often, teachers, psychiatrists, and the rest of us proceed intuitively. Professional ethnographers are different only in that they become disciplined and self-conscious when gathering information about how people think. Rather than roughing out "where a person's head is at," they struggle to rigorously define a person's "categories for action" (Barth, 1969).

Consider the following illustration of what an ethnography attempts to describe. When a scientist publishes a report with special findings, the scientific community has procedures for holding the findings accountable. Were the proper conditions for doing the experiment present? Were the proper statistical analyses performed? Were the interpretations of the data consistent with previous methods used for interpreting similar data? These and many more questions could be legitimate ways to hold a scientist accountable. This is called a methodology, and it constitutes a canon in terms of which scientists make sense of each other. Such a canon is explicit and, ideally, scientists should be aware of the assumptions underlying their methodology and their implications. The point of this illustration is that people in everyday life also have methods for holding each other accountable (Garfinkel, 1968). An ethnography is an attempt to describe a group's methodology; that is, an attempt to describe the procedures natives use to make sense of each other and hold each other accountable to certain culturally sensible ways of behaving (Garfinkel, 1967; Cicourel, 1974; Frake, 1974). Unfortunately, the procedures used in everyday life are never very explicit. Legal norms set limits and etiquette manuals make suggestions, but procedures used in daily life are hidden deep beneath the surface (Malinowski, 1927; Moerman, 1973). For example, how many of us can examine in detail the procedures used in greeting another person or in walking down a street? The first can involve a head toss, a presentation of the palm of the hand, a brief flash of the eyebrows, and a flash of the teeth in a smile (Kendon and Ferber, 1972; Sherzer, 1973); while the second can involve the computation of complex trajectories for people walking in different directions and the discernment of who is with whom in order that collisions be avoided (Goffman, 1971; Ryave and Schenkein, 1974). We can all greet people and we can safely and unobtrusively navigate the streets, but few of us really know just what we are doing.

In science, methodologies have their consequences. A behaviorist studies different problems and develops quite different results than a psychologist following a psychoanalytic canon. So it is in everyday life. The procedures we use in our daily doings have consequences for us and for all those around us. A successful ethnography should help us to become aware of ourselves and the consequences of our actions. If we all walked down the street in the same way or if we all greeted each other without regard for who was involved, then an ethnography of our greeting behavior would be truly uninteresting. But the point is that we are all quite selective about who we interact with and most often for reasons which we ourselves do not understand. Some people attract us and others do not. The question we must face is, "How much of what happens to us every day is in fact caused by us as a product of the unconscious and limited methods we use to handle the world and to hold each other accountable?" How many of us are aware, for example, that when walking through the neighborhood of a different ethnic group we generally display "the posture of territorial behavior"? We lower our heads, curl our shoulders so that our chests do not protrude, bring our hands close to or in front of our bodies, and keep our eyes down (Scheflen, 1972). Such behavior may make us a little less noticeable, but it also cuts off the possibility of communicating with anyone in that neighborhood. In other words, by exhibiting passing behavior we are helping to maintain the very boundaries which are oppressing us. What we know about how to walk through different neighborhoods helps to divide those neighborhoods. What we know has consequences, and an ethnography of what we know should help to sort out what effects we have on the world. As such, good ethnography is a first step to morality and freedom.

Examples are numerous of how we are all embedded in our own procedures and of how our procedures make us very smart in one situation and very blind and stupid in the next. Ethnographers generally specialize in telling delightful stories about how disoriented people can become when they cross even the smallest of cultural borders. In contrast, the following is a not so delightful story from our own culture; the point is the same, however. People develop elaborate procedures for making sense of each other and holding each other accountable in certain situations. These procedures offer people a shorthand, a quick and easy way of dealing which may hide just what the people are really doing to each other. Change either the situation at hand (move from one culture to another) or the procedures used by one of the individuals and, with great pain, the persons involved will discover what their procedures have been hiding. This example comes from a family disrupted by the husband's extreme dependence upon his wife (Watzlawick, Beavin, and Jackson, 1967). All agreed the problem was that because the man was illiterate he had a hard time moving around in everyday life and showed little promise of upward mobility. After extensive therapy and instruction, the man acquired enough reading competence to be more independent. Soon after, the wife filed for divorce. What had happened was that the two people had developed a rather special way of dealing with each other which, unfortunately, left the man dependent. Once this symptom was treated, the whole logic of their relationship was undermined and the marriage dissolved. Apparently, neither of them knew what they were contributing to and what they were getting out of the dependency relationship. Is it possible that the logic of many of our relationships is equally well hidden? An ethnography should help us to take a better look at the consequences of our activities, given the social world in which we are immersed.

Turning now to education, the ethnographic study of classrooms hopefully will allow us to look carefully at what we, as teachers, do unconsciously to our students when we simply try to make sense and hold them accountable to our way of making sense. The problem with common sense, of course, is that sense must be made in common with other people. Accordingly, common sense is a rare achievement. Because of this, teachers and children often work out mutually regressive relations in their classroom for reasons generally unknown to both groups (Henry, 1973). We all lose some students in every class. Talented teachers and intelligent children sometimes wind up on opposite sides of the fence. Neither group knows how to stop, and pain and failure result for all involved. No one quite knows why. Students who go wrong in the early years do not even learn to read. Older students suffer from crippling anxieties and alienation. Some analysts blame the children, their genes, their families, and their television. Others blame the teachers for being lazy, insensitive, prejudiced, or untrained. In most cases, neither the children nor their teachers are to be blamed. Communicative breakdowns always have two sides. The question is not who is at fault, but rather, what underlying logic and methods can be held accountable for student-teacher disputes? What is it about how teachers and children hold each other accountable that has them either making sense of each other or at each others' throats? A good ethnography of classrooms should answer this question.

Elementary but systematic ethnographies can be attempted by anyone willing to explore carefully what is going on around them. One introductory text has included samples of undergraduate attempts, and the results have been relatively impressive. One student ethnographer (Davis, 1972) simply elicited labels for teacher activities from junior high school children. The activities noted by the children stand out as remarkably different from those most likely to be noted by the teachers themselves (see Chart 1). Notice the rich elaboration of the teacher's role as an enemy or suppressor. From these results, it is possible to hypothesize that the children and their teachers are employing different categories in terms of which they are interpreting and generating behavior. In school, at least, the children and their teachers appear to be working from different cognitive systems. They have different methods for holding each other accountable. A teacher may be giving a math lesson but, from the children's viewpoints, the teacher is merely "talking a whole lot" or "picking on kids."

CHART 1

TAXONOMY OF THE DOMAIN OF THINGS TEACHERS DO AT SCHOOL*

THINGS TEACHERS DO	Pick on kids	Beat kids Smack kids in the face Push against wall Have a paddle Hit kids ——— ⌐ Hit with books └ Hit with yardsticks Slam kids' heads down on desks Yell Bitch Send kids to office Send kids to detention center Make whole class stay after Pick kids out who misbehave Act mean Make fun of kids Pick kids out by ability Won't help kids Call kids stupid Lean on kids' shoulder Make kid put nose on wall Cut down kids Assume kids are guilty Keep kids after school Tie kids to desk Embarrass kids Shake kids Make kids sit in a certain seat Give extra assignments Give sentences
	Talk a whole lot	
	Run A.V. equipment	
	Give tests	
	Pile on the work	

*From *The Cultural Experience: Ethnography in Complex Society* by James P. Spradley and David W. McCurdy. © 1972, Science Research Associates, Inc. Reprinted by permission.

CHART 1 (*continued*)

THINGS TEACHERS DO (*continued*)	Keep you in the book		
	Hand out assignments		
	Catch kids	Catch kids fighting Catch kids in the halls Catch kids smoking in the cans	
	Try to be cool	Keep cigarettes in shirt pocket Dress cool Crack dumb jokes Cut down kids Give detention	
	Be nice to kids	Let do something special	Let be pet — Let touch drapes Let read orally Let write on blackboards Let run errands all the time Let put stuff on the bulletin board
			Let turn off lights for movie Let run projector Let off assignments Let run errands Let switch assignments
		Let off easy	Let off detention Let you sleep instead of smacking you to wake you up
		Give good grades Write a note to another teacher telling her you're staying for her Don't yell Call you by your first name	

It must be pointed out that the ethnographies achieved by eliciting labels alone do not come close to describing what people know about how to interpret and generate behavior (Rosaldo, 1972). A good ethnography cannot simply center on the words people have for their activities. Such a procedure is only a beginning point, for people do more with words than

ETHNOGRAPHY OF SPEAKING

merely name events. Most importantly, they do things to each other with their words. Speech not only has a content, but it also has a set of social functions (Hymes, 1974a, b). People use words to make sense of each other, to encourage or hurt each other, to celebrate each other, and to strike each other down (Frake, 1964, 1969). They use words and a myriad of other communicative events (gestures, odors, rhythms, style) to hold each other accountable as rational, commonly sensible people. The classroom ethnography just cited cannot stop at claiming that children and teachers see their respective worlds through different glasses. Rather, it must probe more deeply and discern how such a situation came to be. An ethnography should detail what is going on in the classroom that children and teachers adapt to each other and learn to hold each other accountable in terms of "strict," "mean," and "unfair," on the one hand and "disruptive," "brain damaged," and "emotionally disturbed," on the other.

This section has emphasized a definition of ethnography as an attempt to describe the methods people use to get by in the social world. Further, I have suggested that in the course of getting by, all of us help to create a social world we do not understand; one which has negative consequences for all of us. Accordingly, I have argued that ethnographies of everyday life are an essential first step to our becoming the conscious and responsible persons we would all like to be.

Ethnographies are difficult to achieve. Getting to "the routine grounds of everyday life" (Garfinkel, 1967) is no easy task. If the logic of our relations is as hidden as I suggested with the husband-wife and pupil-teacher examples, then ethnography is barely a possibility. Against this defeatist attitude, we have the important developments in the ethnography of communication to look to for encouragement. In the course of trying to describe how people talk to each other, ethnographers have had to move beyond language to the interpersonal relations underlying talk in particular settings. Before the meaning of specific utterances or movements could be described, they had to first examine what the people were doing to each other in order to define the context or framework in terms of which the people were likely to interpret each other's communicative behavior.

THE ETHNOGRAPHY OF SPEAKING

It follows from the definition of ethnography that an ethnography of speaking should describe what it is people know that allows them to talk sensibly to each other and to hold each other accountable. In years gone by, this task appeared to be within the range of our descriptive powers. Talk was thought to be constituted by language, a finite system of sounds with a finite set of rules for combining these sounds into meaningful units which were, in turn, combined into sentences. The ethnographer had only to describe the rules for putting it all together. Thus, the fact that two Americans could make sense of each other in conversation was simply explained by the fact that they both knew how to speak English. As competent speakers of English, they used the same phonological, morphological, and syntactic rules for producing talk, and common sense developed neatly from their mutual competence.

During the past ten years, however, the rules which supposedly governed language have proven illusive. Indeed, even the units of language have been dissolving under closer scrutiny. As in the case of all social activities, language is not generated according to an "exact calculus" (McHugh, 1968). Some of us are better than others in certain situations, but no one can ever be sure of just what to do next in the social world. Similarly, as competent speakers of English, none of us employs an exact set of rules for speaking. Rather, linguists are now talking of language learning in terms of the "concept of gradatum" which stipulates that all of us learn flexible procedures for interacting and generating various kinds of talk which can be more or less sensible and appropriate depending upon "the relative statuses of the interlocutors, the setting of the speech act, the message, the code (including gestures), the situation, the topic, the focus, and the presuppositions that are paired with sentences" (Shuy, 1973). Accordingly, the ethnography of speaking does more than locate rules for producing sentences. Rather, in order to understand language behavior, ethnographers have to examine what people are doing to each other with their speech.

Every speech act has implications for those involved. Every speech act not only has a content or reference function, but also a social or relational function in that it also helps to define the relations between the participants (Bateson, 1972; Hymes, 1974; Scheflen, 1974). Without specifying the relational context, the referential function of many utterances cannot be understood. The resources people have at their disposal for generating and interpreting speech are not purely linguistic; it has become increasingly clear that the resources people use to handle speech are fundamentally social in nature. Depending upon their experiences in the social world, people develop memories, patterns of selective attention, and goals in terms of which they define any situation at hand. As Malinowski (1922) stressed, it is in terms of the situation at hand and how it is defined and constantly redefined by the participants that speech behavior must be understood.

For example, consider the statement, "Look at that." Try it on a child of two years, and you will notice a confused child scanning the surroundings for a possible "that." Try it on an adult, and the adult will most likely look at whatever you are looking at. What is it that, of all the millions of stimuli available to the eyes at any given time, enables two people to so simplify the world and locate and look at the same "that"? There is more than linguistic competence here. "The utterer of a remark like 'Look at that!' expects that another can solve problems such as what is to be noticed and what to make of it after simply directing his gaze toward the sight" (Twer, 1972). There is a whole social world hidden in the ability of two people to make common sense of a "Look at that!" statement. In acquiring a language, a child necessarily acquires an essential knowledge of the world which stipulates what is important, what is to be looked at, and how all things—objects, events, and people— relate to one another (Cicuorel, 1974). All speakers build on this relational fabric with their every activity when they make sense of one another.

The embeddedness of language behavior in the social world has become apparent in accounts of language learning and should be apparent in accounts of learning to read. By 1960, it was clear that language was not simply programed into children in the same way that feeding habits were programed into laboratory pidgeons (Chomsky, 1959), and the primary problem facing students of language development was that it was not possible to "understand how language gets from outside the child to inside unless it is in some way inside from the beginning" (Church, 1961). This was followed with a decade of claims that language was a species specific, genetically determined phenomenon which developed "naturally" in all children (Lenneberg, 1967). Our present decade, however, is apparently going to place our language genes back into the social arena— the only place any work on human behavior genetics belongs. Workers in at least four fields—anthropology (Bateson, 1971); Condon and Sander, 1974), linguistics (MacNamara, 1972; Halliday, 1973), psychology (Church, 1970, 1971; Lewis and Freedle, 1972), and sociology (Cicourel 1974a, 1974b)—have heralded the primacy of the social experiences in terms of which speech acts, from babbling to oratory and poetry writing, take on meaning. Sounds, words, and statements only make sense in terms of the contexts in which they are uttered and the experiences the participants have had with the particular sounds, words, statements, and contexts employed.

The acquisition of speaking abilities begins immediately after birth, and possibly well before. By its second day, the neonate moves its body in a rhythm with an adult's speech (Condon and Sander, 1974). Before two months, protoconversational sequencing is practiced, by mother-infant pairs (Bateson, 1971). By four months, and possibly long before, cultural differences can easily be observed in the specifics of such sequencing. For example, Japanese babies vocalize less often and at different times than do American babies (Caudill and Weinstein, 1969). The cultural differences make sense in terms of what Japanese and American mothers do with their babies in their first four months. The specifics are not important here. But it is important to realize that what has been demonstrated in all these studies is that parents and children develop ways of relating to each other by integrating their basic biological and interactional rhythms, those involving feeding, sleeping, bodily movements, speech (Byers, 1972). The meanings of speech activities are mapped onto this relational fabric. Just as parents and children work out ways of making common sense and holding each other accountable to particular patterns or rhythms, we all build and maintain our relational patterns in our every utterance.

Not all social experiences can be had in infancy. A person's social world grows with each new day, and so does a person's language. Consider the protoconversational sequencing practiced by mother-infant pairs. We spend the rest of our lives refining these skills in turn taking. Indeed, much of our time in the social world is spent trying to get a word in edgewise (Yngve, 1970). Speaking ability involves more than just having something to say and a language in which to say it. In addition, speaking involves knowing what to say at a particular time, in a particular setting, so others can be held accountable for listening. No one is responsible for listening to a person saying the wrong thing at the wrong time. By knowing how and when to talk and what to say, a person makes demands on people and creates stable relations with them. In American culture, children and old people have to work hardest at saying the right thing at the right time, but we are all involved. Let us consider children first.

Sacks (1972) has offered the following example from the speech corpus of most three-year-olds: "You know what, Mommy?" A child in America has few conversational rights. For the most part, the child has little right to punctuate an adult conversation with a long story. The adult response could legitimately be something like: "I am talking to someone else now, dear. You run along." The child can punctuate the speech stream only to answer questions and to occasionally ask questions. Consider now what an ingenious strategy the "You know what?" question is. It is a question and, therefore, gives the child a right to a speech turn; and it is designed to be answered with a question, which the child is allowed to answer—at great length if necessary. Three-year-olds appear to know the rules and manipulate them brilliantly. Not only stories but commands fit into this question-question-answer form. For example, consider "Daddy, pretend you are a know what?" "What?" "Pretend you are a dog, and you were on the floor, and you . . . ."

Adults also struggle to punctuate the speech stream. Indeed, much of the politics of everyday life is embodied in the struggle over who is to talk, when, and for how long. Turn taking gives us one possible clue to what people are doing to each other in their conversations (Sacks, 1973). If asked, most of us would claim that conversations involve an orderly exchange of information in turns; you tell me something, I tell you something. Two implicit rules appear to be: 1) only one person speaks at a time, and 2) each person's contribution must be related to the previous person's contribution. Such an ideal conversation has been described as a game of catch in which one player throws a ball, a second player catches the ball and throws it back, and so on until the game ends (Fillmore, 1971). In fact, normal conversations seldom go this way. Rather, the rules of conversation depend upon just what the participants are trying to do to

ETHNOGRAPHY OF SPEAKING

each other; that is, just what relations they are trying to establish between each other. As always, rules turn out to be on-the-spot relational imperatives.

Variations are numerous on a game of catch model of conversation. Fillmore (1971) has described a conversational game familiar to teachers —the socratic dialogue. In this game, the first player throws the ball high into the air; the second player watches it fall, picks it up, and carries it back to the first speaker who again throws the ball high into the air. The teacher-student relationship is made clear in the differential rights to talk time. In the Meet the Press game, the first player—a newsperson—throws a direct pitch to the second player—an administration spokesperson. The game continues as "the administration spokesman pretends to catch it, but he takes one of his own balls and throws it in the air.... After three tries, the newsman stops retrieving the same ball and takes out another one" (Fillmore, 1971).

In addition to the rules of the game differing in every conversation, depending upon the relational fabric created, the methods used to create a particular relational fabric differ from one culture to the next. Many Native Americans entertain long periods of silence and seldom interrupt each other's talk (Philips, 1974). Conversely, in many cultures, it is expected that two or more people will speak at one time in certain situations. This is the case for story telling among the Bushmen, arguing among the Yanomamo, and light discourse among Antiguans (Byers, 1972; Reisman, 1974). In American terms, such overlapped talk would be interpreted as chaotic and most likely volatile. New Yorkers would be only a little surprised. Along with the Socratic and the Meet the Press conversational games, Fillmore might have easily included the New York City conversational game. In this game, every participant throws a ball into the air at the same time. The one that looks most interesting is allowed to stay in flight while the others are somehow recalled by their owners. When the chosen ball nears the end of its flight, each participant again throws a ball into the air. One may see in this conversational game one source of New Yorkers' being stereotyped as pushy and aggressive when they are evaluated by outsiders who stick more closely to Fillmore's ideal game-of-catch conversation.

In many classrooms, it appears that turn taking is a key to understanding teacher-student relations. Orderly turn taking—orderly, that is, in terms of a particular community's standards for conversational sequencing—appears to be one good measure of whether people are making sense of each other. Interactions between different ethnic groups and between different social classes abound in examples of sequencing problems (Byers and Byers, 1972; Erickson, 1973a, b; Kochman, 1975). In my own research into the social organization of reading groups in first grade classrooms in suburban New York, it has become apparent that groups marked by turn taking struggles do not do as well in school as do groups which somehow engineer a smooth transfer from one reader to the next. Any classroom with chronic conversational turn taking problems is most likely working with a minimum of: teacher-pupil common sense, good relations, and learning. Classrooms are in trouble when children talk all day long against the expressed wishes of the teacher, or do absolutely no talking despite the urgings of the teacher. The first problem dominates urban schools for minority children, and the second problem flourishes in white schools for Native American children (Dumont, 1972; Philips, 1972; Roberts, 1970; Rosenfeld, 1971). Both populations are marked by a high rate of school failure.

Top and bottom reading groups have been described in terms of how they use different procedures for turn taking (Gumperz and Hernandez-Chavez, 1972; Rist, 1973). In the videotapes I have been analyzing, the top group effects an orderly sequencing procedure: child A reads a page and everyone looks to the teacher who nods her head at child B who is sitting next to child A; child B reads a page and everyone looks to the teacher who acknowledges child C who is sitting next to child B; and so on around the table until the story is complete. In the bottom group, every turn appears to be up for grabs with some children shouting "ME, I want to read" and with others being generally inattentive.

These are the facts. What are we to make of them? Until recently, we might have been told that the children in the bottom group were neurologically impaired, hyperactive, in need of immediate gratification, or just plain hungry; most of the deprivation hypotheses have proven inadequate when put to rigorous testing. More recently, we have been hearing the opposite to the notion that there is something wrong with the children. Now we are offered account after account that there is something wrong with the teachers, that they are working against the children in the bottom group for some reason—be it skin color, dialect, clothes, or records from previous classes. In fact, it is not necessary to blame either side. The behaviors of the children and their teachers makes sense if you look at them in the context in which they occur. In the next section, some reasons for this sequencing situation will be considered. In this section, there is only room for an example of a characteristic turn taking problem between a student and her teacher.

Rosa is one of four Puerto Rican children in an almost all white first grade in a middle-class suburban school in New York. All the Puerto Rican children, one of the two black children, and two of the eighteen white children in the class are in the bottom reading group. The top group is composed of white (mostly Italian and Jewish) children. The reason Puerto Rican children start off in the bottom group is quite clear; their English is not yet fluent and reading is difficult. The question is whether being in the bottom group has to permanently retard a child's progress in the acquisition of literacy. I will argue that 1) given the nature of the educational enterprise in America, with its emphasis on competition and tests which measure a child against other children instead of measuring each child's own progress (Singer in press); and 2) given both the teacher's and the children's own conceptions of how they should succeed in classrooms, placement in a bottom group and participation in the everyday relational give and take of the bottom group are fatal to any child's attempt to learn school material. I will argue this case briefly in an analysis of turn taking in Rosa's bottom group.

Rosa constantly struggles to get a turn to read. Yet day after day, she is passed by. Rosa's problem is simply that her competency in English is quite limited. The teacher's problem is more complex. She is a sensitive woman and worried about calling on Rosa when she would be unable to perform and would, therefore, be embarrassed by her peers. This situation makes an orderly linear turn taking procedure impossible, for Rosa then would be passed by in a way that everyone could see. Accordingly, everyone must volunteer and compete for turns. In addition to taking much more time than the simple head nod needed to effect a turn change in the top reading group, this procedure also makes the bottom group totally dependent upon the teacher for control, and everytime she is interrupted (which is often) the social order of the bottom group must be renegotiated.

These procedural differences make a difference, for the bottom group gets only one-third of the actual reading that the top gets for every twenty minute lesson they have with the teacher. For every day spent in the bottom group, Rosa and her friends fall even further behind their classmates in the top group. After a few years of this differential progress, Rosa most likely will be sufficiently behind to become a "problem," "nonlearner," "dropout," "deprived child," or "bad girl." Who do we blame? Is it Rosa's fault she learned Spanish as a child, and is this any reason for her to be permanently cut off from the rewards of literacy? Of course not. Early bilingualism appears to have primarily positive consequences for cognitive development (Diebold, 1968). Is it the teacher's fault that she refuses to embarrass Rosa by making her read what she is not yet able to read? Of course not. In fact, it is possible to claim that Rosa wants no part of reading, that she is quite content to make believe that she is trying to get a turn. In one videotaped lesson I have analyzed, Rosa raises her hand and calls the teacher at almost every juncture suitable for a turn change. However, she always includes a signal that she does not want to be called, a signal which can be identified by the teacher. Some negative signals include looking away, covering the book with her arm, or turning to the wrong page—all while pleading for a turn to read. The one time she did not include any of these negative signals, the teacher called on her, and she had to admit that she could not read the page. It appears that the teacher and Rosa attend quite carefully to each other and achieve a certain degree of common sense with each other. Nevertheless, they both suffer for their efforts. No one is to blame, yet everyone could be doing a better job if they could deal more carefully with the unstated relations which appear to govern or key (Hymes, 1974a) their interpretations of each other's talk.

The effort of this discussion of the ethnography of speaking has been to show that language behavior is best understood in terms of its social context and that ethnographers have been quite successful in initiating an analysis of how people make sense of each other and hold each other accountable in speech situations. A brief discussion of the social issues involved in conversational sequencing was offered as an example of the social skills which must be developed if a child is to become a competent member of a speech community and as a testament of the kind of progress the ethnography of speaking has been making. The relevance of the turn taking issue for understanding the relations between teachers and children and the consequences of their communicative procedures for classroom learning were considered.

THE ETHNOGRAPHY OF READING

We have considered teacher-student relations as the key to successful classrooms. We have considered ethnography as a way of describing these relations and have given special attention to the ethnography of speaking. Now we must consider the possibility that an ethnography of speaking and an ethnography of reading would locate the same relational system. In other words, we must now consider the hypothesis of this paper that certain ways of speaking in certain situations are related to just what kind of literacy is achieved by particular people. Certainly, Rosa's case indicates that certain ways of calling for a turn to read has devastating consequences for the children of the bottom group, but we need a general framework in order to understand such specific cases.

To a great extent, without using the word, this paper has been about what motivates people to say what they do and why they take what is said to them in the way that they do. Ethnographers of speaking have been locating that people speak for reasons, that they speak in response to something, and that their tiniest utterance ("uh" or "ya know") can be related to the ongoing social fabric in which they suspect they are participating (Jefferson, 1973, 1974). Equivalent accounts for how and why people read cannot be offered yet, but some indications of the reasons for people learning how to read are beginning to appear. Perhaps the most interesting comes from the rugged mountains of the island of Mindoro in the Philippines. There, a small group of people known as the Hanunoo achieve a 60 percent literacy rate on a rare Indic derived script imported centuries ago and virtually unknown to surrounding groups. The Hanunoo receive no formal training in their reading and writing activities and, in fact, ignore literacy until early puberty. At that time, they appear to have the ultimate motivation for learning to read. Literacy is used almost exclusively in courtship among the Hanunoo, and the children work diligently on the script until they can master writing songs in order to support an active love life. They achieve competency within months (Conklin, 1949, 1960). Similarly, remarkable adult learning achievements are on record for people having to master an orthography for social and religious purposes (Basso and Anderson, 1973; Walker, 1972).

For other groups, the desire to read appears to be founded within the social organization of the community. Among the European Jews in Israel, learning to read appears to function as a key milestone in a child's life. "Most first graders did acquire reading without undue difficulty and, by April or May of their first year in school, children used to receive their first reader at a special ceremony attended by their proud parents" (Feitelson, 1973). What is particularly interesting about this Israeli case is that the children were taught how to read using a visual, whole word method. This method is particularly useless for teaching Hebrew which offers a minimal number of word shapes to work with and demands attention to the finest detail. The children appeared to learn, in spite of the method, with massive doses of aid from their families and larger communities. Although the dynamics of this reinforcement of school activities has not been made clear, a similar motivating device was apparently not generated in the communities of the Oriental Jews of Israel who accomplished a high rate of reading failure even after a more phonetic approach was used in the schools.

These two examples emphasize the importance of the social relations which motivate a child's attempts at learning to read; the Hanunoo root their training in the demands of peer group sexuality and the European Jews of Israel in the demands of family and community groups. Groups which show a high rate of functional illiteracy, despite elaborate educational programs, apparently do not produce an equivalent relational fabric for motivating its youth to read. There are two possible explanations for this phenomenon: 1) there is something wrong with the people and their culture, and 2) there is something wrong with the situations in which they are asked to learn to read. In the first case, the problem comes from within the culture in that the parents either place no importance on literacy or they ill equip their children for the kind of thinking they have to do in order to play the reading game. In the second case, the problem comes from the outside, from the group's contacts with the people of another group who are helping (sometimes forcing) their children to read under circumstances not congenial to the enhancement of the children's identities. Each of the possibilities must be considered.

There is little possibility that a large proportion of children would remain illiterate despite intensive educational attempts simply because their parents place little importance on literacy. People are willing to learn the strangest and most complex schemas if they are offered relationally positive environments for learning whatever it is they are asked to learn. Baseball, sex, and drug talk and pig latin and various other specialized codes or games are mastered quickly when introduced by the right people. The same can be true of literacy. Witness the Hanunoo. A good teacher may be able to teach children to read Chinese quicker than a bad teacher can teach the same English speaking children to read English (Rozin, Poritsky, and Sotsky, 1971). The subject matter and its potential relevance to everyday life make no difference. The peasants of rural Greece clamor for the classics in their schools and shun the technical education which could be helpful to them (Friedl, 1964). And the least industrialized people of the world, the Papuans of the New Guinea Highlands, have taken to literacy with a great fervor (Meggit, 1967). The important question to be asked is whether the subject matter is introduced in the proper relational context. If it is, the children will learn. If not, the children will either have to learn it elsewhere, or they will shun it completely.

There is even less possibility that a culture cognitively disables its young and cuts them off from possibly learning to read. In terms of formal psychological operations, reading is no different from any other kind of human behavior. Even if they are illiterate, all people play the same kind of psycholinguistic guessing games and do the same kind of hypothesis testing in their everyday behavior as they would have to do if they were to learn to read. Culturally induced reading failures must develop from some place other than the formal logic embedded in the culture's categories for action, for there are no data to indicate that any one of the world's thousands of cultures logically disables its members from mastering reading skills, once sufficient motivation and adequate presentation of the task are present.

When we look for an explanation of the high rate of school failure among some groups in the situations in which the children are asked to learn, we are on much more interesting ground. Almost invariably, such problems arise when a group in power educates the children of a minority group. The picture is quite uniform. Indian children throughout North and South American schools fail, Mexican children in American Anglo schools fail, African children in Western colonial schools fail, Oriental Jews in European Israeli schools fail, black children in American schools fail, and so on. One good explanation is that people from divergent traditions do not communicate well with each other, they do not establish the proper motivational fabric, the proper relational foundation for the children to throw themselves into learning to read. As much as the Hanunoo and European Israeli children are fired up to read, that is the extent to which minority children for the most part appear turned off by learning to read and sometimes appear to learn not to read; i.e., they appear to struggle to achieve school failure.

The negative relational messages which flow from a dominant to a minority group often flow through the vocal chords, ways of speaking used by teachers and apparently the source of their pupils feeling badly about the educational enterprise. Three kinds of conflict have been described between a teacher's way of talking and a student's way of talking: language conflict, dialect conflict, and sequencing conflict. All three deserve consideration.

Language conflict, perhaps, has the most devastating effects on a child's motivation to read. First of all, it is much harder to decode according to an unknown language. Second, when a foreign tongue is insisted upon in school, it is usually a sign that members of one group are oppressing members of a second group. Also, almost invariably, the teachers are members of the oppressing group who, regardless of their good intentions, generally try to mold minority children to their own images. In terms of the politics of the classroom, this is an explosive situation. Reading skills can often be found in the resulting debris.

Perhaps the finest and most detailed example comes from the Chiapas highlands where Indian children often fail to acquire literacy in Spanish speaking schools run by the Mexican authorities (Modiano, 1973). Superior results were achieved by Indian teachers working in Spanish, and the best results were achieved by Indian teachers working with a bilingual progam. By American standards, this is a curious result in that the Indian teachers had little training compared to the Spanish speaking teachers, and few of them were better than barely literate. By Amish standards, and by the standards developed in this paper, these results are not at all surprising. Indian teachers in bilingual programs are often able to solve two problems that monolingual Spanish speaking teachers may find impossible: 1) they can teach the children to read in their native tongue and then transfer the skills to reading Spanish, and 2) they stand a much better chance of making common sense with the children because of the relational resources given them by their shared tongue.

Much concern has been spent on whether dialect differences interfere with children learning to read. Most of the important work has centered on whether the language printed on a page was suitable for a child decoding according to a slightly different language (Laffey and Shuy, 1973). But there is another issue; whether dialects interfere with teachers and children making common sense together. There is considerable inverse correlation between a child's dialect and school success. For example, the child who speaks a heavy Black Vernacular is less likely to be doing well in school than a black child who speaks a more standardized dialect. The range of school success and failure appears to be neatly marked by language variation in phonology, grammar, and paralanguage (Frender and Lambert, 1973; Labov and Robin, 1969; Piestrup, 1973). The question is "Why?" Does dialect get directly in the way of a child's decoding operations? Or does dialect get the child involved in the dirty side of the politics of the classroom and thereby destroy the motivation to read (McDermott, 1974)?

Consider the following example (Piestrup, 1973):

T   Who can give me a word that begins with н?
C1   Happy.
T   Happy, good. (Writes it on the board.)
C2   House.
T   House! That's a good one, too. (Writes it down under "happy.")
C3   (W) hor'.
T   (Looking deliberately cool, pauses briefly.)
C3   Like you go to a hor' movie.
T   Oh! Horror! Yes. (Writes it.)

Here a slight difference in the rules used to construct words in Black Vernacular English had a teacher misperceive what a child was saying. This is a simple miscommunication, and similar events can occur often between people, without too much difficulty. But such miscommunication can often lead to bad relations. In this case, the difficulty was repaired before serious relational damage was done: before the teacher chased the child out of the room for being fresh, wrote a note home to the parents chastizing the child's obscenity, assumed there was no worthwhile home to write to, or just simply confused the child by saying the answer was incorrect—that the word started with a *w*. This teacher handled it well, but the alternative was obviously a good possibility.

One interesting and important development recent research is beginning to show is that, among many black children, the use of dialect increases as children proceed through school (Hall and Freedle, 1975; Labov and Robins, 1969; Piestrup, 1973). We are even getting some sense of the social processes underlying these trends. Labov and Robins (1969) have shown, for example, that the use of dialect increases as peer group participation increases and school performance decreases. This finding is further illuminated by Piestrup's study (1973) of first grade classrooms in which dialect use either stayed the same or soared in direct proportion to how much the children were hassled for their use of dialect. The more they were corrected, the more they used it; and, in such classrooms, reading scores were low. In classrooms in which they were allowed to express themselves and read orally in dialect, the use of dialect did not increase and their reading scores were higher, with many children above the norms. There, indeed, appears to be a relational politics to dialect use and the interpersonal relatons certainly appear to be important in defining who learns to read and who does not.

As discussed, people in different cultures employ different rules for taking turns in conversations. If the children's procedures for sequencing talk are not taken into consideration, difficult relational problems can arise. Hawaiian children answer adults in chorus and are embarassed terribly by American teachers who single them out to answer in class (Boggs, 1972). Native American children often lack the conversational competitiveness to do anything but remain mute in their classrooms with

Anglo teachers (Dumont, 1972); Philips, 1972). Here, the difficulties go deeper than just differences in the functions of speech. In order to achieve enough of a conversational position to at least attend to one's efforts to take a turn at talking, much postural-kinesic work must be performed with various body parts. This is also quite different across cultures; black American and Eskimo children both appear to have difficulties synchronizing their behaviors with their white teachers, and the teachers have a difficult time synchronizing with the children (Byers and Byers, 1972; Collier, 1973).

All three kinds of speaking conflicts—language, dialect, and sequencing—can cause relational conflicts, and these may help to account for the high rate of school failure among some minority groups. Now we must ask why this is the case. The simplest explanation is that people from different groups have different codes for generating talk, and it is these codes which keep them constantly miscommunicating. This explanation is a little too simple. Certainly, when the communicative resources of two groups are different, the people will generate much miscommunication. But the question is why this keeps them at one another's throats. Why not simply repair the miscommunication? This leads to an even more difficult question, "Why are there communicative codes? If the data of Labov and Robins (1969) and Piestrup (1973) are a reflection of what happens in our schools, then perhaps different communicative codes represent political adaptations. Further, this means that in the course of talking in one way rather than another we not only suffer from communicative conflicts, we help to make them and are somehow rewarded for our efforts. Our communicative codes, as persuasive and entrapping as they are, do not turn us into communicative robots incapable of coming to grips with other people simply because they communicate differently. The social world is subject to much more negotiation. If codes exist, it is because we all help create them. If codes are keeping us apart, it is because we are allowing them to do so because we have an interest in maintaining the social order buried in the codes and because we are getting something from our behavior, no matter how painful the consequences. Remember the person walking through the "wrong" neighborhood displaying passing behavior. Such a person attempts to achieve safety. But also, such a person is helping to make the boundary which is making the painful passing behavior necessary. We all do this with our speech behavior. Our ways of speaking harbor a political system which we all help to recreate with our every utterance (Hymes, 1961, 1973). Thus, it is no accident that there is a marked relation between ways teachers talk in their classrooms and the success and failure of different types of students in American classrooms. Our vocal chords constitute some of the materials on the basis of which failing self-fulfilling prophecies work (Jansen, 1974; Rist, 1973, 1974). In talking the way we do, we relate to different types of children in different ways; create environments unsuitable for encouraging the learning of reading by some children;

unintentionally encourage the development of divergent communicative codes; fail more children of one group than another; and, in the end, socialize a new group of minority children into the pariah status we were hoping to eliminate. In short, in talking the way we do, we are as much a part of the school problem as failing children are.

CONCLUSION

Two major claims have been made: that teacher-student relations are the key to understanding who learns what in a classroom, and that the ways teachers and students speak to one another in classrooms is a key to understanding who learns to read. An attempt was made to point out that we are equally responsible (in the sense that we help to create them) for both the successful and the unsuccessful students in our classrooms, and it was suggested that we all attempt ethnographies in order to locate and possibly improve the relational fabric in terms of which students decide whether to learn in our classrooms.

REFERENCES

Barth, F. "Introduction," in F. Barth (Ed.), *Ethnic Groups and Boundaries.* Boston: Little, Brown, 1969.

Basso, K., and N. Anderson. "The Western Apache Writing System: The Symbols of Silas John," *Science*, 1973, 180, 1013-1021.

Bateson, G. *Steps to an Ecology of Mind.* New York: Ballantine, 1972.

Bateson, M. "The Interpersonal Context of Infant Vocalization," MIT Research Laboratory of Electronics, *Quarterly Progress Report*, 1971, 100, 170-176.

Boggs, S. "The Meaning of Questions and Narratives to Hawaiian Children," in C. Cazden, V. John, and D. Hymes (Eds.), *Functions of Speech in the Class-room.* New York: Teachers College Press, 1972.

Byers, P. "From Biological System to Cultural Pattern," unpublished doctoral dissertation, Columbia University, 1972.

Byers, P., and H. Byers. "Nonverbal Communication and the Education of Children," in C. Cazden, V. John, and D. Hymes (Eds.), *Functions of Language in the Classroom.* New York: Teachers College Press, 1972.

Caudill, W., and H. Weinstein. "Maternal Care and Infant Behavior in Japan and America," *Psychiatry*, 32 (1969), 12-43.

Chomsky, N. "Review of B. F. Skinner, Verbal Behavior," *Language*, 35 (1959), 26-58.

Church, J. *Language and the Discovery of Reality.* New York: Random House, 1961.

Church, J. "Techniques for the Differential Study of Cognition in Early Child-hood," *Cognitive Studies*, 1 (1970), 1-23.

Church, J. "The Ontogeny of Language," in H. Moltz (Ed.), *Ontogeny of Verte-brate Behavior.* New York: Academic Press, 1971.

Cicourel, A. *Cognitive Sociology.* New York: Free Press, 1974 (a).

Cicourel, A. "Gestural Sign Language and the Study of Nonverbal Communication," *Sign Language Studies*, 4 (1974), 35-76 (b).

Collier, J. *Alaskan Eskimo Education*. New York: Holt, Rinehart and Winston, 1973.

Condon, W., and L. Sander. "Neonate Movement is Synchronized with Adult Speech," *Science*, 183 (1974), 99-101.

Conklin, H. "Bamboo Literacy on Mindoro," *Pacific Discovery*, 2 (1949), 4-11.

Conklin, H. "Maling, a Hanunoo Girl from the Philippines," in J. Casagrande (Ed.), *In the Company of Man*. New York: Harper and Row, 1960.

Davis, J. "Teachers, Kids and Conflict," in J. Spradley and J. McCurdy (Eds.), *The Cultural Experience: Ethnography in Complex Society*. Palo Alto: SRA, 1972.

Diebold, R. "The Consequences of Early Bilingualism in Cognitive Development and Personality Formation," in E. Norbeck, D. Price-Williams, and W. McCord (Eds.), *The Study of Personality*. New York: Holt, Rinehart and Winston, 1968.

Downing, J. *Comparative Reading*. New York: Macmillan, 1973.

Dumont, R. "Learning English and How to Be Silent: Studies in Sioux and Cherokee Classrooms," in C. Cazden, V. John, and D. Hymes (Eds.), *Functions of Language in the Classroom*. New York: Teachers College Press, 1972.

Erickson, F. "Talking to the Man," paper presented at the American Educational Research Association Meeting, New Orleans, March 1973.

Erickson, F., and J. Shultz. "Talking to an 'Us' or a 'Them,'" paper presented at the American Anthropological Association Meeting, New Orleans, December 1973.

Feitelson, D. "Israel," in J. Downing (Ed.), *Comparative Reading*. New York: Macmillan, 1973.

Fillmore, C. Deixis II. Unpublished manuscript, University of California, Santa Cruz, 1971.

Frake, C. "How to Ask for a Drink in Subanum," *American Anthropologist*, 66 (1964), 127-132 (a).

Frake, C. "Notes on Queries in Anthropology," *American Anthropologist*, 66 (1964), 132-145 (b).

Frake, C. "Struck by Speech," in L. Nadar (Ed.), *Law in Culture and Society*. Chicago: Aldine, 1969.

Frake, C. "Plying Frames Can Be Dangerous," unpublished manuscript, Stanford University, 1974.

Frender, R., and W. Lambert. "Speech Style and Scholastic Success," in R. Shuy (Ed.), *Sociolinguistics: Current Trends and Prospects*. Washington, D.C.: Georgetown University Press, 1973.

Friedl, E. "Lagging Emulation in a Post-Peasant Society," *American Anthropologist*, 66 (1964), 569-586.

Garfinkel, H. *Studies in Ethnomethodology*. Englewood Cliffs, New Jersey: Prentice-Hall, 1967.

Garfinkel, H. "Comments," in R. Hill and K. Crittenden (Eds.), *Proceedings of the Purdue Symposium on Ethnomethodology*. Purdue University: Department of Sociology, 1968.

Goffman, E. *Relations in Public*. New York: Harper and Row, 1971.

Green, G. "How to Get People to Do Things with Words," in R. Shuy (Ed.), *Some New Directions in Linguistics*. Washington, D.C.: Georgetown University Press, 1973.

Gumperz, J., and E. Hernandez-Chavez. "Bilingualism, Bidialectalism, and Classroom Interaction," in C. Cazden, V. John, and D. Hymes (Eds.), *Functions of Language in the Classroom*. New York: Teachers College Press, 1972.

Hall, W., and R. Freedle. *Culture and Language: The Black American Experience*. New York: Halsted, 1975.

Halliday, M. "Early Language Learning," paper presented at the International Congress of Anthropological and Ethnological Sciences, Chicago, 1973.

Henry, J. *Sham, Vulnerability, and Other Forms of Self-Destruction*. New York: Vintage, 1973.

Hostetler, J. "Education in Communitarian Societies," in G. Spindler (Ed.), *Education and Cultural Process*. New York: Holt, Rinehart and Winston, 1974.

Hostetler, J., and G. Huntington. *The Hutterites of North America*. New York: Holt, Rinehart and Winston, 1967.

Hostetler, J., and G. Huntington. *Children in Amish Society*. New York: Holt, Rinehart and Winston, 1971.

Hymes, D. "Functions of Speech: The Evolutionary Approach," in F. Gruber (Ed.), *Anthropology and Education*. Philadelphia: University of Pennsylvania Press, 1961.

Hymes, D. "Introduction," in C. Cazden, V. John, and D. Hymes (Eds.), *Functions of Language in the Classroom*. New York: Teachers College Press, 1972 (a).

Hymes, D. "The Use of Anthropology: Critical, Political, Personal," in D. Hymes (Ed.), *Reinventing Anthropology*. New York: Vantage, 1972 (b).

Hymes, D. "Speech and Language: On the Origins and Foundations of Inequality in Speaking," *Daedalus*, 102 (1973), 59-86.

Hymes, D. *Foundations in Sociolinguistics*. Philadelphia: University of Pennsylvania Press, 1974 (a).

Hymes, D. "Linguistics, Language, and Communication," *Communication*, 1 (1974), 37-53 (b).

Jansen, M. "Denmark," in J. Downing (Ed.), *Comparative Reading*. New York: Macmillan, 1973.

Jansen, M., P. Jensen, and P. Mylov. "Teacher Characteristics and Other Factors Affecting Classroom Interaction and Teaching Behavior," *International Review of Education*, 8 (1974), 529-540.

Jefferson, G. "A Case of Precision Timing in Ordinary Conversation," *Semiotica*, 9 (1973), 47-96.

Jefferson, G. "Error Correction as an Interactional Resource," *Language in Society*, 3 (1974), 181-199.

Kendon, A., and A. Ferber. "A Description of Some Human Greetings," in P. Michael and J. Crook (Eds.), *Comparative Ecology and Behavior of Primates*. London: Academic Press, 1973.

Kochman, T. "Orality and Literacy as Factors of 'Black' and 'White' Communicative Behavior," *International Journal of the Sociology of Language*, 3 (1975), 95-118.

Labov, W., and C. Robins. "A Note on the Relation of Reading Failure to Peer Group Status in Urban Ghettos," *Florida FL Reporter*, 7 (1969), 54-57, 167.

Laffey, J., and R. Shuy. *Language Differences: Do They Interfere?* Newark, Delaware: International Reading Association, 1973.

Lenneberg, E. *Biological Foundations of Language*. New York: Wiley, 1967.

Lewis, M., and R. Freedle. "Mother-Infant Dyad: The Cradle of Meaning," paper presented at a Symposium on Language and Thought, University of Toronto, March 1972.

MacKay, R. "Conceptions of Children and Models of Socialization," *Recent Sociology*, 5 (1973), 27-43.

MacNamara, J. "Cognitive Basis of Language Learning in Infants," *Psychological Review*, 79 (1972), 1-13.

Malinowski, B. "The Problem of Meaning in Primitive Language," in C. Ogden and I. Richards (Eds.), *The Meaning of Meaning*. New York: Harcourt Brace Jovanovich, 1923.

Malinowski, B. *Crime and Custom in a Savage Society*. Totowa, New Jersey: Littlefield, 1972 (1927).

McDermott, J. "Introduction," in M. Montessori (Ed.), *Spontaneous Activity in Education*. New York: Schoken, 1965.

McDermott, R. "Achieving School Failure: An Anthropological Approach to Illiteracy and Social Stratification," in G. Spindler (Ed.), *Education and Cultural Process*. New York: Holt, Rinehart and Winston, 1974.

McDermott, R., and J. Church. "Making Sense and Feeling Good: The Ethnography of Communication and Identity Work," *Communication*, in press.

McHugh, P. *Defining the Situation*. Indianapolis: Bobbs-Merrill, 1968.

Meggitt, M. "Uses of Literacy in New Guinea and Melanesia," in J. Goody (Ed.), *Literacy in Traditional Societies*. London: Cambridge University Press, 1968 (1967).

Miller, R. "Levels of Speech (*keigo*) and the Japanese Response to Modernization," in D. Shively (Ed.), *Tradition and Modernization in Japanese Culture*. Princeton: Princeton University Press, 1972.

Mishler, E. "Implications of Teacher Strategies for Language and Cognition," in C. Cazden, V. John, and D. Hymes (Eds.), *Functions of Language in the Classroom*. New York: Teachers College Press, 1972.

Modiano, N. *Indian Education in the Chiapas Highlands*. New York: Holt, Rinehart and Winston, 1973.

Moerman, M. "The Use of Precedent in Natural Conversation: A Study in Legal Reasoning," *Semiotica*, 9 (1973), 193-218.

Montessori, M. *Spontaneous Activity in Education*. New York: Schoken, 1965 (1917).

Passin, H. "Intrafamilial Linguistic Usage in Japan," *Monumenta Nipponica*, 12 (1968), 97-113.

Payne, J. "Analysis of Teacher-Student Classroom Interaction in Amish and Non-Amish Schools," *Social Problems*, 19 (1971), 79-90.

Philips, S. "Participant Structures and Communicative Competence," in C. Cazden, V. John, and D. Hymes (Eds.), *Function of Language in the Classroom*. New York: Teachers College Press, 1972.

Philips, S. "The Role of the Listener in the Regulation of Talk: Some Sources of Cultural Variability," paper presented at American Anthropological Association Meeting, Mexico City, November 1974.

Piestrup, A. *Black Dialect Interference and Accommodation of Reading Instruction in First Grade*. Berkeley: Language Behavior Research Laboratory, 1973.

Reisman, K. "Noise and Order," in W. Gage (Ed.), *Language in Its Social Setting*. Washington: Anthrological Society of Washington, 1974.

Rist, R. *The Urban School: A Factory of Failure*. Cambridge: Massachusetts Institute of Technology, 1973.

Rist, R. "Becoming a Success or Failure in School," unpublished manuscript, Portland State University, 1974.

Roberts, J. *Scene of the Battle: Group Behavior in the Classroom*. New York: Doubleday, 1970.

Rosaldo, M. "Metaphors and Folk Classification," *Southwestern Journal of Anthropology*, 28 (1972), 83-99.

Rosenfeld, G. "Shut Those Thick Lips", *A Study of Slum School Failure*. New York: Holt, Rinehart and Winston, 1971.

Rozin, P., S. Poritsky, and R. Stotsky. "American Children with Reading Problems Can Easily Learn to Read English Represented by Chinese Characters," *Science*, 171 (1971), 1264-1268.

Ryave, A., and J. Schenkein. "Notes on the Art of Walking," in R. Turner (Ed.), *Ethnomethodology*. Baltimore: Penguin, 1974.

Sacks, H. "On the Analyzability of Stories by Children," in J. Gumperz and D. Hymes (Eds.), *Directions in Sociolinguistics*. New York: Holt, Rinehart and Winston, 1972.

Sacks, H. "On Some Puns with Some Intimations," in R. Shuy (Ed.), *Sociolinguistics: Current Trends and Prospects*. Washington, D.C.: Georgetown University Press, 1973.

Sadock, J. "Whimperatives," in J. Sadock and A. Vanek (Eds.), *Studies Presented in R. Lees*. Edmonton: Linguistic Research, 1969.

Sapir, E. "Cultural Anthropology and Psychology," in D. Mandelbaum (Ed.), *Culture, Language, and Personality*. Berkeley: University of California Press, 1966 (1932).

Scheflen, A. *Body Language and the Social Order*. Englewood Cliffs, New Jersey: Prentice-Hall, 1972.

Scheflen, A. *How Behavior Means*. New York: Anchor, 1974.

Shands, H., and J. Meltzer. *Language and Psychiatry*. The Hague: Mouton, 1974.

Sherzer, J. "Verbal and Nonverbal Deixis: The Pointed Lip Gesture among the San Blas Cuna," *Language in Society*, 2 (1973), 117-131.

Shuy, R. "Some Language and Cultural Differences in a Theory of Reading," in K. Goodman and J. Fleming (Eds.), *Psycholinguistics and the Teaching of Reading*. Newark, Delaware: International Reading Association, 1969.

Shuy, R. "The Concept of Gradatum in Language Learning," paper presented at the American Sociological Association Meeting, Montreal, 1973.

Siegel, B. "Defensive Structuring and Environmental Stress," *American Journal of Sociology*, 76 (1970), 11-32.

Singer, H. "Measurement of Early Reading Ability," in Proceedings of the National Reading Conference, 1973, in press.

Spindler, G. "Beth Anne" in G. Spindler (Ed.), *Education and Cultural Process.* New York: Holt, Rinehart and Winston, 1974 (a).

Spindler, G. "Why Have Minority Groups in North America Been Disadvantaged by Their Schools?" in G. Spindler (Ed.), *Education and Cultural Process.* New York: Holt, Rinehart and Winston, 1974 (b).

Thorndike, R. *Reading Comprehension in Thirteen Countries.* New York: Halsted, 1973.

Twer, S. "Tactics for Determining Persons' Resources for Depicting, Contriving, and Describing Behavioral Episodes," in D. Sudnow (Ed.), *Studies in Social Interaction.* New York: Free Press, 1972.

Walker, W. "Notes on Native Systems and the Design of Native Literacy Programs," *Anthropological Linguistics*, 11 (1969), 148-166.

Watzlawick, P., J. Beavin, and J. Jackson. *Pragmatics of Human Communication.* New York: Norton, 1967.

Yngve, V. "On Getting a Word in Edgewise," *Papers from the Sixth Regional Meeting, Chicago Linguistic Society.* Chicago: Chicago Linguistic Society, 1970.